HOW TO COLLECT
STAMPS

SEVENTH EDITION

H.E. Harris & Co.®
Serving the Collector Since 1916

www.whitman.com

Copyright © 2023 Whitman Publishing, LLC
1974 Chandalar Drive • Suite D • Pelham, AL 35124

All Rights Reserved.

Designed in U.S.A. Printed in China
ISBN: 0794846432

CONTENTS

Introduction 1

History of Stamp Collecting 4

History of Postage Stamps 6

Famous Rarities 10

History of First Day Covers 14

Cachets 18

How to Begin 23

Accessories 28

Catalogs 33

Albums 36

United States Stamp Identifier 41

Step-by-Step Identification-A Standard Procedure 53

Collector's Dictionary 61

Worldwide Stamp Identifier 97

Foreign Numerical Tables 160

Philatelic History by Country 164

Vanished Lands 181

Map Index 201

Map Section 207-219

Key Map 207

Map No. 1: North & Central America 208

Map No. 2: Caribbean Seas & West Indies 209

Map No. 3: South America 210

Map No. 4: Atlantic Ocean 211

Map No. 5: Europe 212

Map No. 6: German States 213

Map No. 7: Italian States 214

Map No. 8: The Near East 215

Map No. 9: Africa 216

Map No. 10: West Indian Ocean & Arabian Sea 217

Map No. 11: The Far East 218

Map No. 12: Australia & South Pacific Ocean 219

COLLECTING IS
THE OLDEST HOBBY!

Man is a born collector – since time immemorial, he has been collecting all sorts of things, for all sorts of different reasons. The first collector was probably a caveman who found some unusually attractive rocks and decided to take them home or it may have been bones to which he attached some supernatural significance, or some shells, or feathers – no matter. What is important is that today, more people are collectors than any other type of hobbyist; and more people by far collect stamps than any other object.

Why stamps? Think of all the different things that people collect – antiques, magazines, bottles, coins, rocks, automobiles, works of art, even autographs – and the reasons why they collect them – aesthetic appeal, cultural or historical significance, curiosity, nostalgia value, pride of ownership, or just plain whimsy – and you'll find that stamp collecting offers all these attractions combined and more!

Aesthetic appeal? You would need a museum larger than the fabulous Louvre to house all the marvelous paintings, magnificent statues, and other great works of art to be found on stamps. The Mona Lisa, Venus de Milo, Rodin's "The Thinker," Rembrandts, Michelangelos, Picassos, Van Goghs–they're all here. Many collectors consider stamps themselves, with their finely executed designs and exquisite details, to be miniature works of art in their own right.

1

Cultural and historical significance? Through stamps you will gain knowledge about the manners, customs, dress, traditions, and folklore of people in all parts of the globe. You will witness events which shaped the world as it is today, meet heroic figures of the past, and catch futuristic glimpses of things to come.

Curiosity? Nothing will whet your curiosity like the hundreds of strange and unknown people, events, and other subjects you will find on stamps. You'll delve through history, geography, science, sports, every subject known to man seeking the answers to questions posed by your stamps.

Nostalgia? Antique autos, people dressed as they were years ago, old buildings long since torn down, figures from the past – they are all on stamps. Pride of ownership? Just watch a stamp collector beam as they regard a new acquisition or straighten out the volumes in their collection. Whimsy? There are stamps picturing scenes from fairy tales, cartoon characters, imaginary space creatures, and more.

And stamp collecting has other virtues, too. It offers relaxation, rejuvenation of the spirit, an escape from the cares of the everyday world. It offers the excitement of the hunt, the unknown, as you pore through a pile of stamps hoping to find something of value, perhaps even great rarity!

Through stamp collecting, too, you can make new friends, and strengthen existing relationships. One of the pleasures of stamp collecting is meeting with other collectors, to swap stamps, discuss finer philatelic points, and in general share your interest in the hobby. Families find that stamp collecting offers an excellent way to

spend time together, and stamp collectors in their neighborhood, city, state, other states, even other countries. Stamp collecting provides a common ground for understanding between peoples, near and far. As stamp collector Lily Pons, the famed opera star said, "Stamp collecting, like music, makes one part of a great worldwide fraternity knowing no bounds of nationality."

It is no wonder, then, that famous people from every walk of life – presidents, kings and queens, businessmen, movie stars, religious leaders – have all been avid stamp collectors.

As president Franklin D. Roosevelt said, "Stamp collecting dispels boredom, enlarges our vision, broadens our knowledge, makes for better citizens, and in innumerable ways enriches our life."

A BRIEF HISTORY
OF STAMP COLLECTING

Who was the first stamp collector? No one knows for sure, but it couldn't have been too long after the first stamps were issued that someone thought it would be a grand idea to collect these little bits of postal paper as novelties or souvenirs. As more countries adopted the new postal system, and the number of different stamps from different countries began to grow, other people took interest, and the hobby of philately was under way.

Of course, it was easier to collect stamps then. There were no decisions that had to be made over what countries or topics to collect – nearly everyone was a worldwide collector. Ten years after the introduction of the Penny Black, the world's first postage stamp, only 153 more stamps had been introduced; in 1860, the total number of stamps was still under 1,000. But the number of stamps and stamp-issuing countries and colonies increased rapidly thereafter, and today there are well over 400,000 different stamps – not including all of the minor varieties, errors, reprints, and so forth.

Then, as today, people gathered stamps for many different reasons: one woman advertised for used Penny Blacks to paper her walls; another wanted to use the stamps to decorate lampshades. The first known advertisement for stamps for actual hobby-collecting purposes appeared in the *London Family Herald* in 1851. It was probably through such advertisements that stamp collectors first contacted each other and formed the first stamp clubs and philatelic societies. The very first philatelic society on record was called the Omnibus Club and was formed in the United States in 1856. Today, there are many different philatelic societies in many countries, and an international society called FIP – the Fédération Internationale de Philatélie, founded in 1926.

As for the use of the word "philately" to describe stamp collecting, it first appeared in an article written in 1864 by a French stamp collector named Herpin for a French stamp magazine. Derived from two Greek roots, *philo*, meaning "love," and *atelos*, meaning something exempt from "taxes," i.e., a letter with postage stamps. The term gained such widespread popularity – many people must have thought it described exactly the way they felt – that it was incorporated into common usage.

Some people in those early days of philately may have thought that stamp collecting was just a passing fancy, a short-lived fad – time has proven them very wrong. Interest in stamp collecting has grown steadily through the years until today countless people throughout the world – and more than 5 million in the United States alone – turn to stamp collecting for both recreation and pleasure, making it truly "The World's Most Popular Hobby."

H.E. Harris & Co. Archives
Circa 1935

A BRIEF HISTORY OF
POSTAGE STAMPS

The first organized system for carrying written messages was established by the Persians under Darius, who created a network of mounted couriers stationed at various points throughout his vast empire, ready to speed letters to any part of the country. These early "Pony Express" riders were so efficient that they inspired the ancient Greek historian Herodotus to coin the famous phrase which appears on the facade of the New York City post office building: "Neither snow nor rain nor heat nor gloom of night stays these couriers from the swift completion of their appointed rounds."

Darius' system was adopted and expanded upon by Caesar Augustus, whose *Cursus Publicus* included couriers on foot, on horseback, and in carriages, traveling well-maintained highways connecting Rome with every outlying territory of the Roman Empire. The *Cursus Publicus* was known familiarly as the "post" system because of the waystations, or posts, established at regular intervals along each route to provide the couriers with food and fresh horses.

The first postal system open to the public (the earlier ones had all been exclusively for royal use) was established in 1505 by the Thurn and Taxis families of Austria, who offered to carry letters and parcels anywhere in continental Europe for anyone who could pay the fee. Organized under a royal license, the Thurn and Taxis system survived for more than 350 years, well into the modern postal era.

The Thurn and Taxis system was privately-owned, and so was the London Penny Post when it was inaugurated in 1680 by a businessman named William Dockwra. But the Penny Post proved to be so profitable that the government, seeing in it an ideal source of internal revenue, decided to take over its operation for itself. Thus, in 1698, the first postal system was born.

Dockwra's Penny Post was a model of Postal efficiency, and it remains so even to this day. Letterboxes were posted at hundreds of points throughout London, and branch offices were established in every district. For one penny, a letter or parcel deposited at a letter box or branch station would be picked up, hand stamped to indicate the time of collection and certify that the postage had been paid, then delivered to any address in the city. Deliveries were made every hour in the business district and from four to eight times a day in the outlying sections.

In colonial America, meanwhile, the first post office had been established at Boston in 1639, and by 1691 a uniform postal service was in operation throughout the colonies. The first postal system of the new government of the United States went into operation in 1775, with Benjamin Franklin as the first Postmaster General.

Until 1840, however, all these systems operated without the benefit of a postage stamp. Items were hand stamped mostly to show receipt at a post office, and postage was collected from the addressee upon delivery. Many people developed secret codes by which they could cheat the postal services: secret marks on the outside of the envelope conveyed the sender's message, and all the addressee had to do was to read the secret message on the envelope, then refuse to accept the letter and pay the fee.

To counter this trend, Sir Rowland Hill, the British Postmaster General, created the first adhesive postage stamp in 1840 – and the modern postal era was born. The stamps were to be bought beforehand by the person wishing to send a letter, then affixed to the letter, indicating that the postage had been paid. The stamps were designed by Hill himself, and bore a profile likeness of the Queen Victoria, who had just come to the throne three years before. Because they were printed in black, the one-cent stamps became known as "Penny Blacks" – and were the first government-printed postage stamp.

This new postal system of collecting the postage in advance proved immensely popular, and it was not long before all the civilized countries in the world had instituted like systems. The United States itself issued its first stamps in 1847, a 5¢ Franklin and a 10¢ Washington.

As more and more nations joined the postal fraternity, the frontiers between them began to cause numerous difficulties. Different nations had different postal rates, transportation fees, and internal conditions, so the delivery of mail over international boundaries involved the negotiation of complicated and confusing bilateral written treaties. Mail from Spain to Germany, for example, had to travel from Spain to France under one treaty, and from France to Germany under another – and might be stopped altogether if the treaty expired while the mail was en route. An obvious need existed for a broad international postal system to replace the multitude of bilateral treaties.

One of the early leaders in the movement for an international postal organization was Montgomery Blair, the U.S. Postmaster General. It was mostly through Blair's efforts that the first international postal conference was convened in Paris in 1863, attended by the United States and 15 European Nations. Though an international postal organization was not founded in Paris, many of the proposals forwarded at the conference, such as standardization of postal weights and rates, influenced the agreement which finally emerged 12 years later.

In the following years, the initiative in the international movement was taken over by the German Postmaster General, Dr. Heinrich von Stephan, who worked hard to draft proposals which would make the flow of mail between countries as simple and efficient as the flow of mail within countries. His years of labor bore fruit in October 1874, when twenty-two countries met in the first Postal Congress in Berne, Switzerland, and founded the Universal Postal Union. The final agreement, which took place in July 1875, included such principles as a unified rate for letters, the principle that the postage is paid by the sender, standardized delivery and transportation fees, and more.

Today, all civilized nations of the world belong to the U.P.U. In addition to expediting the worldwide distribution of mail, the U.P.U. also regulates international organizations, the U.P.U. is the one body which comes closest to successfully fulfilling its original goals.

FAMOUS RARITIES

Mention stamp collecting to the average noncollector, and chances are the first thing that will come to his mind will be some story he has heard in the past about a rare stamp being sold for a fabulous amount of money. And in truth, such tales are as much a part of the hobby as are the stamps themselves.

For example, every collector, and many non- collectors as well, knows the story of the 1856 British Guiana one cent magenta, the world's rarest stamp. Found in the attic by an English schoolboy in 1873 and sold to a friend for a $1.50, this one stamp is valued at $9,500,000.

Other famous rarities include the 1847 Mauritius 1¢ and 2¢ issues, accidentally printed "Post Office" instead of "Post Paid," and are valued over $1,250,000 apiece (all values given here are 2022 Standard Catalog or realized auction prices); the 1851 2¢ Hawaiian Missionary stamp (valued at $625,000), Spain's 1851 2 reale stamp, printed in blue instead of red (valued at $23,000), and another color error, the 1851 Baden 9 kreuzer green – which should have been red (valued at $1,300,000).

Famous United States rarities include most of the 1846-47 Postmaster's Provisionals, particularly the Alexandria, VA, 5¢ Blue Boy stamp (valued at $1,180,000), the Boscawen, NH, 5¢ stamp (valued at $300,000), and the Lockport, NY, 5¢ stamp (valued at $120,000). Also included are the 1869 "Landing of Columbus" 24¢ and "Shield, Eagle, and Flags" 30¢ stamps with inverted vignettes (valued at $750,000). The most famous U.S. rarity of all is the 1918 "Curtis Jenny" 24¢ airmail with inverted center (valued at $800,000).

What makes these little pieces of paper worth so much money? The answer lies in the age-old law of supply and demand: in the more than 100 years since the 1856 British Guiana was discovered, no other copy has come to light. Meanwhile, the number of collectors in the world has grown into the tens of millions, all of whom would like to own this one stamp. It's no wonder then that the price has risen to such astonishing heights!

Of course, the chance of finding any of the really old, rare stamps grow slimmer each day, with so many millions of collectors engaged in the search; but important philatelic finds are still being made, usually as they have always been made in the past: by someone browsing through a collection of old letters, cleaning out an attic, thumbing through a pile of old documents, etc.

The best place to look for valuable stamps is anywhere mail has been saved or accumulated for many years. Attics, basements, storage rooms, etc., often yield old trunks or bundles containing letters from grandparents or even great-grandparents. Among these letters there is always the possibility that a valuable stamp will be found.

Many businesses, banks, and other financial concerns, schools, country courthouses, churches, and others store their correspondence and records for years; some of the greatest stamp finds have been made among such ancient papers.

A stamp does not necessarily have to be very old, however, to be extremely valuable – the law of supply and demand applies to modern stamps as well as to ancient ones.

For example, in 1954 a copy of the newly minted Kenya 5¢ stamp picturing the Owen Falls Dam was found to have a picture of the dam inverted. Millions of "correct" copies of this stamp were printed in 100-stamp sheets, four sheets to a pane. But no other copy of the stamp with the "upside-down dam" has ever turned up, the one-of-a-kind stamp was eventually purchased by a wealthy Indian maharajah for a price estimated to be around $10,000, and its value today is considered to be many times that.

In 1962, a sheet of Canal Zone "Thatcher Ferry Bridge" 4¢ stamps was found which had the picture of the bridge erroneously omitted. Sixty years later, these stamps are now valued at $8,000 each.

CORRECTLY PRINTED

ERROR

This last case, incidentally, was one of significant importance to all collectors. The Thatcher Ferry Bridge find was made by H.E. Harris, founder of the stamp firm which bears his name, and one of the great pioneers of the stamp hobby. When Canal Zone postal authorities learned of Harris' discovery, they proposed to print millions of additional stamps with the bridge omitted – deliberate "errors" which would have rendered Harris' copies worthless as rarities.

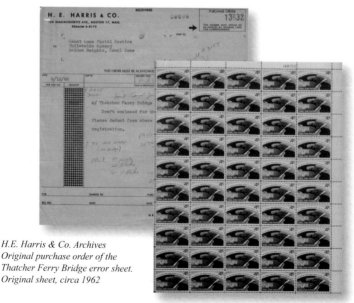

H.E. Harris & Co. Archives
Original purchase order of the
Thatcher Ferry Bridge error sheet.
Original sheet, circa 1962

Harris went to court to protect his find, and in a landmark decision, the postal authorities were enjoined from any action which would devalue genuine errors. This decision set a legal precedent which assures every collector who even dreams of finding a valuable error that any such discovery cannot be rendered worthless through deliberate government interference.

This hope of someday discovering a rare stamp, no matter how remote the chances may be, adds much to the excitement of stamp collecting – but it is still only a small part of the large pleasures the hobby has to offer. What makes a stamp valuable is the fact that, though millions of people may want one, only a very select few collectors will ever be privileged to own a copy of it, thus, a collector whose only interest in the hobby lies in the acquisition of great rarities is almost certain to be disappointed.

Obviously, then, the millions of people in the world today who collect stamps must do so for some reason other than the simple acquisition of rarities. And, although much has been said time and again about the many virtues of the hobby – it is educational, it brings people together, it is relaxing, it teaches good habits, etc. – the one overriding fact that remains is this: stamp collecting is fun!

HISTORY OF
FIRST DAY COVERS

If you are a stamp collector, you probably have a few First Day Covers (FDC's) in an album or shoe box. For most collectors a FDC is a cacheted envelope with a new stamp and a "First Day of Issue" postmark. Some might also have a First Day Program, outlining the Ceremony held on the First Day in the official First Day city.

First use of First Day Issue cancellation

First Day Cover collecting, as we know it today, did not start until the 1920s and 1930s. Between July 1922, and Sept. 1923, the first official First Day of Issue, the First Day Ceremony and program and the first commercial FDC cachet all appeared.

It was not until 1937 that the familiar "First Day of Issue" slogan was first used. Since then, these basic elements of FDC collecting have changed very little.

"First Day of Issue" slogan

14

When considering FDC's before 1922, all the rules change. Collectors accustomed to an official First Day for each new stamp will be surprised to learn there were only nineteen Designated First Days for all U.S. stamps issued before 1922. These official dates were designated by the Post Office in either PO instructions for stamp sale, with the PO announcement of the new issue, or by the Congress in the bill which authorized the stamps.

Even with these few cases, First Day Covers do not exist for all issues with Designated First Days. Often the stamp was not available for sale until after Designated First Day, and in at least one case there is evidence that a stamp sold before the Designated First Day.

"Earliest Dated Cover" without cachet

First Day Covers for most issues before 1922 are more properly called "Earliest Dated Covers." An Earliest Dated Cover is one with the earliest known postmark for the particular issue on the cover.

The history of First Day Cover collecting changed when the USPOD designated the first official First Day of Issue on July 12, 1922. This was the First Day of E12, the 10¢ Special Delivery stamp.

The next stamp issued with an official First Day was the 11¢ Hayes regular issue, on October 4, 1922, in Washington, D.C., and Fremont, OH. This FD included several new firsts: the first FD city outside Washington, D.C., the FD ceremony, and the FD program.

Linprint cachet

On September 1, 1923, George Linn serviced the first commercially produced US FDC cachet. Linn printed a simple five line cachet on a black bordered, mourning envelope. Several hundred of these cacheted FDC's were prepared and offered for sale in philatelic journals of the period: *Collector's Club Philatelist*, *Meekel's Weekly Philatelic Gossip*, as well as his own paper, *Linn's Weekly Stamp News*.

From a simple start of one cachet in 1923, cachet making grew in popularity to over thirty different cachets per issue for the Clark and Sullivan commemoratives of 1929, and nearly one hundred different cachets per issue for many of the three cent purples of the 1930s.

Cover addressed to C.E. Nickles

Cacheted FDC's before 1935 were made in very small quantities and they are getting harder to find every year. Because of this, many collectors are happy to have uncacheted covers in this period.

Covers with addresses of prominent FDC enthusiasts, Adam Bert, C.E. Nickles, Henry Hammelman, Philip Ward and Edward Worden are highly sought after by many FDC specialists.

Introduction to Cachet Collecting

Today, many FDC collectors are really cachet collectors. The thrill of the hobby is in finding a scarce cachet for their collection. Up to one hundred different cachets exist for many stamp issues from mid-1930s up to the present.

Some collectors enjoy the challenge of collecting different cachets for a stamp or a set that they will like; some will collect by topic, such as U.S. history, Masonic history, or a professional topic. Topical collections can be researched, written up and mounted on pages to produce a personalized album or exhibit. Others collect by cachet, trying to put together a collection of all the cachets produced by a cachetmaker they like.

JVC cachet

CACHETS

Grimsland cachet

ENGRAVED CACHETS have always been immensely popular with collectors. Four popular engraved cachets are Grimsland, House of Farnam, ArtCraft, and Artmaster. Henry Grimsland of Chicago, Illinois, produced engraved cachets from 1933 until 1951. Most are one color cachets, with many in the color of the stamp. Most are signed "Grimsland" in the design.

House of Farnam cachets have been produced for every issue from the TIPEX Souvenir sheet of 1936 up to the present. Farnam cachets are engraved usually in one color; many are signed "House of Farnam" or "HF."

ArtCraft Cachets have been continually produced by the Washington Stamp Exchange since 1939. The first ArtCraft, prepared for the World's Fair issue of 1939, is an unsigned engraved design, in blue. Most ArtCraft cachets are black, signed with the ArtCraft pallet and brushes trademark.

Artmaster Cachets have been produced for all new U.S. stamps since the Honorable Discharge Commemorative of 1946. Artmaster cachets are engraved cachets usually in a dark green or gray color and are signed "Artmaster."

COLORED CACHETS appeal to many FDC collectors. Ioor, Grandy, Staehle and Boll all produced colored cachets. Harry Ioor produced two-colored cachets from 1929 until 1951. In the 1940s and early 50s most Ioor cachets were signed, but before 1940 they were unsigned.

W.M. Grandy produced one or more cachet designs per issue from 1935 until 1957. They are all two color cachets, usually signed "W.M. Grandy," or "WMG."

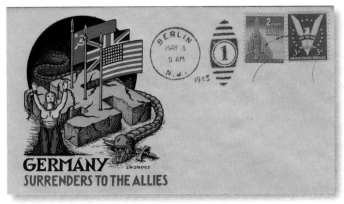

Ludwig W. Staehle cachet

Ludwig W. Staehle was one of the most prolific U.S. cachet makers, usually producing three or more cachet designs for each issue. Staehle cachets are known for the vivid use of color, often with three or more colors on the design. Staehle produced designs from the late 30s until the early 50s.

Cachet Craft produced from the late 1930s until the early 1970s. During the 1940s Cachet Craft produced attractive two color cachet designs by both L.W. Staehle and Ken Boll. Several popular lines of cachets have been produced from original artwork. C. Stephen Anderson designed cachets from 1933 until his death in 1978. Anderson cachets are usually one color line drawings, with an illustration above, and historical text below. Most are signed "C. Stephen Anderson" or "CSA."

Aristocrat Cachets have been continually produced since 1936. Most Aristocrat cachets will capture the interest of FDC collectors. Fulton, Fluegel, Crosby and "Silk" cachets are very popular for these reasons.

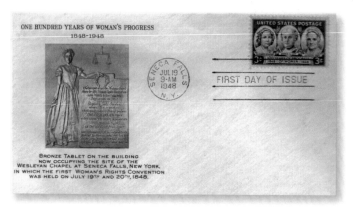

Fulton cachet

Fulton Cachets are finely engraved cachets, usually printed in color rather than black. Because Fultons were produced only from 1947 to 1950, they offer an opportunity to assemble a complete collection of very attractive cachets. While many Fultons can be located with some persistence, a few, such as the foreign issues and the U.S. Utah cachet, are quite difficult to find.

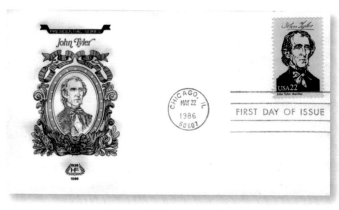

House of Farnam cachet

Fluegel cachet

Fluegel Covers are attractive, multicolored cachets produced from 1945 until 1968. Attractive use of color is being appreciated more and more by the cachet collector, and all Fluegel cachets are becoming harder and harder to find.

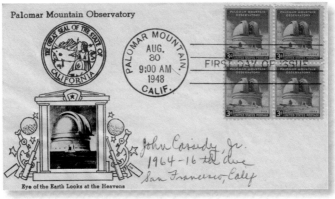

Crosby cachet

One of the most intriguing cachetmakers of the 1930s and 1940s is W.G. Crosby. Crosby produced cachets using a raised print, with a space in the printed design for a small photo to be posted on the cover. Crosby produced many varieties of his cachet by changing the printed design and the photo. Over twenty-five different Crosby cachet varieties are known to exist on the Navy issue of 1945.

"Silk" cachets have been produced in the United States only since 1971. However, since that time, they have become the most popular and fastest growing cachet on the market. As new collectors have gone back to buy the early "Silk" Cachets, the demand has far exceeded the supply. Today, many early "Silk" Cachets are bringing high prices when they appear on the market.

"Silk" cachet

Another exceedingly popular area of FDC collecting is First Cachets. A First Cachet is the very first cachet produced by any cachetmaker. Very often the first cachets were produced in small quantities. First cachets by the popular cachetmakers such as ArtCraft, Colorano, Farnam, Fluegel, Fulton and others are difficult to locate, and sell for ten to fifty times the price of a common cachet on the same issue.

HOW TO BEGIN

Stamps can be obtained from any sources. First of all, save them from your own incoming mail, and have your friends, relatives, and business acquaintances do the same. Servicemen and others visiting foreign countries can bring back many interesting stamps. You can swap stamps with friends or "pen pals," exchanging your duplicates for others that you do not have.

The best way to obtain a goodly number of all-different stamps for a reasonable price is by purchasing a large stamp packet at a local stamp or hobby store or department store. Bags or boxes of "mixture" – that is, stamps still on paper, unpicked and unsorted – are quite different; their cost per stamp is much less but you will likely receive many duplicates of quite common stamps, although you will probably also find a few good commemorative stamps or others to add to your collection.

As your collection grows, you may wish to add more packets – available for many different countries and topics – or stamps purchased from a reputable mail-order house such as Harris. Through stamp mail order catalogs, retail stores, and the internet, you can buy stamps in sets, packets, and individually.

You will probably want to keep your stamps in an album, and you will find helpful hints as to album selection in the *Albums* section in this book. Duplicate stamps and those you have not yet mounted in your album are usually kept in glassine envelopes or stock books (see *Accessories* section.)

NEVER paste, glue, or tape stamps down in an album; always use an approved stamp mounting such as hinges.

In the earliest years of stamp collecting, stamps were merely glued down, often with their own gum. Then collectors began to preserve most of the original gum by using "stamp hinges," little gummed pieces of paper or glassine that are folded in the middle and act like a hinge, one part attached to the back of the stamp, the other to the album page, as described under "Hinges." In recent years however, most collectors prefer to keep the gum on mint stamps intact by using the so-called "hingeless" mounts, which protect the stamp completely, but from which the stamp can be removed, if desired. (Note: Most **mounts** are **not** peelable, while better grades of stamp hinges **are** peelable and can be removed from the album page and stamp with little trace.)

Very old and rare stamps, such as found once in a blue moon on old correspondence, plus those with special postal markings such as "First Day of Issue," are likely to be worth more if left on their original envelopes. But nearly all stamps – and especially those which the beginning collector is likely to acquire through buying "mixture" lots or from his own current mail – should be cleanly separated from any attached paper before being mounted in the collection.

Place the stamps in cold or lukewarm (but not hot) water for five or ten minutes, and you will find that the paper peels off easily. Then place the stamp face down on a clean blotter and let it dry thoroughly before you mount it in your album. If the stamps curl, they may be straightened by drying them between blotters on which a book has been placed, or by using a "stamp press."

NOTE: A few stamps have ink which will run or disintegrate when placed in water. The best guide to these stamps is the *Scott Standard Postage Stamp Catalogue*, which may be purchased from almost any stamp dealer or can be found in the reference section of most public libraries. If you buy, or have access to, a Scott Catalogue, you will find a wealth of information at the beginning of each volume as to how stamps are printed, the various types of paper, printing, etc.

Most collectors acquire duplicate stamps; many wonder what to do with them. First of all, you will want the best possible copy of each stamp for your collection, so if you acquire a second copy, check with the one you already have and mount the best one in your album. (Some collectors even maintain two collections, one for unused and one for used stamps.) Duplicate stamps may be used for trading with other collectors, while a small packet of one's duplicates and an inexpensive album make a wonderful gift for a youngster who has not yet started this fascinating hobby.

After collecting stamps of the world for a while, enjoying the romance of acquiring these fascinating and colorful little pieces of paper that move the world's mail, many enthusiasts begin to narrow their collecting interests to a particular country or topic, and here is where stamp collecting can become truly personal, for there are almost as many ideas about collecting as there are collectors. Some keep right on collecting stamps of the entire world, others may specialize in airmails, British Empire stamps, or those of some particular country. They may prefer to choose art on stamps, sports on stamps, or animals, birds, or flowers; or any one of a thousand or more other topics. Whatever appeals to you – whatever strikes your fancy – that is what you should collect, for that is what will surely give you the most pleasure.

There is also a whole fascinating micro-world in stamps – secret marks, minor varieties and the like, as seen through a magnifying glass (see U.S. Identifier section for examples.) There are stamps that can be told apart only by their perforations as measured in a space of two centimeters, or by whether they are printed on watermarked or unwatermarked paper. (See further information elsewhere in this book.) You can spend hours, like Sherlock Holmes with his magnifying glass, tracking down the identity of a single stamp, or you can let your imagination roam the whole world as you leaf through your stamp album. The choice is yours!

The Best Practices of Stamp Collecting:

- NEVER PASTE, GLUE OR TAPE A STAMP DOWN. Always use stamp hinges or other approved stamp mounts.

- ALWAYS USE STAMP TONGS TO HANDLE MINT STAMPS. In fact, it is a good idea to use tongs when handling all stamps.

- HANDLE YOUR STAMPS CAREFULLY AT ALL TIMES. Do not cram them into a box so that they may become torn, creased or otherwise damaged and thus destroy their value.

- USE VERY LITTLE MOISTURE WHEN USING ANY KIND OF STAMP MOUNT. This applies to all mounts – hinges or any other type of mounting.

- BEWARE OF HUMIDITY. Stamp gum is made to stick, and stamps with gum will stick to almost anything if moisture is introduced, and there is no absolutely sure way to unstick them. If you are in a humid area, keep your stamp collection in as cool and dry a place as possible.

- ONCE YOU HAVE DECIDED WHAT YOU WILL COLLECT, BUY THE BEST (Largest) ALBUM YOU CAN AFFORD. Buying a too-small album will only require transferring stamps to new album pages later – a time- consuming and expensive process.

- NEVER SEAL A STAMP MOUNT COMPLETELY. Paper may disintegrate if kept absolutely air tight.

- DO NOT SOAK A STAMP OFF A COVER (ENVELOPE) UNTIL YOU FIND OUT WHETHER IT HAS ANY SPECIAL POSTAL MARKINGS OR OTHER REASON THAT WOULD MAKE IT MORE VALUABLE IF LEFT "ON COVER." For instance, a cover stamped "First Day of Issue" would be more desirable than the stamp by itself. Generally speaking, common ordinary stamps may be soaked off without any further checking; older covers should be checked with the *Scott Standard Postage Stamp Catalogue* first, or better yet, with a qualified cover expert.

- REMEMBER THAT A FEW STAMPS HAVE "FUGITIVE" INKS, AND THESE INKS WILL RUN IF PUT IN WATER OR IN WATERMARK DETECTION FLUID. If in doubt, check the Scott Catalogue first.

- ENJOY YOUR HOBBY TO THE FULLEST! It can bring you a whole lifetime of enjoyment.

ACCESSORIES

STAMP TONGS

To avoid getting your stamps soiled or creased, you should never handle them with your fingers, or with anything other than a clean pair of good quality stamp tongs. These handy tweezer-like instruments are easy to use, and come in assorted styles, allowing you to choose according to your own personal preference. A good pair of stamp tongs should be thin enough to pick up a stamp from a flat surface, should have slightly rounded ends, and highly polished edges and surfaces to avoid damaging the stamp.

PERFORATION GAUGE

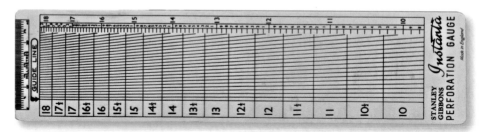

Measuring the number of perforation holes in a two-centimeter space along the edge of a stamp is often the only way to tell the difference between two stamps that may look exactly alike but belong to different issues. By placing a stamp on a perforation gauge and moving the stamp up and down until the dots on the gauge perfectly fit the holes along the edge of the stamp, you can tell exactly what the "perf. number" is.

MAGNIFIERS

Magnifying glasses enable you to examine stamps closely and identify details too small to be seen easily with the naked eye. Magnifiers come in many unique styles, ranging from small, folding pocket magnifiers to large battery-powered "flashlight" types and stand-type magnifiers which leave both hands free.

WATERMARK TRAY AND FLUID

Watermarks on stamps (see pgs. 56 and 95) are often very difficult to see clearly, so stamp collectors use various methods to make them easier to detect. The most common method is to place the stamp face down in a black tray or dish and pour a few drops of detector fluid onto the stamp, making the watermarked design stand out against the black background. CAUTION: Watermark detection fluids may react unfavorably with some inks and dissolve them, so extreme care should be taken in their use.

STAMP LIFT FLUID

The stamp lift is a fluid used to remove old hinges and separate stuck-together or stuck-down mint stamps while preserving most of the original gum.

UV LAMP

Ultraviolet lamps are used to make phosphor tags (see pg. 94) visible, and can be obtained either as complete units, or as ultraviolet bulbs which will fit into regular fluorescent or incandescent fixtures. Direct ultraviolet light can damage the eyes, so you should take care not to look directly into an ultraviolet lamp.

STAMP PRESS

A stamp press is used to flatten out folds and creases in stamps, and to prevent them from curling while they are drying after having been soaked. These can be found in manual or electric.

GLASSINE ENVELOPES

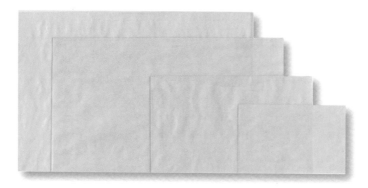

Many collectors use glassine envelopes to keep their stamps sorted, identified, clean, and undamaged prior to mounting them in an album, or to package and prepare them for sale or trading. Glassines are translucent and come in a wide range of sizes.

STOCK BOOKS

Stock books are temporary albums used to keep stamps for preliminary sorting or accumulation prior to mounting, or to keep duplicates for sale or trade. The pages have long, shallow pockets into which stamps can be slipped; they are then held reasonably secure but can be quickly and easily removed when necessary. Stock books may have either stiff manila pocket pages or transparent plastic pockets on black backing, to show off your stamps better; they may be inexpensive, and small enough to fit into your pocket or purse, or as large and luxurious as any standard stamp album.

HINGES

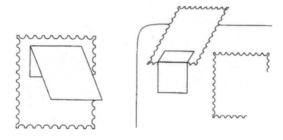

Stamp Hinges are small pieces of gummed glassine paper used to mount stamps in your album. The shiny side is gummed; keep it outside as you fold the hinge.

Just moisten the upper half of the gummed side of the hinge and attach it to the back of the stamp; then moisten the other half and attach it to the album page. It's easy! (Remember to leave the stamp, where it is hinged in the album, until dry; otherwise, if you try to remove the stamp, you may damage it.)

MOUNTS

- Insert stamp in tube.
- Trim tube close to stamp with scissors.
- Moisten gum, then fasten to album.
- Fold back upper part of tube and crease so stamp will lie flat.

Another method of mounting stamps in an album is to use plastic strips or tubes, which can be cut to an exact fit. Stamps thus mounted are well-protected by the tough plastic shell but remain completely visible. Use of plastic mounts instead of hinges also means that the original gum on mint stamps remains intact. There are many different mounts available.

CATALOGS

A catalog is an illustrated list of stamps, usually arranged in sets according to face value, and listed in order of the date of issue. Besides helping to identify stamps and giving the current market values, catalogs also provide other information: color and design variations, watermarks, perforation numbers, type of printing used, etc. Both general worldwide and specialized catalogs are available.

WORLDWIDE CATALOGS

The worldwide catalog most widely used in the United States is the *Scott Standard Postage Stamp Catalogue* (U.S.). Other highly regarded worldwide catalogs include *Stanley Gibbons* (Great Britain), *Michel* (Germany), and *Yvert & Tellier* (France).

In these publications, the individual stamps in the set are listed, with the index, or catalog, number, design-type number (referring to the illustration with that number), denomination, color (if two or more colors are used, the color of the frame or border is given first, then the colors of the central, or vignette portion of the design), and the prices for unused and used copies of the stamp. Minor variations are denoted by a lowercase alphabet letter.

SPECIALIZED CATALOGS

Specialized catalogs deal with specific topics, countries, or types of issues. The largest selling catalog for U.S. and Canada stamps is the H.E. Harris Reference Catalog of Postage Stamp Prices of the United States, Canada, and Provinces. Other prominent specialized catalogs include the *Scott U.S. Specialized Catalogue*, *Sanabria's World Airmail Catalog* (for collectors who specialize in airmail issues), and many country and regional catalogs. It is also possible to get listings of issues on specific topics from some of the topical collecting societies.

Reproduced at left is part of a page from the Scott Standard Catalogue. Under the illustration of the stamp and description of the other designs in the set are given the date of issue, type of printing process used and perf. number.

Reproduced at right is a page from the 2022 H.E. Harris US/BNA Postage Stamp Catalog. Under each illustration is a listing by Scott Catalogue number of the individual stamps having that design.

ALBUMS

The best way to keep your stamp collection organized, well protected, and beautifully displayed is to mount your stamps in an album.

In choosing an album, carefully consider your own interests and needs – are you interested in collecting stamps from around the world, or from one specific country; or are you interested in a specific topic, like sports or flowers, or a specific type of stamp, like air mails or special deliveries? Whatever your interests, albums come in such a wide range of classes, prices, sizes, and types that there is bound to be one that is just right for you.

Choice of an album is a very personal matter, but there are some helpful guidelines. If the user is to be a youngster, then the amount of time and money he or she will be able to spend on the hobby, and whether there will be adult supervision, should be considered. A youngster "on his own" or carrying a heavy school and extra-curricular schedule would become frustrated by a too-large album for which he has too little time. If an adult will be aiding their stamp collecting, or better yet, if it is going to be a real "family hobby," then a larger album is desirable. An adult may wish to start with a moderate-sized or larger album.

Most collectors start with a worldwide album and then, later – sometimes many years later – narrow their collecting interests to a single country or topic, at which time they can choose one of the many excellent specialized albums on the market.

Loose-leaf albums, especially, are virtually necessary because they allow you to add or rearrange pages whenever it becomes necessary. Most album manufacturers publish annual supplements for their loose-leaf albums, allowing you to keep your collection up to date with the latest issues.

There are two general classes of albums, those in which the pages have ruled spaces for the stamps (often illustrated), and those in which the pages are blank. Within the ruled-space category one finds the general worldwide albums, plus most single-country specialized albums; blank albums are generally for collectors with very specialized interests, or very advanced collectors who wish to design their own albums.

Worldwide albums can range in size and comprehensiveness from the very smallest beginner's album costing about $10.00 to the huge 50+ Volume International, costing more than $10,000.00. The larger the album, of course, the more complete it will be, but all worldwide albums, regardless of size, are by necessity abridged to a degree. To be truly complete, an album would have to include every stamp ever issued by every country in the world since Great Britain issued the first adhesive postage stamp, the famous "Penny Black," back in 1840. This would not only require many, many volumes, but would also mean providing spaces for many rare stamps which are today essentially unobtainable to all but the very wealthiest collectors – if they are obtainable at all. The most popular worldwide albums today are those which concentrate on the easily obtainable low- and medium-priced stamps which the average collector is most likely to have in abundance.

Specialized albums concentrate on stamps from specific areas – individual countries, like the United States or France, or groups of countries, like the British Commonwealth; individual topics, like sports, space, or flowers; and individual types of issues, like airmails, special deliveries, or postage dues. Individual country albums usually have spaced and illustrated pages; other specialty albums usually have blank pages with simple titles.

Some excellent examples of specialized single-country albums, all loose-leaf, are pictured here. The U.S. Liberty Album is 100% illustrated and virtually complete for issues of the United States and Confederate States. It includes not only regular postage and airmails, but also special deliveries, postage dues, hunting stamps, revenues, and more. For beginning U.S. collectors, the Patriot Album offers a selection of most U.S. commemorative and regular issues a collector would easily find. The 3-Volume U.S. Plate Block Album is 100% illustrated and is specifically designed for collectors of United States plate blocks.

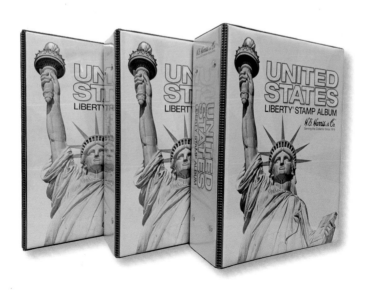

Blank albums are primarily for collectors who cannot find exactly what they want in a standard ruled-space album, or who want to arrange their stamps themselves, rather than mount them according to a pre-arranged order or pattern. They are particularly suitable for topical collectors.

The pages themselves may be entirely blank, or they may have a faint blue or gray quadrille-type ruled background, to help the collector arrange the stamps in a balanced pattern. The ruling may be standard 1/4 -,1/5-, or 1/8-inch squares; also available are the Harris "Speed-rille" ruled pages, which have faint gray lines dividing the pages into various equal sections – fifths, sixths, sevenths, etc. – to make it easier to evenly space out a row of stamps.

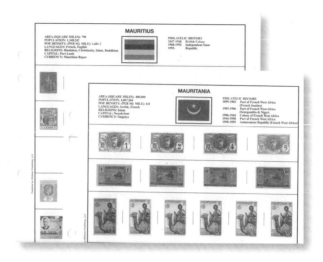

Often, the pages will also have decorative ruled borders, and may come with separate printed titles which are gummed and may be affixed to the pages as the collector desires. In the case of blank albums designed for specific topics or countries, the pages may not only have decorative ruled borders, they may also have fancy titles and illustrations.

Blank albums for topical collections will usually come in matched sets of binder and pages, with extra pages available separately; but you can also select a binder and pages separately, to suit your own tastes. There is a wide variety of binders available, in different sizes and of different constructions, as well as many different styles and sizes of blank pages.

If you decide to mount your collection in a blank album, some accessories you may find helpful are: stamp positioner to help you space out your stamps on non-ruled pages; stencil guides, for writing descriptive captions for the stamps; and decorative gummed flags of various countries and states, to add a colorfully attractive touch to your blank pages.

Special albums are also available for collectors of first day covers and mint sheets. Cover albums have cover-sized transparent plastic pockets into which the covers are slipped, while mint sheet albums have whole pages made of sheets of plastic, open at the top and one side, and closed at the bottom and the binder side, so the sheets can easily be inserted and removed, yet will not fall out.

Most of the larger stamp companies today produce large, highly illustrated supply catalogs and would be pleased to send you their latest catalog.

THE
UNITED STATES
Stamp Identifier

SHOWS YOU HOW TO DISTINGUISH BETWEEN THE RARE AND COMMON UNITED STATES STAMPS THAT LOOK ALIKE

What does " Grill with points up" mean? "Single line watermark?" How can I tell whether my 15¢ "Landing of Columbus" stamp of 1869 is worth $3,250.00 (Type I), $975.00 (Type II), or the newly discovered Type III.

At one time or another, every collector of United States stamps ask questions like these. For very often, it is a minute difference in design that deteremines not only whether a stamp is Type I, II, or III, but whether it is a great rarity or just another common variety. The different varieties of the 1¢ Franklin design of 1851-56, for example, range in price from $95.00 to $69,000.00. So it pays to know

how to tell the correct types of your stamps! To enable you to do so easily and quickly is the purpose of this U.S. STAMP INDENTIFIER.

Other seemingly identical but different United States stamps may be told apart by differences in perforations, watermarks, grills, or methods in printing. These terms are fully explained in the glossary of terms section in this book. Charts are included to make it easy for you to quickly identifiy the many Bank Note varieties and the most troublesome of U.S stamps — the hard-to-classify regular issues of 1908 to 1923.

Scott catalogue numbers are from the Standard Postage Stamp Catalogue, by special permission of the publishers, Amos Press Inc.

FIRST UNITED STATES POSTAGE ISSUE OF 1847

#1

#1,3

#2,4

#2

#3

#4

The first stamps of the United States Government, the 5¢ and 10¢ designs were placed in use in July 1847, superseding the Postmasters' Provisionals then being used in several cities. In 1875, official reproductions (#3 and #4) were made from newly engraved printing plates.

In the original 5¢ design, the top edge of Franklin's shirt touches the circular frame about at a level with the top of the "F" of "FIVE", while in the 1875 reproduction it is on a level with the top of the figure "5."

In the original 10¢ design, the left edge of Washington's coat points to the "T" of "TEN," and the right edge points between the "T" and "S" of

"CENTS." In the reproductions, the left and right outlines of the coat point to the right edge of "X" and to the the center of "S" in "CENTS" respectively. Also, on the 1875 reprints, the eyes have a sleepy look and the line of the mouth is straighter.

The 1947 "Cipex" Souvenir Sheet, issued on the hundredth anniversary of United States stamps, features reproductions of the two original designs. Stamps cut out of souvenir sheet are, of course, valid for postage. However, no difficulty in identification should be encountered since the 1947 reproductions are light blue (5¢) instead of the original red brown and brownish orange (10¢) instead of the original black.

TYPES OF THE 1¢ FRANKLIN DESIGN OF 1851-60

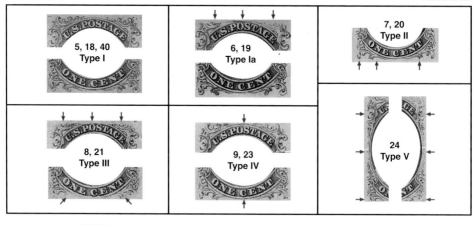

TYPE I has the most complete design of the various types of stamps. At the top and bottom there is an unbroken curved line running outside the bands reading "U.S. POSTAGE" and "ONE CENT". The scrolls at bottom are turned under, forming curls. The scrolls and outer line at top are complete.

TYPE Ia is like Type I at bottom but ornaments and curved line at top are partly cut away.

TYPE Ib (not illustrated) is like Type I at top but little curls at bottom are not quite so complete nor clear and scroll work is partly cut away.

TYPE II has the outside bottom line complete, but the little curls of the bottom scroll, and the lower part of the plume ornaments are missing. Side ornaments are complete.

TYPE III has the outside lines at both top and bottom partly cut away in the middle. The side ormaments are complete.

TYPE IIIa (not illustrated) is similar to Type III with the outer line cut away at top or bottom, but not both.

TYPE IV is similar to Type II but the curved lines at top or bottom (or both) have been recut in several different ways, and usually appear thicker than Type II.

TYPE V is similar to Type III but has the side ormaments partly cut away. Type V occurs only on perforated stamps.

TYPES OF 3¢ WASHINGTON DESIGN OF 1851-60

10, 11, 25, 41
Type I

26
Type III

Type IV

TYPE I has a frame line around the top, bottom and sides.

TYPE II (not illustrated) is like Type I, but with the inner lines at the sides added by recutting on the plate.

TYPE III has the frame line removed at top and bottom, while the side frame lines are continuous from the top to bottom of the plate.

TYPE IV is similar to Type III, but the side frame lines were recut individually, and therefore are broken between stamps.

TYPES OF THE 5¢ JEFFERSON DESIGN OF 1851-60

Type I

Type II

TYPE I is a complete design with projections (arrow) at the top and bottom as well as at the sides.

TYPE II has the projections at the top or bottom partly or completely cut away.

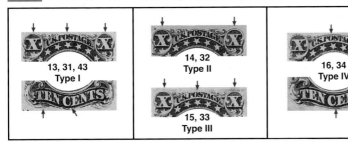

13, 31, 43
Type I

14, 32
Type II

16, 34
Type IV

15, 33
Type III

35
Type V

TYPE I has the "shells" at the lower corners practically complete, while the outer line below "TEN CENTS" is very nearly complete. At the top, the outer lines above "U.S. POSTAGE" above the "X" in each corner are broken.

TYPE II has the design complete at the top, but the outer line at the bottom is broken in the middle and the "shells" are partially cut away.

TYPE III has both top and bottom outer lines cut away; similar to Type I at the top and Type II at the bottom.

TYPE IV has the outer lines at the top or bottom of the stamp, or at both place, recut to show more strongly and heavily.

Types I, II, III and IV have complete ornaments at the sides and three small circles or pearls (arrow) at the outer edges of the bottom panel.

TYPE V has the side ornaments, including one or two of the small "pearls" partly cut away. Also, the outside line, over the "X" at the right top, has been partly cut away.

Types of the 12¢ Washington Issues of 1851-60

Plate 1

Plate 3

1875 Reprint

PLATE 1 has stronger, more complete outer frame lines than does Plate 3. Comes imperforate (#17 or perf #36).

PLATE 3 has uneven or broken outer frame lines that are particularly noticeable in the corners. The stamps are perf 15. (#36b)

1875 REPRINT plate is similar to plate 1, but the reprint stamps are greenish black and slightly taller than plate 1 stamps (25mm from top to bottom frame lines versus 24.5 mm). The paper is whiter and the perforations are 12 gauge.

TYPES OF THE 1861 ISSUE, GRILLS & RE-ISSUES

Shortly after the outbreak of the Civil War in 1861, the Post Office demonitized all stamps issued up to that time in order to prevent their use by the Confederacy. Two new sets of designs, consisting of six stamps shown above plus 24¢ and 30¢ denominations, were prepared by the American Bank Note Company. The first designs, except for the 10¢ and 24¢ values, were not regularly issued and are extremely rare and valuable. The second designs became the regular issue of 1861.

The illustrations on the following page show the first (or unissued) designs, which were all printed on thin, semi-transparent paper, as well as the second (or regular) designs. #55-62 are now considered to be essays or trial color proofs.

43

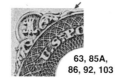

55

63, 85A, 86, 92, 103

63 shows a small dash (arrow) under the tip of the ornaments at the right of the figure "1" in the upper left-hand corner of the stamp.

56

64-66,79, 82, 83, 85, 85C, 88, 94, 104

64, 66, etc., 3¢ value, shows a small ball (arrow) at each corner of the design. Also, the ornaments at the corners are larger than in the first design.

3¢ 1861 PINK (Scott #64) — It is impossible to describe a "pink" in words, but it might be helpful to remember that this stamp is usually rather heavily inked, and has a tinge of blue or purple which makes it stand out from the various shaded of rose to red brown for which it is sometimes mistaken.

57

67, 75, 76, 80, 95, 105

64, 75, etc., 5¢ value has a leaflet (arrow) projecting from the scrolled ornaments at each corner of the stamp.

58, 62B

58, 62B has no curved line below the row of stars and there is only one outer line of the ornaments above them.

68, 85D, 89, 96, 106

68/106 have a heavy curved line below the row of stars (arrow); ornaments above the stars have double outer line.

59

69, 85E, 90, 97, 107

59 has rounded corners. **69/107** has a oval and a scroll (arrow)in each corner of the design.

62

62 does not have the row of dashes or spot of color present in **72/111**

72, 101, 111

72/111 have a row of small dashes between the parallel lines of the angle at the top center of the stamp. There is also a spot of color (arrow) in the apex of the lower line of the single.

TYPES OF THE 15¢ "LANDING OF COLUMBUS" DESIGN OF 1869

118: Type I

119:Type II

118-119
Type I, II

129
Type III

118, TYPE I has the central picture without the frame line shown in Type II.

119, TYPE II has a frame line (arrows) around the central picture: also a diamond shaped ornament appears below the "T" of "Postage".

129, TYPE III is like Type I except that the fringe of brown shading lines which appears around the sides and bottom of the picture on Types I and II has been removed.

44

Description and Identifying Features	1¢	2¢	3¢	5¢	10¢	12¢	15¢	24¢	30¢	90¢
1861. National. First designs. Thin, semi-transparent paper. No grill.	55^4		56^4	57^4	58^1 $62B^4$	59^4		60^4	61^4	62^4
1861-62. National. Modified designs³. Thicker, opaque paper. No grill.	63		64^2, 65^2 66^2	67	68	69		70^2	71	72
1861-66. National. Thicker, opaque paper. No grill. a. New designs.		73					77			
b. Same designs, new shades.			74^2	75^2, 76^2				78^2		

1867. National. Grills. All on thick, opaque paper.

Grills	Pts. as seen from stamp face	Area of covered Horiz. x Vert.	# of rows of Pts.	1¢	2¢	3¢	5¢	10¢	12¢	15¢	24¢	30¢	90¢
A	Up	All over	—					79	80			81	
B	Up	18 x 15 mm	22 x 18				82						
C	Up	c. 13 x 16 mm	16-17 x 18-21				83						
D	Down	c. 12 x 14 mm	15 x 17-18			84	85						
Z	Down	c. 11 x 14 mm	13-14 x 17-18	85A	85B	85C		85D	85E	85F			
E	Down	c. 11 x 13 mm	14 x 15-17	86		87	88	89	90	91			
F	Down	c. 9 x 13 mm	11-12 x 15-17	92	93	94	95	96	97	98	99	100	101

Description	1¢	2¢	3¢	5¢	10¢	12¢	15¢	24¢	30¢	90¢
1875. National. Re-issues. Hard, white paper. White crackly gum. No grill.	102	103	104	105	106	107	108	109	110	111

FOOTNOTES:
1. 58 does not exist used. Unused, it cannot be distinguished from 62B.
2. Different from corresponding 1861-66 issues only in color.
3. See diagrams for design modification.
4. 1861 National first designs are now considered to be essays or trial color proofs. (55-62)

The stamps of the 1870-71 issue were printed by the National Bank Note Company. The similar issue of 1873 was printed by the Continental Bank Note Company. When Continental took over the plate previously used by National, they applied so called "secret marks" to the design of the 1¢ through 15¢ denominations by which the two issues can be distinguished as shown below. The illustrations at the left show the original designs of 1870-71; those at the right show the secret marks applied to the issue of 1873.

ISSUE OF 1870-71	ISSUE OF 1873-87	ISSUE OF 1870-71	ISSUE OF 1873-87

134, 145	**156, 167, 182, 192**	**135, 146**	**157, 158, 178, 180, 183, 193, 203**
156/192 has a small curved mark in the pearl at the left of the figure "1".		**135** and **146** are red brown. 157 and later numbers have a small diagonal line under the scroll at the left of the "U.S." (arrow). 135, 146, 157, 168, and 193 are various shades of brown. 178, 180, 183, and 203 are shades of vermilion.	

134, 145 _(138, 149)_	**160, 171, 196**	**139, 150, 187**	**161, 172, 188, 197**

136, 147	**158, 169, 184, 194**	**137, 148**	**159, 170, 186, 195**
158 and later numbers have a heavily shaded ribbon under the letters "RE".		**159** and later numbers have the first four vertical lines of shading in the lower part of the left ribbon greatly strengthened.	

138, 149	**160, 171, 196**	**139, 150, 187**	**161, 172, 188, 197**
160 and later numbers have two tiny semicircles drawn around the end of the lines which outline the ball in the lower right-hand corner.		**161, 172, 188,** and **197** have a small semicircle in the scroll at the right-hand side of the central design.	
140, 151	**162, 173, 198**	**141, 152**	**163, 174, 189, 199**
162 and later numbers have the "balls" at the top and bottom on the figure "2" crescent-shaped (right) instead of nearly round as in **140** and **151**.		**163** and later numbers have strenghtened lines (arrow) in the triangle in the upper left-hand corner, forming a "V".	

46

The 1¢, 3¢, 6¢, and 10¢ denominations of the 1873 & 1897 issues, shown above were re-engraved in 1881-82. The new plates resulted in four variations described below. The background shading lines in all four of these stamps appear stronger and more heavily inked than in the earlier designs.

1¢

206

6¢

208

206 has strengthened vertical shading lines in the upper part of the stamp, making the background appear almost solid. Lines of shading have also been added to the curving ornaments in the upper corners.

208 has only three vertical lines between the edge of the panel and the outside left margin of the stamp. (In the preceding issues, there were four such lines.)

207, 214

10¢

209

207 and 214 has a solid shading line at the sides of the central oval (arrow) that is only about half the previous width. Also a short horizontal line has been cut below the "TS" of "CENTS". **207** and **214** can be told apart by their colors.

209 has only four vertical lines between the left side of the oval and the edge of the shield. (In the preceding issues there were five such lines.) Also, the lines in the background have been made much heavier so that these stamps appear more heavily linked than previous issues.

TYPES OF TH REGULAR ISSUES OF 1890-98

1890-93. This issues, printed by the American Bank Noted Company, consists of a 1¢, 2¢, 3¢, 4¢, 5¢, 6¢, 8¢, 10¢, 15¢, 30¢, and 90¢ denominations.

1894-98. This issue — and all subsequent regular United States issues — were printed by the Bureau of Engraved and Printing, Washington, D.C. In more recent years, starting in 1943, some commemorative issues were printed by priviate firms. The 1894-98 "Bureau" issue is similar in design to the issue of 1890 but triangle (arrows) were added to the upper corners of the stamps and there are some differences in denominations.

2¢ "CAP OF 2" VARIETY OF 1890

Plate defects in the printing of the 2¢ "Washington" stamp of 1890 accounts for the "Cap of left 2" and "Cap on both 2s" varieties illustrated.

Cap on left "2"

Cap on right "2"

47

IDENTIFIER CHART
1870-1887 Bank Notes

Description and Identifying Features	1¢	2¢	3¢	5¢	6¢	7¢	10¢	12¢	15¢	21¢	30¢	90¢
1870-71. National. No secret marks. White wove paper, thin to medium thick. With grills.	134	135	136		137	138	139	140	141	142	143	144
1870-71. National. As above, except without grills.	145	146	147		148	149	150	151	152	153	154[2]	155[2]
1873. Continental. White wove paper, thin to thick. No grills. a. With secret marks.	156	157	158		159	160	161	162	163			
b. No secret marks.											165[2]	166[2]
1875. Continental. Special Printing. Same designs as 1873 Continental. Hard, white wove paper. No gum.	167	168	169		170	171	172	173	174	175	176	177
1875. Continenal. New color or denomination. Hard yellowish, wove paper.		178		179								
1875. Continental. Special printing. Same designs as 1875 Continental. Hard, white wove paper. No gum.		180		181								
1879. American. Same designs as 1873-75. Continental. Soft, porous paper.	182	183[3]	184[3]	185	186[3]		188		189[3]		190[3]	191[3]
a. Without secret mark.							187[3]					
1880. American. Special printing. Same as 1879 issue. Soft, porous paper. No gum.	192	193 203[3]	194[3]	204	195[3]	196	197[3]	198	199[3]	200	201[3]	202[3]
1881-82. American. Designs of 1873. Re-engraved[4]. Soft, porous paper.	206		207[5]		208		209					
1887. American. Same designs as 1881-82. New colors.		214[5]									217	218

FOOTNOTES:

1. See diagrams for secret marks.
2. Corresponding denominations differ from each other only in color.
3. Corresponding denominations differ from each other only in color and gum. The special printings are slightly deeper and richer. The lack of gum is not positive identifier because it can be washed from the 1879 issues.
4. See diagrams for re-engravings.
5. Corresponding denominations differ from each other in color.

TYPE OF THE
2¢ WASHINGTON DESIGN
OF 1894-98

The triangles in the upper right and left corners of the stamp determine this type.

248-250, 265
Type I

251, 266
Type II

252, 267, 279B
Type III

TYPE I has horizontal lines of the same thickness within and without the triangle.

TYPE II has horizontal lines which cross the triangle but are thinner within it than without.

TYPE III has thin lines inside the triangle and these do not cross the double frame line of the triangle.

10¢ WEBSTER DESIGN
OF 1898

282C
Type I

283
Type II

TYPE I has an unbroken white curved line below the words "TEN CENTS".

TYPE II shows white line is broken by ornaments at a point just below the "E" in "TEN" and the "T" in "CENTS" (arrows).

$1 PERRY DESIGN OF 1894-95

261, 276
Type I

261A, 276A
Type II

TYPE I shows circles around the "$1" are broken at point where they meet the curved line below "ONE DOLLAR" (arrows).

TYPE II shows these circles complete.

2¢ COLUMBIAN
"BROKEN HAT" VARIETY OF 1893

As a result of a plate defect, some stamps of the 2¢ Columbian design show a noticeable white notch or gash in the hat worn by the third figure to the left of Columbus. This "broken hat" variety is somewhat less common than the regular 2¢ design.

231

Broken Hat variety,
231c

4¢ COLUMBIAN BLUE ERROR

Collectors often mistake the many shades of the normal 4¢ ultramarine for the rare and valuable blue error. Actually, the "error" is not ultramarine at all, but a deep blue, similar to the deeper blue shades of the 1¢ Columbian.

2¢ WASHINGTON ISSUE OF 1903

319, 319g, 320
Die I

319f, 320a
Die II

The rounded inner frame line below and to the left "T" in "TWO" has a dark patch of color that narrows, but remains strong across the bottom.

Perforation	Watermark	Other Identifying Features	1¢	2¢	1¢	2¢	3¢ thru $1 denominations	8¢ thru $1 denominations
PERF. 12	USPS	White paper	331	332			333-42	422-23
	USPS	Bluish gray paper	357	358			359-66	
	USPS	White paper	374	375	405	406	376-82, 407	414-21
COIL 12	USPS	Perf. Horizontal	348	349			350-51	
	USPS	Perf. Vertical	352	353			354-56	
	USPS	Perf. Horizontal	385	386				
	USPS	Perf. Vertical	387	388			389	
IMPERF.	USPS		343	344			345-47	
	USPS	Flat Plate	383	384	408	409		
	USPS	Rotary Press				459		
	Unwmkd.	Flat Plate			481	482-82A	483-85	
	Unwmkd.	Offset			531	532-34B	535	
COIL 8-1/2	USPS	Perf. Horizontal	390	391	410	411		
	USPS	Perf. Vertical	392	393	412	413	394-96	
PERF. 10	USPS							460
	USPS				424	425	426-30	431-40
	Unwmkd.	Flat Plate			462	463	464-69	470-78
	Unwmkd.	Rotary Press			543			
COIL 10	USPS	Perf. Horizontal — Flat		441	442			
	USPS	Perf. Horizontal — Rotary		448	449-50			
	USPS	Perf. Vertical — Flat			443	444	445-47	
	USPS	Perf. Vertical — Rotary			452	453-55	456-58	
	Unwmkd.	Perf. Horizontal			486	487-88	489	
	Unwmkd.	Perf. Vertical			490	491-92	493-96	497
PERF. 11	USPS			519				
	USPS					461		
	Unwmkd.	Flat Plate			498	499-500	501-07	508-18
	Unwmkd.	Rotary Press			*544-45	546		
	Unwmkd.	Offset			525	526-28B	529-30	
Perf. 12-1/2	Unwkmd.	Offset			536			
11 x 10	Unwkmd.	Rotary			538	539-40	541	
10 x 11	Unwkmd.	Rotary			542			

* Design of #544 is 19mm wide x 22-1/2mm high. #545 is 19-1/2 to 20mm wide x 22mm high.

Size of Flat Plate Design
22mm
18-1/2 to 19mm

Stamps printed by rotary press are always slightly wider or taller on issues prior to 1954. Measurements do not apply to booklet singles.

HOW TO USE THIS IDENTIFICATION CHART

Numbers referred to herein are from Scott's Standard Postage Stamp Catalog. To identify any stamp in this series, first check the type by comparing it with the illustrations at the top of the chart. Then check the perforations, and whether the stamp is single or double line watermarked or unwatermarked. With this information you can quickly find out the Standard Catalog number by checking down and across the chart. For example, a 1¢ Franklin, perf. 12, single line watermark, must be Scott's #374.

During the year 1912 through 1920, the 2¢ Washington design pictured below was issued and re-issued with slight variations which give rise to the many different types of this stamp. Certain of these types, as you will see by consulting the price in this catalog, are far more valuable than others. The several variations in actual design are pictured and described below. For perforation, watermark, and printing variations, see the handy identification chart on the preceding page.

Between 406 and 499
Type I

Type I where the ribbon at left above the figure "2" has one shading line in the first curve, while the ribbon at the right has one shading line in the second curve. Bottom of toga has a faint outline. Top line of toga, from bottom to front of throat, is very faint. Shading lines of the face, terminating in front of the ear, are not joined. Type I occurs on both flat and rotary press printings.

482A, 500
Type Ia

Type Ia is similar to Type I except that all of the lines are stronger. Lines of the Toga button are heavy. Occurs only on flat press printings.

454, 487, 491, 539
Type II

Type II has ribbons shaded as in Type I. Toga button and shading lines to left of it are heavy. Shading lines in front of ear are joined and end in a strong vertically curved line (arrow). Occurs only on rotary press printings.

450, 488, 492, 540, 546
Type III

Type III where ribbons are shaded with two lines instead of one; otherwise similar to Type II. Occurs on rotary press printings only.

526, 532
Type IV

Type IV where top line of toga is broken. Shading lines inside the toga bottom read "Did". The Line of color in the left "2" is very thin and usually broken. Occurs on offset printings only.

527, 533
Type V

Type V in which top line of toga is complete. Toga button has five vertical shaded lines. Line of color in the left "2" is very thin and usually broken. Nose shaded as shown in illustration. Occurs on offset printings only.

528-534
Type Va

Type Va is same as Type V except in shading dots of nose. Third row of dots from bottom has four dots instead of six. Also, the Overall height of Type Va is 1/3 millimeter less than Type V. Occurs on offset printings only.

528A, 534A
Type VI

Type VI is same as Type V except that the line of color in left "2" is very heavy (arrow). Occurs in offset printings only.

528B, 534B
Type VII

Type VII in which line of color in left "2" is clear and continuous and heavier than Types V or Va, but not as heavy as in Type VI. There are three rows of vertical dots (instead of two) in the shading of the upper lip, and additional dots have been added to hair at top of the head. Occurs on offset printings only.

51

Between 333 and 501
Type I

484, 494, 502, 541
Type II

TYPE I in which the top line of the toga is weak, as are the top parts of the shading lines that join the toga line. The fifth shading line from the left (arrow) is partly cut away at the top. Also the line between the lips is thin. Occurs on flat and rotary press printings.

TYPE II where top line of toga is strong and the shading lines that join it are heavy and complete. The line between the lips is heavy. Occurs on flat and rotary press printings.

529
Type III

530, 535
Type IV

TYPE III in which top line of toga is strong, but the fifth shading line from the left (arrow) is missing. The center line of the toga button consists of two short vertical lines with a dot between them. The "P" and "O" of "POSTAGE" are separated by a small line of color. Occurs on offset printings only.

TYPE IV in which the shading lines of the toga are complete. The center line of the toga button consists of a single unbroken vertical line running through the dot in the center. The "P" and the "O" of "POSTAGE" are joined. Type IV occurs only in offset printings.

TYPES OF THE 2¢ WASHINGTON DESIGN OF 1922-29

Between 554 and 634
Type I

TYPE I has thin hair lines at the top center of head.

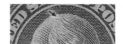

599A, 634A
Type II

TYPE II has three heavy hair lines (arrow) at top.

TYPES OF THE 15¢ OLIVER WENDELL HOLMES DESIGN

1288, 1305E
Original

1288d, 1305Ei
Revised

1288B
Booklet

ORIGINAL has the vertical bar of the "¢" symbol pointing to the left part of the "E" in "POSTAGE." In the necktie area, there are complete downward sloping hatch lines which touch the right-hand side of the tie.

REVISED has the vertical bar of the "¢" symbol pointing to the center of the "E" in "POSTAGE." In the tie, the downward sloping hatch lines are almost eliminated, while the lines angling upward do not touch the lower right-hand side of the tie. The third line from the bottom is very short, leaving a colorless spot.

BOOKLET SINGLE has the vertical bar of the "¢" symbol pointing more toward the "G" in "POSTAGE." The necktie is 4-1/2 milimeters long and is straightened down the center of the rob. The overall design size is smaller both vertically and horizontally. All copies have at least one straight edge.

THE STAMP COLLECTING PYRAMID

How do you begin separating your stamps and putting them where they belong in your album? The answer is in the stamp collecting pyramid – it contains the tools and procedure you need to build a collection that will give you a lifetime of fun, knowledge, and satisfaction.

THE TOOLS

The most basic tools of collecting are stamp albums and they have been designed to fit specific levels of collecting.

Beginning albums contain only a selected number of stamps that were issued by any given country. These stamps are usually very common and easily obtainable.

Intermediate albums contain a larger percentage of the total number of stamps that have been issued by any given country and usually provide spaces for both common and harder to obtain stamps.

Advanced albums provide spaces for the majority of stamps issued by a country and spaces for all but the rarer issues.

Comprehensive albums provide spaces for virtually every stamp issued by a particular country and provide spaces for many extremely rare issues.

IDENTIFICATION TOOLS

These are the basic tools one needs to properly handle and identify stamps that form the foundation of the collecting pyramid:

Stamp Tongs: used to pick up and handle stamps. Their proper use will keep you from bending, tearing, or disturbing the gum on your stamps.

Perforation Gauge: used to measure the various distances between the holes punched around stamps to make their separation easier.

Watermark Tray & Fluid: used to distinguish between the types of paper on which some stamps have been printed.

Magnifying Glass: used to observe small engraving marks that distinguish between stamps with the same general appearance.

IDENTIFICATION

You now have all the essential tools and it's time to identify the building blocks of the pyramid: your stamps. Here is a procedure for you to follow.

1. Identify the country of issue

2. Identify the denomination and date of issue

3. Measure the perforations

4. Find a watermark (if any)

5. Look for distinguishing marks (if any)

Note: On difficult to identify stamps, the denomination can sometimes help you narrow the search for issue date, as postal rates tended to stay stable.

To identify the easier stamps, you may only need to look at them. Look for the country and any dates – usually the latest date is the date of issue. With this information, you can go directly to the appropriate space in your album. (Note: In beginning albums, not all stamps are illustrated but you can still place them in their logical date of issue position.)

Stamps that are harder to identify will have the country plainly visible, yet no date as a reference. In this case go to your catalog and look for a picture that matches your stamp. The catalog will list the catalog number and date of issue. With this information you can go to the appropriate place in your album.

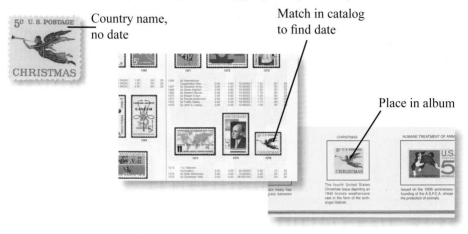

Country name, no date

Match in catalog to find date

Place in album

Difficult to identify stamps include stamps that look alike but may have different perforations, watermarks, or special markings. To identify these stamps, you must first gather information using your stamp collecting tools.

Perforations: To measure the perforations of a stamp place it on a perf gauge as shown below. Be sure the perf gauge lines up properly or you will have a wrong piece of information. Remember to measure the perfs both across (horizontal) and up and down (vertical) – they can be different measurements.

Correct Reading

(Perf. 11.5) All in line

Wrong Reading

(Not perf. 11.25) Out of line

Watermarks: Place the stamp face down in a black watermark tray. Place a few drops of watermark fluid on the stamp – observe and note what you see.

Watermark

Special markings: Some stamps that look alike have only slight line or "secret mark" differences. Refer to the identification section of your catalog.

Once you have gathered this information, match your stamp with the pictures in the catalog. When you find a match, look for the catalog numbers (in Harris) listed underneath illustration or (in Scott) under description type. These are all the possible varieties. Match you list against each catalog number until you find a match.

Scott's
Catalog

H.E. Harris
Catalog

This should enable you to identify even the most difficult stamps.

The more stamps you try to identify the easier it becomes. Don't get disappointed – it takes thinking, observing, and practice. The reward is the satisfaction of building your collection block by block. It's a hobby that can be enjoyed for a lifetime.

GLOSSARY OF TERMS COMMONLY USED IN IDENTIFYING U.S. STAMPS

BOOKLET PANES are small sheets of stamps sold by the Post Office in booklet form. United States postage and airmail booklets can consist of 5 stamps up to 20 stamps per pane. Booklet panes are usually collected unused, with the tab, or binding edge, attached. On recent self-adhesive issues, stamps can be found on both sides of the booklet.

COIL STAMPS are stamps which come in long rolled strips, especially for use in vending machines, automatic affixing machines, etc. They have straight edges on two opposite sides and perforated edges on the other two sides. If the straight edges run up and down, the stamps are called "endwise coils"; if they run from side to side, they are called "sidewise coils". Coils are generally collected in singles or pairs. They are also collected in Line Pairs with a "line" separating the two stamps. More recent issues also have a plate number under every 20-25 stamps – these are collected in strips of 3 or 5 with the number under the center stamp. These are called *Plate Number Coils.*

GRILLS are raised impressions made in a stamp by pointed metal rollers, resembling the impressions made in a waffle by a waffle iron. The theory behind the grills used on the United States postage issues of 1867-71 was that the cancelling ink would soak into the broken fibers of the paper, thus preventing the stamp from being washed clean and used over again. If the grill impression is made from behind, so that the points show on the face of the stamp, the grill is said to be "points up". If done the opposite way, the grill is said to be "points down". Grills are further classified as "Grill A", "Grill B", etc., according to the type and size of the grill marks on the stamp. It should be remembered that a complete grill is not always found on any one stamp. Major varieties with grills are 79-101, 112-122 and 134-144.

Regular Grill   *Continuous Marginal Grill*   *Split Grill*

PERFORATIONS around the edges of a stamp are measured by the number of perforation holes in a space of two centimeters, as "Perf. 11", "Perf 12", etc. This sounds complicated, but collectors use a simple measuring device called a *perforation gauge* which readily gives this information about any stamp. Where a stamp is identified by only one perforation number, it is perforated the same on all four sides; if two numbers are shown (e.g., Perf 11 x 10 1/2), the first number indicates the top and bottom; the second indicates the sides. (See also ***Die Cutting*** in the *Collector's Dictionary* on page 71.)

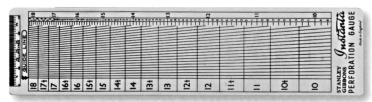

Perforation Gauge (Not Actual Size)

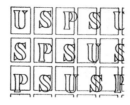

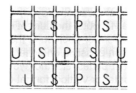

Double line watermark
PERIOD OF USE
Postage 1895-1910

Single line watermark
PERIOD OF USE
Postage 1910-1916

WATERMARKS are faint markings impressed into the paper during manufacture to help detect counterfeiting. Practically all United States postage stamps issued between the years 1895-1916 are watermarked "USPS" (United States Postal Service), either in single line or double line letters, as illustrated. Before 1895 and since 1916, all postage issues, except for Scott's #519 and some copies of the $1 "Presidential" – an error – are unwatermarked.

To see a watermark, place the stamp in a *watermark tray* and add a few drops of watermark fluid. The watermark – if there is one – will usually show clearly. From the illustrations it can be seen that frequently only a part of a letter will appear.

HOW TO DISTINGUISH BETWEEN
FLAT, ROTARY AND OFFSET PRINTINGS

FLAT PLATE means printed from flat metal plates or engravings.

Left: rotary press issue slightly taller than corresponding flat press design.

Right: rotary press stamp slightly wider than the same design printed from flat plates.

ROTARY PRESS means printed from plates that are curved to fit around a cylinder. In the curving process, the designs of the stamp stretch slightly in the direction that the plate is curved, so that rotary press stamps issued prior to 1954 are always either slightly wider or slightly taller than the same designs printed from flat plates. Also, on rotary printings, one or more ridges have been forced into the paper to keep it from curling, and these usually show across the back of a stamp. No such ridges are found in flat press stamps.

OFFSET is a method of printing in which the plate transfers or "offsets" the design onto a rubber blanket which, in turn, transfers it to the paper. On stamps printed from flat press or rotary press plates (that is, engraved stamps), a relatively large amount of ink is deposited on the paper, giving the stamps a "rough" feeling. If you run a fingernail or metal edge lightly across the lines on such stamps, you can actually feel the ridges of ink. Offset stamps, on the other hand, have a smooth or "soapy" feeling. The ink lies down uniformly on the surface of the paper, and no ridges can be felt.

SPECIAL PRINTINGS are reprints, either from the original or from new engravings, of stamps previously issued. They are usually printed in limited quantities and for specific purposes, and can almost always be distinguished from the originals by differences in color, perforations, gum, type of paper, etc. The largest single group – the Special Printings of 1875 – consist of a complete set of all designs issued up to that date. They were prepared for display by the government at the Philadelphia Centennial Exposition of 1876. Another good example of a Special Printing is the 1947 "CIPEX" souvenir sheet, shown below, which was printed as a souvenir of the Centenary International Philatelic Exposition held in New York in May 1947.

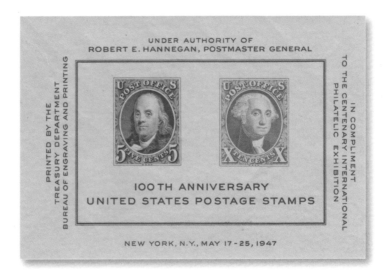

COLLECTOR'S DICTIONARY

Acknowledgment of Receipt Stamp. A stamp used to pay the extra fee that is sometimes required when the sender of a postal item requests a receipt, signed by the addressee, acknowledging the item's safe delivery.

Adhesives. All stamps intended to be affixed to postal matter, as distinguished from postage printed or hand-stamped directly on cards or covers.

Aerogramme. The official Universal Postal Union name for air lettersheets, which are usually carried for less than the normal airmail rates.

Aero-Philately. The collecting of airmail stamps and other airborne mail items; one of the most popular collecting specialties.

Air Cover. See *Flight* or *Flown Cover.*

Airmail. Postal matter carried by aircraft.

Airmail Stamp. A stamp intended specifically for use on airmail items.

Albino. The uncolored impression of a stamp (usually embossed on the envelope).

Aniline Inks. Extremely bright water-soluble inks derived from coal-tar. Used extensively in stamp printing because they are easily damaged by rubbing and run when wet, thus discouraging attempts to remove cancellations or other markings.

Approval Selections or **"Approvals".** Stamps sent by dealers to collectors, usually in sheets, books, envelopes, or cards, for free examination. The collector selects the stamps he wishes to purchase and returns the balance to the dealer along with his payment for the stamps he has kept. One of the easiest, quickest, and most popular ways to build a collection.

Arc or **Serrated Roulette.** A roulette in which the slit is curved in a semi-circle.

Arms Types. Stamps bearing coats-of-arms or other heraldic devices; a popular subject among typical collectors.

Arrow Block. A block of stamps containing the arrow-shaped markings used to guide the pane-separator and perforator.

"As is." A term used when selling stamps to indicate that there is no guarantee of condition. Such items should always be carefully inspected before buying, as they are usually non-returnable.

Auction. A public sale at which various lots of stamps are sold to the highest bidder. When the sale is an important one, an Auction Catalog describing the various lots is printed and distributed in advance, so collectors at distant points may submit bids on a stamp.

Backprint. Any printing on the back of a stamp.

Backstamp. A postmark applied to the back of an envelope to indicate the date of arrival at the post office of destination, the location of the post office, and sometimes the exact time of receipt.

Bank Mixture. Mixed stamps, usually still on paper, collected from the incoming mail of banks and other financial institutions. Usually, this is a reliable source of a wide range of foreign stamps.

Bantams. The name given to miniature stamps, especially the war-economy and war-tax issues of South Africa.

Bars. Bars or parallel lines are sometimes used to cancel stamps to indicate that they are invalid, especially in the case of government remainders. They may also be used to obliterate the face value or other details when overprinting.

Bicentennial. A two-hundredth anniversary or its celebration.

Bicolor. A stamp printed in two colors. See *Duty Plate.*

Bilingual. A stamp inscribed in two languages (Canada, Belgium, etc.).

Bilingual Pair. Two joined stamps identical to each other, except that the inscription is in a different language on each stamp (South Africa, South West Africa, etc.).

63

Bisect. A stamp cut in half vertically, horizontally, or diagonally to be used as two separate stamps, each equal to one-half the value of the whole stamp. Often used in emergencies when stamps of lower denominations are unavailable.

Block. Four or more unseparated stamps forming a square or rectangle; generally understood to consist of four stamps unless otherwise specified, as "block of six," etc.

Bogus Stamps. Imaginary stamps from real or imaginary countries, counterfeited and circulated by swindlers who hope unwary collectors will purchase them as genuine postal issues.

Booklets. Small convenient books containing stamps of one or more denominations. They are often sold through vending machines.

Booklet Pane. A block of stamps, usually six, which originally formed a page in one of the small booklets of stamps sold by the post office.

Border. The outer part or edge of a stamp design.

Bourse. An organized meeting of stamp dealers and/or collectors, at which stamps are sold or traded.

Branding. See *Perforated Initials*.

Broken or **Incomplete Set**. A group of stamps containing some, but not all, of the stamps in a particular issue or series.

"Bulls-Eye" or **"Socked-on-the-Nose."** A colloquialism used to indicate a stamp with a perfectly centered and completely legible postmark, usually one with a full town and date cancel.

Bureau Prints or **Precancels**. Stamps printed or precanceled at the United States Bureau of Engraving and Printing in Washington, D.C., where most U.S. issues have been printed since 1894.

Burelage. A pattern of fine dots or lines on the face (under the design) or back of a stamp to discourage removal of the cancellation or counterfeiting.

Burr. A raised bit of metal on an engraving plate, caused by the engraving tool. If it is not smoothed out or removed, a burr can appear on a sheet of stamps as a printing flaw.

Cachet. A picture, design, or inscription printed or rubber-stamped on an envelope to describe or explain the occasion on which the envelope was mailed, such as the first flight over a new airmail route, first day of issue of a new stamp, the event being commemorated by the new stamp, etc.

Canceled-to-Order or **C.T.O.** Canceled without having been used for postal purposes. Government remainders are often C.T.O. before sale to dealers, as are many speculative issues.

Cancellation. The ink mark or other defacement (cuts, holes, etc.) on a stamp to show that it has been used once and may not be used again.

Carrier's Stamps. Used in the United States from 1851-63 to pay the delivery fee on postal items from the postal receiving station to the addressee, or from one address to another within the same postal delivery zone, as during those years ordinary stamps only paid the postage from one post office to another.

Catalog Number. The identifying number assigned to each individual stamp of a country by the publisher of a postage stamp catalog.

Catalog Value. The value or "price" assigned to a stamp by the publisher of a postage stamp catalog, usually based on current market conditions.

Centenary or **Centennial.** A one-hundredth anniversary or its celebration.

Centering. The placement or location of a stamp design with reference to the piece of paper on which it is printed. If the design is squarely in the center, as shown by equal margins of paper on all sides, it is said to be perfectly centered. If one or more margins are much larger than the others, the stamp is said to be *Off-Center,* and is generally regarded as less desirable and valuable than a well-centered copy.

Center Line Blocks. Blocks of stamps with horizontal and vertical lines intersecting the middle of the block.

Centimeter or **cm.** A unit of measurement in the metric system. 2.54 centimeters equal one inch; 100 centimeters equal one meter.

Certified Mail. First class mail for which the sender is given a receipt certifying that the item has been mailed. If desired, a receipt signed by the addressee can also be requested, as proof of safe delivery. There is no compensation for loss of Certified Mail, thus distinguishing it from **Registered Mail.**

Chalky or **Coated Paper.** A highly surfaced chalk-coated paper designed to make it impossible to clean off the postmark without removing the stamp design; also used in some humid countries to prevent sheets of stamps from sticking together.

Charity Stamps. See *Semi-Postal Stamps.*

"Chop." Japanese characters overprinted, hand-stamped, or handwritten on stamps of territories occupied by Japanese troops during World War II; used until official Japanese occupation stamps became available.

Classic. A stamp, chiefly one issued before 1870, which has gained universal popularity and reputation through widespread philatelic acceptance.

Cleaned. In philately, the term implies that a stamp has had a cancellation or other marking removed for fraudulent re-use or resale as an unused item.

Coarse Perforation. A perforation with large holes and the teeth far apart.

Coil Line Pair. A pair of stamps from a rotary coil showing a colored line caused by a gap where the curved printing plate is joined. Coil line pairs are a favorite specialty item. Also called *Joint Line Pair* or *Line-Gap Pair.*

Coil Stamps. Stamps which are issued in long, coiled strips, especially for use in vending or affixing machines. Coil stamps have straight edges on two opposing sides, and perforations on the other two. If the straight edges run up and down, the stamps are called "vertical coils"; if they run from side to side, the stamps are called "horizontal coils."

Collateral Materials. Relevant literature and illustrations exhibited with a stamp display to provide additional background information about the stamps in the display.

Color Changeling. A stamp whose color has been altered, either accidentally or intentionally, by chemicals, heat, sunlight, or moisture.

Column. A complete vertical row of stamps from a sheet.

Comb Perforation. A perforation made by a machine which perforates three sides of each stamp in a row at the same time.

Combination Cover. A cover bearing stamps from two countries (*Mixed Postage*); necessary when mail travels between two non-U.P.U. nations. The first stamp pays postage within the country of origin, the second within the country of destination.

Commemorative Stamp. A stamp issued in remembrance of an event, or as a memorial to some person.

Complete Set. A group of stamps including all the stamps in a particular series or issue.

Compound Perforations. Perforations of two different measurements on the same stamp. A stamp, for example, which is Perf. 12 on the top and bottom, and Perf. 11 on the sides is described as Perf. 12 x 11. See *Perforations.*

Condition. The state of being, character, or quality of a stamp, as determined by centering, cancellation marks, cleanliness, etc. Generally recognized grades are: 1. Superb; 2. Very Fine; 3. Fine; 4. Average; 5. Second Grade; 6. Damaged.

Condominium. A territory ruled by more than one power. Condominium issues may be bilingual, or they may be separate issues of the same design, printed in different languages (Anglo-French New Hebrides, Anglo-Egyptian Sudan, etc.).

Constant. The term used to describe a minor variety which appears in the same place on the sheet throughout multiple printing runs of a stamp.

Control Mark. A letter or numeral placed in the sheet margin or overprinted on the front or back of a stamp for accounting purposes.

Copyright Block. Beginning in 1978, the U. S. Postal Service replaced the "Mail Early" slogan with the standard copyright inscription as seen in copyrighted publications, etc. This was a legal move to protect the design from copyright infringement. Copyright Blocks are collected as blocks of four.

Corner Block. A block of stamps originally located at one of the four corners of a sheet or pane of stamps and having intact sheet margins on two adjacent sides.

Counterfeit. See *Forgery*.

Counterfoil. Some European stamps, especially parcel post issues (Italy, San Marino, etc.), are printed in two parts, one to be affixed to the item being mailed, and the other, known as a counterfoil, being kept by the sender as a receipt.

Coupon. A postally invalid label or tag attached to a postage stamp, usually carrying a slogan, propaganda matter, or design related to the stamp.

Cover. A complete envelope or card with stamp(s) and cancellation intact.

"Crash" Cover. A cover which has been salvaged from a wreck or crash and delivered to the addressee, usually containing an official inscription explaining the delay.

Crease. A line or mark on a stamp, caused by folding or wrinkling.

Current. The term used to describe stamps which are presently available at the post office.

Cut Cancellation. A cancellation which cuts through the stamp.

Cut Close. A stamp –usually imperforate– with one or more edges trimmed close to the design, leaving an inadequate margin.

Cut Square or **Envelope Square Cut.** An embossed or printed envelope, post-card, wrapper, lettercard, or lettersheet stamp cut in a squared shape (allowing ample margin) from the entire piece for the sake of convenience. Cut squares are worth more than the same items cut to their exact shape but are not worth as much as the entire envelope or piece.

Dead Country. A country which no longer issues stamps, either because it has ceased to exist or because it has changed its name.

Dedication Covers. Covers that are mailed from a place where a special event has occurred such as inaugural covers.

Definitives. Stamps used for ordinary postage and kept in general circulation for a number of years, as distinguished from provisionals, commemoratives, or special purpose stamps. Also called *General* or *Regular Issues.*

Demonetized. A stamp is demonetized when it has been declared no longer postally valid by the issuing authority.

Denomination. The monetary and postal value of a stamp, as "1 cent," "2 shil-lings," etc.

Departmental Stamps. Official stamps intended for use by one particular govern-ment office alone.

Design. The printed portion of a stamp, as distinguished from the surrounding mar-gin of blank paper.

Diamond or **Lozenge Roulette.** A roulette in which the slits are X-shaped, thus creating a diamond-shaped space between them.

Die. The piece of metal or other material on which the original engraving of a stamp design is made. Multiple reproductions are then taken of the die and put together to form the plate used to print a complete sheet of stamps.

Die-cutting. A modern method of stamp separation where a die is created in a straight or wavy pattern. This method is used in the production of self-adhesive postage stamps.

Documentaries. Revenue stamps, formerly used on numerous types of documents (mortgages, wills, bills of lading, etc.) in payment of a government tax.

Double Impression or **Double Transfer.** The term used when a stamp shows a second impression of the design distinctly overlapping part or all of the first impression.

Dry Printing. A printing method developed in the United States in the 1950's, in which special inks and greater printing pressure allow the use of heavier, stiffer paper with a low moisture content, creating a whiter, high-sheen printing surface which makes the stamp design stand out sharply.

Dues. See *Postage Due Stamps*.

Dumb Cancellation. A postmark which gives neither the date nor the place of cancellation. The term "dumb" is also used to describe stamps which do not outwardly indicate the country or place of origin, and sometimes even the face value.

Duplex Cancellation. A cancellation given in two parts – a cancellation, and a postmark – to ensure the legibility of the date and place name on the postmark.

Duplicate. An additional copy of a stamp. Duplicates should be carefully examined to make sure they are not actually minor varieties.

Duty Plate. One of the two plates used in printing bi-colored stamps. The duty plate prints the changing part of the design, usually the value alone, but sometimes other elements as well. The unchanging part of the design is printed by the *Key Plate.*

Electrotype. A method of producing replicas of a die for printing, by applying a coating of copper to a mold taken from the die.

Elusive. The term given to a stamp which is not generally considered to be rare or scarce, but which nonetheless is hard to find.

Embossed stamps. Stamps in which part or all of the design is raised above the surface of the paper on which they are printed, most commonly used on pre-stamped envelopes.

Engraving. Method of printing using a metal plate into which the stamp design has been cut or etched.

Entire. A stamped envelope, wrapper, postcard, or other postal stationery in its entirety, as sold by the post office.

Envelope Stamp. A stamp printed directly on an envelope, as distinguished from the separately printed or "adhesive" stamp.

Errors. Stamps with wrong designs, colors, printing, paper, perforations, or over-printing, unwittingly issued by the post office.

Expertize. To make an expert examination of a stamp and render an opinion as to its genuineness.

Express. Special Delivery.

Face Value. The postal value of a stamp as indicated by the figures, words, or abbreviations in the design or surcharge.

Facsimile. An exact imitation or close likeness of a genuine stamp; often created so many collectors can have souvenir or specimen copies of a very rare stamp. Unlike forgeries, facsimiles are openly acknowledged as being only imitations (usually by an inscription on the back) and are not intended to deceive or defraud.

Fake. An originally genuine stamp that has been illegitimately altered by adding or removing perforations, surcharges, overprints, or cancellations, or by changing the color or the value, etc., to increase its philatelic value.

Fine Perforation. A perforation with small holes and the teeth close together.

First Day Cover. An envelope bearing a cancellation date representing the first day of issue of the stamp affixed thereon, and which is usually mailed from the postal station where the stamp was first put into circulation.

First Flight Cover. A cover carried on the inaugural flight over a new airmail route, or an extension of an existing route.

Fiscal. See *Revenue Stamps*.

Flat Plate. A stamp printed on a press with flat plates, as opposed to those printed on a rotary press with curved plates.

Flaw. See *Freak*.

Flight or **Flown Cover**. An airmail cover.

Forgery. An imitation of a genuine postage stamp, made with intent to deceive or defraud.

Format. The general physical characteristics of a stamp: size, shape, dimensions, etc.

Frame. The outer part or border of a stamp design.

Frank. A mark or label indicating that postage either has been paid or is free. Most often associated with government or military mail.

Freak. A stamp which shows a production flaw which is not a constant error, such as an ink smudge, a fold or crease in the paper, crooked or off-center perforations, etc. An inconstant minor variety.

Fugitive Inks. Generally aniline inks, used to discourage fakes, forgeries, and fraudulent erasures. They run when wet and become easily damaged by rubbing, so great care is necessary when dealing with such stamps.

General Collector. One who collects all kinds of stamps from different countries, as opposed to a *Specialist.*

General Issue. See *Definitive.*

Granite Paper. A type of safety paper, with tiny colored fibers running through it, to deter forgery.

Grill. A network of embossed or raised impressions made in a stamp by a metal roll with points. The grill is said to be "points up" if they show on the face of the stamp, and "points down" if they show on the back. Grilling was used on some early United States issues to help the stamp absorb the canceling inks, thus discouraging fraudulent cleaning.

Groundwork. The background of a stamp design, against which the principal subject is shown.

Guide Dots or **Lines**. Markings made on the printing plate to guide the pane-separator and perforator.

Gum. The adhesive coating on the backs of most unused, adhesive postage stamps.

Gutter. The space between panes on a sheet of stamps.

Handstamped. Stamped or canceled by hand, usually with a rubber stamp but sometimes hand-written, instead of by a machine.

Harrow Perforation. A perforation produced by a machine which perforates the entire sheet of stamps in one operation.

Heliogravure. An early type of photogravure still used in some countries for stamp printing.

Humidor or **"Stamplift."** A device used to remove stamps from paper without immersing them in water. The stamps are placed on a shelf above the water, then covered. The humidity slowly loosens the paper. Preferable to soaking, especially when dealing with old stamps or fugitive inks.

Hyphens. Rectangular-shaped perforations used on some stamps.

Imperforate or **"Imperf."** Printed without perforations.

Imprint Blocks. A block of stamps with a portion of the sheet margin bearing the printer's inscription, usually his name or initials, but sometimes technical data or other notations.

Inconstant. The term used to describe a minor variety which does not appear in the same place on the sheet through multiple printing runs of a stamp.

Inscription. The letters, characters, or words appearing on a stamp as an integral part of the overall design.

Inscription Block. A block of stamps bearing a marginal inscription relating either to the stamps or to general postal matters, such as "Use Zip Code" or "Mail Early in the Day."

Insured Mail. See *Registered Mail*.

Intaglio. Line-engraving, or recess-printing, so-called because the design is cut into the printing plate and thus is recessed below the surface of the plate. The ink which collects in the recessed design is then transferred to the paper. Line-engraved stamps are easily discernible by feeling with the fingers for the raised ridges caused by the ink making up the design.

Interleaves. Translucent tissue on thin plastic sheets placed between the pages of an album to prevent rubbing. Necessary in albums with stamps mounted on both sides of the pages.

Interrupted or **Syncopated Perforations.** Used by some countries on stamps intended for use in coil-vending machines. One or more of the hole punches in the perforation machine are removed leaving a paper "bridge" between the stamps for added strength.

Interverted. The term used to describe a pair of stamps, or a stamp and counterfoil or label, printed or cut in the wrong sequence.

Invalidated. No longer valid for postal use.

Invert. A stamp which has part of the design (usually the central portion) upside down in relation to the rest of the design.

Irregular Perforation. The term used when the perforations on any one side of a stamp are not evenly lined up, or are of different sizes, etc.

Issue. A stamp; also, a related series of stamps, released by a government post office at one time or during a certain period.

Journal Stamps. Stamps used to pay bulk postage and sometimes tax on newspapers, magazines, and other periodicals.

Jubilee. A 25th (silver), 50th (golden), 60th (diamond), or 70th (platinum) anniversary of a ruler's reign or a country's independence, usually the occasion for issuance of a commemorative set.

Key Plate. See *Duty Plate*.

Keytype. A stamp design used in two or more colonies, with only the name and sometimes the value being changed, either by using a different duty plate, or by overprinting. So-called because the common elements of the design are the ones on the key plate.

"Killer" Cancellation. A cancellation which is very heavy and/or covers most of the stamp, effectively disfiguring or obliterating the design.

Label Coupon. Also used as a disparaging term to describe stamps of dubious philatelic value, as many speculative issues.

Laid Paper. One of the two principal types of paper used for printing stamps. Distinguished by closely parallel horizontal and/or vertical lines created during the paper's manufacture.

Last Day Cancellation. A cancellation made at a discontinued post office on the last day of operation.

Late Fee Stamps. Stamps used to pay the additional postage which is sometimes required when an item is mailed after normal postal hours.

Letterpress. Typography, or relief-printing. The stamp design or a photograph of it (**Photoengraving**) is transferred onto a metal plate with a greasy ink; the rest of the plate is etched away, leaving only the raised design. Letterpress-printed stamps can be detected by an impression of the design "standing out" on the back, the result of the raised portions of the plate being pressed into the paper.

Lettersheet. A sheet of writing paper with a stamp already printed on it, so that the sheet can be folded, addressed, and mailed without the necessity for a separate envelope.

Line-Engraving. See *Intaglio*.

Line Pair. A pair of stamps showing a line of color between them, usually the guideline. See ***Coil Line Pair.***

Line Perforation. A perforation made by a machine which only perforates one line at a time.

Line Roulette. The most common type of roulette, consisting of ordinary straight slits.

Lithography. A flat-surface printing method in which the design is drawn, photographed (***Photolithography***) or otherwise transferred to a stone or metal plate, and fixed there via treatment with acid to accept a greasy ink, the rest of the plate being kept damp to reject the ink. Lithographed stamps are distinguished by their generally flat surface.

Local Stamps. Stamps issued for use only in a certain city, town, or district not good for postage elsewhere.

Local Precancels. Stamps intended for bulk mailings, precanceled at a local post office to speed mail processing.

Luminescent Stamps. Stamps treated with a phosphorescent substance (***Phosphor Tagged***) or printed on fluorescent paper or with fluorescent ink. Used with electronic machines to speed mail processing.

Maiden Voyage Covers. Covers transported on a ship's first voyage and so designated by a special postmark.

"Mail Early" Inscription Block. A block of U.S. stamps containing the "Mail Early in the Day" inscription on the sheet margin.

Major Varieties. Stamps differing in one or more major respects – design, color, denomination, shape, size, paper, perforations, watermarks, imprints, inscriptions, etc. – either in the same issue or in different issues.

Manuscript Cancellation. See *Pen Cancellation*.

Margin. The unprinted paper surrounding the design of a stamp; also, the blank paper bordering a sheet of stamps, sometimes called the *Selvedge.*

Marginal. The term used to describe a stamp taken from the extreme top, bottom, left, or right rows of stamps in a sheet, i.e., the rows which directly adjoin the sheet margins.

Master Plate. A printing plate kept as a "master" from which additional printing plates may be made.

Maximum Card. A pictorial postcard showing a stamp design or other subject, bearing either the stamp pictured or a stamp related to the design, and bearing a postmark related to the stamp or subject.

Memorials. Stamps issued to honor prominent persons. The U.S. by policy does not honor persons until after death.

Meter Cancellation. A design printed directly on an envelope or strip of gummed paper (for affixing to mail) by postage meter machine and used as a substitute for postage stamps. Meter postage is paid in advance, and thus differs from a *Permit.*

Military Stamps. Issued for use by a country's army and military personnel, usually during time of war only.

Millimeter or **mm.** A unit of measurement in the metric system, equal to one-tenth of a centimeter, and often used in expressing stamp measurements.

Miniature Sheet. A smaller-than-regular-size sheet of stamps; often a *Souvenir Sheet.*

Minor Varieties. Seemingly similar stamps which differ in minor respects such as shade of color or of paper; imperfections in design, printing, or perforations; positioning of watermark or overprint; etc. See *Major Varieties.*

Mint or **Mint Condition.** A stamp which is in the same physical condition as when it left the mint or printing source or supply; with full, original gum and never hinged, canceled, soiled, stained, creased, marked, or torn.

Mirror Print. An error in which part or all of a stamp is reversed, as in a mirror.

Mission Mixture. Mixed stamps, usually still on paper, collected by mission houses and other charitable organizations. Usually, a reliable source of a wide variety of foreign stamps and has come to signify any bulk mixture of unsorted stamps.

Mixed Postage. Stamps of two different countries used on the same postal item. See *Combination Cover.*

Mixture. A miscellaneous lot of unsorted stamps, usually containing many duplicates and with the stamps frequently on bits of paper, just as torn from envelopes and wrappers.

Multicolored. A stamp printed in three or more colors.

Multiple. A group of stamps from the same sheet, unseparated, numbering more than two but less than a full sheet.

Multiple Watermarks. A popular form of watermarking, in which a design is repeated so frequently on a sheet that partial watermarks may appear several times on a single stamp.

Mute Cancellation. See *Dumb Cancellation.*

Name Block. A block of stamps on whose margins appears a name rather than a number.

Net. Clear of or free from all deductions.

New Issue. The latest stamp or series of stamps issued currently by a country.

Newspaper Stamps. See *Journal Stamps*.

New Value. An additional value (denomination) added to an existing series; also, a new value surcharged on a stamp of different original value, creating a "revalued" stamp.

Oblique Roulette. A roulette consisting of parallel diagonal slits.

Obliteration. An overprint used to blot out unwanted parts of a stamp design. See *Bars*.

Obsolete. No longer in use; a term applied to stamps that are no longer being issued or distributed by the post office.

Occupation Stamps. Stamps issued by one country for use in conquered or occupied territory of another country.

Off Center. See *Centering*.

Off Paper. The term used to describe a used stamp which has been removed from the piece of paper to which it was affixed.

Official Seal. See *Post Office Seal*.

Official Stamps. Stamps used by some countries for use on official government mail.

Offset. A type of lithography in which the design is first transferred from the printing plate to a rubber roller, then from the roller to the paper. See *Lithography*.

Omnibus Issues. A group of stamps, usually sharing a common design, issued by several different postal authorities to mark the same occasion. Usually issued by all the colonies of one country, or all the countries in a commonwealth or union (British Commonwealth of Nations, EUROPA, etc.)

On Cover. A stamp still affixed to the entire piece of mail, usually an envelope, on which it was originally used.

On Paper. A stamp still affixed to enough of the paper on which it was originally used, to provide philatelic evidence of authenticity, such as a postmark.

Original. A stamp that is not a reprint, forgery, or facsimile.

Original Gum or **O.G.**. The unimpaired gum with which the stamp was originally issued.

Overprint. Any additional printing (surcharging, hand-stamping, overprinting, etc.) on a stamp after the stamp itself has been printed.

Oxidation. An unintended chemical process by which the original color of a stamp changes, usually through exposure to the elements.

Packet. An envelope or package of stamps, as offered for sale by a dealer. Properly, a packet contains all different stamps as distinguished from mixtures, which usually contain duplicates.

Packet Cancellation. A special postmark applied to mail carried on a ship maintained or chartered by a government or post office. Differs from a **Ship Cancellation,** which is a postmark applied to mail carried on a private vessel. Both postmarks usually include the name of the ship and/or shipping line.

Pair. Two unseparated stamps; a "vertical pair" when one stamp is above the other, a "horizontal pair" when side by side.

Pane. The so-called "sheets" of stamps sold by post offices are more correctly termed "panes." Most stamps are printed in much larger-sized sheets, which are then divided into smaller units, or panes, for distribution at post offices.

Parcel Post. A class of postal service reserved for the sending of packages or parcels, sometimes requiring special *Parcel Post Stamps.*

Part-Perforate. Perforated on two or three sides only. Most coil stamps are perforated on two opposing sides – top and bottom or left and right; booklet pane stamps are perforated on two or three connecting sides, depending on the location of the stamp in the pane.

Patriotic Covers. Covers on which patriotic pictures and slogans appear. These are generally used during a period of war and were prominent on both sides during the Civil War.

Pen Cancellation. A cancellation drawn by hand with a pen or pencil. Also called a *Manuscript Collection*.

Perforated Initials or **Perfins**. Holes punched in a stamp to form letters of a design, used to advertise or to prevent theft. Also called *Branding* or *Punch Perforating*.

Perforations. The holes punched between the rows of stamps in a sheet to facilitate separation. Usually round, but may be square, rectangular, diamond-shaped, etc.

Perforation or **Perf. Number.** The number of perforated holes in a space of 2 centimeters along the edge of a stamp, determined by using a perforation gauge.

Permit. A postal system used to facilitate bulk mailings. The sender is licensed to use a registered permit number on his mail in lieu of stamps. He is then charged for the total number of items on which his permit number appears.

Philatelic Agency. A bureau or central point maintained by a government for selling current issues of stamps in quantity to dealers, and in some cases, also to collectors.

Philatelist. A person who collects and studies stamps.

Philately. The technical name for stamp collecting.

Phosphor Tagged. See *Luminescent Stamps*.

Photoengraving. See *Letterpress*.

Photogravure. A popular method for printing stamps, in which a photograph of the stamp design is etched into a metal plate, usually for use on a rotary press (when the process is called *Rotogravure*). Photogravure stamps have the general impression of a photograph, with the design made up of fine dots which can be clearly seen with a magnifier.

Photolithography. See *Lithography*.

Pictorials. Stamps bearing pictures, such as landscapes, animals, flowers, etc., as distinguished from those bearing portraits or symbols.

Pin Roulette. A roulette consisting of tiny pinholes, with no paper removed.

Plate Number. A file or index number engraved in a plate from which stamps are printed. This number is used to help keep track of the plates and is usually found in a corner margin of the sheet.

Plate Number Block. A block of stamps with an attached portion of the sheet margin bearing the plate number. A popular collecting specialty.

Plate Number Coil or **Strip**. A strip of three (some collectors prefer five) containing a tiny plate number below the center stamp.

Position Blocks. Blocks of four or more stamps which have markings, usually on an attached portion of sheet margin, indicating a position on the sheet, such as plate number blocks, arrow blocks, inscription blocks, etc.

Post Office Seals. Postally-invalid adhesive labels used to re-seal letters or parcels damaged in transit or opened for inspection, or to seal registered items to prevent tampering.

Postage and Revenue. An inscription meaning that the stamps so inscribed can be used for either postage or revenue purposes.

Postage Due Stamps. Special stamps affixed by postal clerks to mail on which the postage was underpaid by the sender. The amount indicated by the stamps is then collected from the addressee upon delivery.

Postal Cancellations. Cancellations showing that a stamp has been used for postal rather than revenue purposes.

Postal-Fiscal. See *Revenue Stamps.*

Postal Stationery. Envelopes, postcards, lettersheets, wrappers, lettercards, etc. with stamps officially printed or embossed on them.

Postally Used. Used for postage, as distinguished from stamps used for non-mail purposes, or canceled-to-order.

Postmark. A cancellation which usually gives the place and date, and sometimes the exact time of cancellation.

Postmasters' Provisionals. Stamps issued by individual postmasters in various towns and cities, with or without official Post Office sanction, and used locally before general postal issues were made available.

Pre-Adhesive. A postal item dating from the period prior to the use of adhesive stamps in a particular country.

Precancels. Stamps canceled in advance of use, usually with the name of the place where they are to be used, to facilitate the handling of large mailings.

Printed on Both Sides. An error which occurs when a sheet of stamps is accidentally turned over and run through the printing press a second time, so that both sides are "correctly" printed. Not to be confused with *Set-Off*, in which the impression on the back of the stamp is a reverse, or "mirror" image.

Printing. The four most common methods used in printing stamps are: Line-engraving (*Intaglio*, or recess-printing); *Lithography* (usually *Offset* photolithography); *Photogravure*; and *Typography* (*Letterpress*, usually photoengraving). See separate listings.

Proof. A trial impression taken at various stages of the printing process to make sure that the colors are correct, design is satisfactory, etc. before the actual printing run begins.

Protectorate. A country governed, guided, or protected by a larger, stronger country.

Provisionals or **Provisional Issues**. Stamps issued or overprinted for temporary use until regular issues are available.

Punch perforating. See *Perforated Initials.*

Quadrille. Paper containing intersecting vertical and horizontal lines forming small squares or rectangles.

Quartz Lamp. See *Ultraviolet Lamp.*

Railroad Cancellation. A cancellation used on a railway mail car, usually while the mail is in transit.

Recut or **Re-Engrave**. To remake part or all of a printing plate, to make additions or alterations without materially changing the design.

Redrawn. A redrawn stamp design usually retains all the main characteristics and essential elements of its type but exhibits minor variations.

Registered Mail. First class mail for which the sender is given a numbered receipt by the post office, ascribing a specific monetary value to the item being mailed (for purposes of compensation in event of loss). A signed receipt is also required of the addressee, certifying safe delivery of the item. Insured Mail is similar but is sent third class.

Registration Stamps. Stamps issued by some countries exclusively for use on registered mail.

Regular Issue. See *Definitives*.

Reissue. A stamp which has been withdrawn from circulation may later be reprinted and reissued by postal authorities.

Remainders. The stamps left on hand in government offices after an issue of stamps has been discontinued. Remainder stocks are usually destroyed but are sometimes canceled-to-order and sold to stamp dealers.

Repaired or **Mended.** Stamps that are damaged (thin spots, creases, tears, etc.) are sometimes very cleverly repaired to hide the damage, usually for fraudulent resale as better-quality items.

Reprint. A stamp printed from the original plates (usually after an issue has become obsolete) but not intended for postal use.

Retouching. Minor repairs made to a printing plate, to mend damaged or worn portions. Usually involves less severe alterations than does recutting.

Revenue Stamps or **Fiscals.** Stamps affixed to playing cards, tobacco, wines and other spirits, documents, stock certificates, patent medicines, etc., to show that the required government tax on these items has been paid. Revenue stamps used for regular postage are called *Postal-Fiscals*; regular stamps used for revenue purposes are called *Fiscal-Postals.*

Rotary Press. A printing method using curved plates; stamps printed on a rotary press are slightly higher or wider than those printed with flat plates on a flat-bed press, due to the plates stretching slightly when they are being curved.

Rough Perforation. A perforation with jagged holes.

Rouletting. A method of stamp-separation in which slits or pinholes of various sizes and shapes are made between the rows of stamps without removing any of the paper, thus differing from perforating. See *Arc (Serrated), Diamond (Lozenge), Line, Oblique, Pin, Sawtooth, Serpentine,* and *Zigzag (Point) Roulette* listings.

Safety or **Security Paper**. Special paper used to make forgery or fraudulent alterations of a stamp more difficult. See *Chalky* and *Granite Papers.*

Sawtooth Roulette. A roulette which leaves angular pointed edges.

Se-tenant. A term applied to two or more unseparated stamps having different values, overprints, or designs, and printed that way intentionally (usually as part of the same set) rather than through an error.

Seals. Postally-invalid adhesive labels usually sold to raise money for various charities. Not to be confused with ***Post Office Seals.***

Secret Marks. Microscopic or hidden marks placed in a stamp design by the artist or engraver for identification or reference.

Selvedge. See ***Margin***.

Semi-Postal Stamps. Stamps surcharged, overprinted, or inscribed (as above) to obtain funds for various charities, in addition to the usual postal fee.

Separation. See ***Perforations*** and ***Rouletting***.

Series. All the denominations of stamps belonging to a certain issue, as the United States Bicentennial Era Series, often released at different times over a period of months or years.

Serpentine Roulette. A roulette consisting of wavy lines.

Service. When surcharged on a stamp, usually means "on government services," and indicates that the stamp is for use only by a government official.

Sesquicentennial. A 150th anniversary or its celebration.

Set. A number of stamps belonging to a particular issue or series.

Set-Off. A reverse impression on the back of a sheet of stamps, occurring when the sheet has been laid on another sheet whose ink is still wet. Also, reverse impression transferred to the back of an album page by the stamps on the following page, occurring when the album has been kept for a long time under great pressure. Avoidable through the use of interleaves.

Shade. Slight variations of colors; in philately, taken to mean any variation from the normal color of a stamp.

Sheet of Stamps. The complete sheet as it comes off the printing press. See *Pane.*

Ship Cancellation. See *Packet Cancellation.*

Short Set. A group of stamps from a particular issue or series, usually including all the stamps except for the higher values.

"Sleeper." An unexpectedly elusive or otherwise surprisingly desirable issue.

Soaking. The process of immersing a stamp in water to remove any attached bits of paper; somewhat fallen into disfavor now with the growing use of fugitive inks. If soaking is unavoidable, salt should be added to the water to help retard any running of colors.

"Socked-on-the-Nose." See *"Bullseye."*

Souvenir Sheet. A sheet of one or more stamps specifically printed by a government for a specific event or purpose; the margins are usually extra-wide, carrying inscriptions describing the purpose of the issue, and the stamps may be perforate or imperforate.

Space Filler. An inferior copy of a stamp, used to fill an album space only until a better copy can be obtained.

Special Delivery Stamps. For use when the sender of a postal item wants it delivered immediately by special messenger, upon its arrival at the post office.

Special Handling Stamps. Stamps for use on fourth class mail, entitling it to the same priority given first class mail.

Specialist. One who collects stamps in a restricted field, such as United States or German stamps only, airmail or revenue stamps only, sports or floral stamps only, etc.

"Specimen" or **"Sample."** An overprint or perfin applied to postally-invalid samples of a new stamp issue, for distribution to postmasters, philatelic agencies, etc.

Speculative Issues. Many countries today issue stamps less for any legitimate postal use they may see, than for the revenue they will generate through sales to collectors. These stamps are known as speculative issues.

Split. A stamp which has been cut into two or more pieces, each piece to be used as a separate stamp. See *Bisect.*

Split Grille. The term used when a stamp shows parts of two separate grills.

Spurious. A term used to describe items that are not completely genuine and are used to defraud, such as *Fakes, Forgeries, Bogus Stamps,* etc. *Facsimiles* are generally excluded, as they are not issued for fraudulent purposes.

Stampless Covers. Envelopes, or sheets folded into envelope form with the written message on the inside, which were sent through the mails in the early days before stamps came into use. These covers usually bear postal markings indicating the date the item was mailed and the post office from which it was mailed.

Straight Edge. A stamp with one or two adjacent sides without perforations, caused by cutting the sheet into panes.

"Strike." The impression of a handstamp on an envelope or cover.

Strip. Three or more unseparated stamps in a row, either side by side (*horizontal strip*) or one above the other (*vertical strip*).

Stuffed Cover. An envelope which has had a card or other stiffening material inserted for protection during cancellation and while in transit.

Subject Collecting. See *Topical Collecting.*

Surcharge. An overprinted revaluation of a stamp, which may include blocking out the original denomination (*Face Value*).

Surtax. The added fee on *Semi-Postal Stamps.*

Syncopated Perforations. See *Interrupted Perforations.*

Tab. See *Coupon*.

Teeth. The projections between perforation holes on a stamp.

Telegraph Stamps. Stamps used to pay telegraph charges or tolls.

Tercentenary. A three-hundredth anniversary or its celebration.

Tete-Beche. The term used to describe a pair of unseparated stamps arranged so that one is printed upside-down in relation to the other. The usual method of printing triangular stamps.

Thematic Collecting. See *Topical Collecting.*

"Tied To" or **"On Cover."** A stamp affixed to an envelope, card, or wrapper, with a postmark extending over the stamp onto the cover to prove that cover and stamp belong together, and that the stamp was not affixed at another time in a fraudulent attempt to increase its value.

Topical Collecting. The increasingly popular practice of collecting only stamps relating to a single subject or theme, such as Sports, Flowers, Animals, etc.

Torn Stamps. Slightly torn stamps are generally acceptable as space-fillers but should otherwise be rejected. An exception are certain issues of Afghanistan, which were canceled by having the post office clerk tear off a piece of the stamp.

Town or **Office Cancellation**. The most common type of postmark, giving the name of the post office where (and usually also the date when) the item was mailed.

Typeset stamps. Stamps printed from regular printer's type, rather than from engraved designs.

Typography. See *Letterpress.*

Ultraviolet, UV or **Quartz Lamp**. A lamp producing strong ultraviolet rays, used by experts to check for tampering, aniline inks, or phosphor tags in postage stamps.

Underprints. As an anti-forgery measure, a light color tint or fine repeat design or pattern is sometimes applied underneath the main design of a stamp. See *Burelage.*

Ungummed. Some countries with hot, humid climates issue stamps without gum, as gummed stamps would be too prone to stick together. Other ungummed stamps are normally gummed issues which have, for one reason or another, lost their adhesive, and usually much of their philatelic desirability as well.

Universal Postal Union or **U.P.U.** An international organization formed in 1874, and of which virtually all countries are members. The purpose of the U.P.U. is to regulate   international postal matters and facilitate cooperation on such issues as worldwide mail distribution, international postal rates, etc.

Unperforated. Imperforate.

Unused. Not canceled or otherwise defaced, but not necessarily still in mint condition or with original gum.

Unwatermarked. A term applied to stamps printed on unwatermarked paper.

Used. The term implies a stamp which has been postally-used, as distinguished from canceled-to-order.

Value. *Face Value*, when referring to the amount of money for which the stamp was sold at a post office and for which postal service will be rendered; *Market* or *Monetary Value,* when referring to its worth as a philatelic commodity.

Varieties. Two or more stamps that are not duplicates. See *Major* and *Minor Varieties.*

Varnish Bars. Lines or bars of clear varnish, sometimes applied to the face of a stamp to make fraudulent removal of cancellation difficult.

Vignette. The main portion of a stamp design, usually the portrait or picture inside the border.

"Wallpaper." A disparaging term used to describe sheets of stamps which have little or no philatelic market value.

Want List. One of the most effective ways for a collector to obtain the stamps he needs is to submit a want list to a dealer, specifying the catalog number, country, value, desired condition, and quantity of each item wanted.

War Tax Stamp. Stamps issued during wartime by some countries and required to be used on mail in addition to regular postage, the money thus raised being used to help pay the costs of war.

Watermark. A design, characters, letters, numerals, or words impressed into paper during its manufacture, and visible in part or whole on each stamp printed on such paper, though usually only with the aid of a watermark detecting device.

Wove Paper. The most popular used for printing stamps. Distinguishable by its finely netted texture, created during the paper's manufacture.

Wrapper. A sheet of paper, gummed at one end and printed with a stamp, to be used for wrapping and mailing periodicals.

Zeppelins. Stamps issued for use on and more recently to commemorate the German Airship Graf Zeppelin.

Zigzag or **Point Roulette.** A roulette which leaves evenly shaped pointed teeth along the edges of a stamp.

"Zip Code" Inscription Block. A block of United States stamps containing the sheet margin inscription, "Use Zip Code."

WORLDWIDE STAMP IDENTIFIER

By choosing a word, sign, or symbol on a stamp of unknown origin and finding it in the index, the collector will be swiftly guided, in most cases, to the stamp's country of origin.

Only relatively difficult-to-classify stamps have been indexed. If the country name in its English form appears anywhere on the stamp, no identifying words are necessary. Likewise, such words as "postage" and "pence," which are quite common, would provide little to no guidance. If you run into trouble, try referencing other words on the stamp until the indexing word is found.

Some European stamps contain special characters that are easily mistaken as others. For example, the character Π represents the Cyrillic letter "Pe" on stamps of Slavic origin or the Greek letter "Pi." These characters can be easily mistaken as H or N, depending on the stamp's design. Some Austrian and German stamps use the old Latin form of "long S" which is represented as either "ſ" or "ʃ" which can be mistaken as "f." A few of these examples have been demonstrated in this index.

Some stamps (e.g., early Afghanistan and Egypt, certain Indian Native States, and others) are printed entirely in Arabic or other Oriental characters and cannot be indexed. To help you with these, see the illustrated section, "OTHER HARD-TO-IDENTIFY STAMPS" at the end of the regular listings.

A.B. on stamps of Russia: **Far Eastern Republic.**
АВИОПОЧТА: Russia.
A.C.C.P.: Azerbaijan.
АСОБНЫ АТРАД: Belarus – White Russia.
AÇORES: Azores.
A.D. HALL: United States – Gainesville, Alabama.
ADMIRALTY OFFICIAL: Great Britain.
A.E.F. ("Afrique Equatorial Française") on stamps inscribed "Centenaire du Gabon":
    French Equatorial Africa.
ΑΕΓΤΑ: Greece.
ΑΕΠΤΑ: Epirus.
AFGHAN, AFGHANES: Afghanistan.
AFRICA CORREIOS: Portuguese Africa.
AFRICA OCCIDENTAL ESPAÑOLA: Spanish West Africa.
AFRICA ORIENTALE ITALIANA: Italian East Africa.
AFRIQUE EQUATORIAL FRANÇAISE: French Equatorial Africa: on stamps
    inscribed "Moyen Congo": **Middle Congo;** plus "Tchad": **Chad;** with bars
    through "Gabon" and value: **French Equatorial Africa;** on stamps of Gabon:
    Gabon.
AFRIQUE EQUATORIALE GABON: Gabon.
AFRIQUE OCCIDENTALE FRANÇAISE: French West Africa.

ΛΗΜΝΟΣ: on stamps of Greece: **Greece – Aegean Islands – Lemnos.**

AITUTAKI on stamps of New Zealand or Cook Islands: **Aitutaki.**

ALAOUITES on stamps of France and Syria: **Alaouites.**

ALBANIA on stamps of Italy: **Italy – Offices in Turkey – Albania.**

ALBANY GA.: United States – Albany, Georgia.

ALDERNEY: Great Britain – Alderney.

ALERTA: on stamps of Peru: **Peru – Ancachs.**

ALEXANDRIA: United States – Alexandria, Virginia.

ALEXANDRIE: France – Offices in Egypt – Alexandria.

ALGERIE: on stamps of France: **Algeria.**

ALLEMAGNE DUITSCHLAND on stamps of Belgium: **Germany – Belgian occupation.**

A.M.G. - F.T.T. on stamps of Italy: **Trieste – Zone A.**

A.M.G. - V.G. on stamps of Italy: **Italy – Venezia Giulia – Allied occupation.**

A.M. POST: Germany – Allied occupation.

AMTLICHER VERKEHR: Germany – Württemberg.

ANDERSON C.H.S.C.: United States – Anderson Court House, South Carolina.

ANDORRA on stamps of Spain: **Andorra – Spanish Administration.**

ANDORRE on stamps of France: **Andorra – French Administration.**

ANNA: British East Africa, India, Indian States, Mesopotamia, Pakistan, Zanzibar.

ANNAPOLIS: United States – Annapolis, Maryland.

ANTIGUA: Antigua & Barbuda.

ANTIOQUIA: Colombia – Antioquia.

A.O. on stamps of Congo Democratic Republic (ex-Belgian): **German East Africa.**

A.O.F. on stamps of France: **French West Africa.**

A.O.I. on stamps of Italy: **Italian East Africa.**

A PAYER TE BETALEN ("postage due"): **Belgium.**

A PERÇEVOIR: Belgium, France, many **French Colonies.**

APURIMAC on stamps inscribed "Franqueo": **Peru – Apurimac.**

АРЖАВА: Yugoslavia.

A.R.: Colombia, Montenegro, Panama, Chile.

ARMY OFFICIAL: Great Britain; Sudan.

ARABIE SAOUDITE: Saudi Arabia.

ARCHIPEL DES COMORES: Comoro Islands, Grand Comoro.

A RECEBER: Portugal, Portuguese Colonies.

ARRIBA on stamps of Spain: **Spain – San Sebastian.**

ASCENSION on stamps of St. Helena: **Ascension.**

ASSISTENCIA D.L. No. 72 on war tax stamps of Portuguese India: **Timor.**

ATHENS S.A.: United States – Athens, Georgia.

ATLANTA GA. or GEO.: United States – Atlanta, Georgia.

ATT, ATTS: Siam.

A & T on stamps of French Colonies: **Annam and Tonkin.**

AUNUS on stamps of Finland: **Russia – Finnish occupation.**

AUR: Iceland.

AUSTIN, MISS.: United States – Austin, Mississippi.

AUSTIN, TEX.: United States – Austin, Texas.

AUSTRALIAN ANTARCTIC TERRITORY: Australia – Australian Antarctic Territory.

AVISPORTO: Denmark.

AVO, AVOS: Macao, Timo

A.W. McNEEL P.M.: United States – Autaugaville, Alabama.

AYACUCHO: Peru – Ayacucho.

ΑΥΤΟΝΟΜΟΣ: Epirus.

AZERBAIDJAN: Azerbaijan.

B

B in an oval, on stamps with no country name: **Belgium** – parcel post stamps; on stamps of Straits Settlements: **Bangkok.**

B.A. ERITREA, B.A. SOMALIA, or B.A. TRIPOLITANIA on stamps of Great Britain: **Great Britain – Offices in Africa – Eritrea, Somalia, Tripolitania.**

BADEN: Germany – Baden – French occupation.

BAGHDAD on stamps of Turkey: **Mesopotamia.**

BAHAWALPUR: Pakistan – Bahawalpur.

BAHRAIN: on stamps of Great Britain or India: **Bahrain.**

BAHT: Siam.

БАНДЕРОЛЬНОЕ ОТПРАВЛЕНІЕ: Russia – Offices in Turkey

BAJAR PORTO: Indonesia.

BAMRA: India – Bamra.

BÁNÁT BÁCSKA on stamps of Hungary: **Hungary – Serbian occupation – Banata, Bacaska.**

BANI: Romania; on stamps of Austria: **Romania – Austrian occupation.**

BARANYA on stamps of Hungary: **Hungary – Serbian occupation.**

BARBUDA on stamps of Antigua or Leeward Islands: **Barbuda.**

BARCELONA: Spain.

BARWANI: India – Barwani.

BASEL: Switzerland – Basel.

BASUTOLAND on stamps of South Africa: **Basutoland.**

BATAAN on stamps with inscriptions in oriental characters: **Philippines – Japanese occupation.**

BATON ROUGE, LA.: United States – Baton Rouge, Louisiana.

БАТУМ. ОБ., БАТУМ ОБЛАС, БАТУМ.ОБЛ., БАТУМСКАЯ ПОЧТА, БАТУМЪ ОБЛ. on stamps of Russia: **Batum.**

BAYERN, BAYR: Bavaria.

B.C.A. on stamps inscribed "British South Africa Company": **British Central Africa.**

B.C.M., BRITISH CONSULAR MAIL: Madagascar – British Consulate.

B.C.O.F.–JAPAN 1946 on stamps of Australia: **Australia.**

B DPTO. ZELAYA: Nicaragua – Zelaya.

BEAUMONT: United States – Beaumont, Texas.

BECHUANALAND on stamps of South Africa: **Bechuanaland.**

BECHUANALAND PROTECTORATE on stamps of Great Britain: **Bechuanaland Protectorate.**

ВЕНДЕНСКАЯ: Russia – Wenden.

BELGIAN EAST AFRICA: Ruanda – Urundi.

BELGIE: Belgium.

BELGIEN on stamps of Germany: Belgium – German Occupation.

BELGIQUE: Belgium.

BELGISCH CONGO: Belgian Congo.

BELIZE: British Honduras.

BENADIR: Somalia.

BENGASI on stamps of Italy: Italy – Offices in Africa – Bengasi.

BENIN on stamps of French Colonies: Benin.

BERLIN on stamps of Germany: Germany – Berlin.

BEYROUTH on stamps of Russia: Russia – Offices in Turkey.

BHOPAL: India – Bhopal.

BHOR: India – Bhor.

BIAFRA on stamps of Nigeria: issued by revolutionary forces in 1968-69.

BIJAWAR: India – Bijawar.

B.I.O.T. on stamps of Seychelles: British Indian Ocean Territory.

BISHOP'S: United States – Cleveland, Ohio.

B.M.A. ERITREA, B.M.A. SOMALIA, or B.M.A. TRIPOLITANIA on stamps of
  Great Britain: Great Britain – Offices in Africa – Eritrea, Somalia, or
  Tripolitania.

BMA MALAYA: Straits Settlements.

BOARD OF EDUCATION: Great Britain, official stamps.

ВОСТОЧНАЯ КОРРЕСПОНДЕНЦІЯ: Russia – Offices in Turkey.

BOFTGEBIET on stamps of Germany: Lithuania – German occupation.

BOGCHAH or BOGACHES: Yemen.

BÖHMEN UND MÄHREN: Czechoslovakia – Bohemia and Moravia.

BOHΘEITE: Greece.

BOLIVAR: Colombia – Bolivar.

BOLLO DELLA DI SICILIA: Two Sicilies – Sicily.

BOLLO POSTALE: San Marino.

BOSNIEN–HERCEGOVINA or BOSNIË I HERZEGOWINA: Bosnia and
  Herzegovina.

BOYACÁ: Colombia – Boyacá.

BRASIL: Brazil.

BRATTLEBORO VT.: United States – Brattleboro, Vermont.

BRAUNSCHWEIG: Brunswick.

BRIEFPOST: Germany – French occupation.

BRITISH BECHUANALAND on stamps of Cape of Good Hope or Great Britain:
  Bechuanaland.

BRITISH EAST AFRICA COMPANY on stamps of Great Britain: British East
  Africa.

BRITISH NEW GUINEA: Papua New Guinea.

BRITISH OCCUPATION on stamps of Russia: Batum.

BRITISH PROTECTORATE OIL RIVERS on stamps of Great Britain: Niger Coast
  Protectorate.

BRITISH SOMALILAND on stamps of India: Somaliland Protectorate.

BRITISH SOUTH AFRICA COMPANY: Rhodesia.

BRITISH VICE CONSULATE: Madagascar – British Consulate.

100

BR. or **BRITISH VIRGIN ISLANDS:** Virgin Islands.

BROWN & McOILLS: United States – Louisville, Kentucky.

BRUNEI on stamps of Labuan: **Brunei.**

BRUXELLES, BRUSSEL: Belgium.

BUCHANAN (Liberian city): **Liberia, registration stamp.**

BUENOS ARIES: Argentina – Buenos Aires; with "Agosto de 1921": **Argentina.**

BUITEN BEZIT on stamps inscribed "Netherlandsch – Indie": **Dutch Indies.**

BULGARIE: Bulgaria.

BUNDI: India – Bundi.

BURKINA FASO: Upper Volta or **Burkina Faso.**

BURMA on stamps of India: **Burma.**

BUSHIRE on stamps of Persia: **Bushire.**

BUSSAHIR: India – **Bussahir.**

C

c preceded by numeral value, on stamps with Japanese characters: **Ryukyu Islands.**

CABO: Nicaragua – Cabo Gracias a Dios.

CABO JUBI, CABO JUBY on stamps of Rio de Oro, Spain, or Spanish Morocco: **Cape Juby.**

CABO VERDE: Cape Verde.

САНАТОРИУМЬ: Bulgaria.

CACHES on stamps of France or French Colonies: **French India.**

CADIZ on stamps of Spain: **Spain – Cadiz.**

САНАТОРИУМЬ: Bulgaria.

CALCHI on stamps of Italy: **Italy – Aegean Islands – Calchi.**

CALIMNO or **CALINO** on stamps of Italy: **Italy – Aegean Islands – Calimno.**

CAMBODGE: Cambodia.

CAMEROONS U.K.T.T. on stamps of Nigeria: (British) **Cameroons.**

CAMEROUN on stamps of Gabon or Middle Congo: **Cameroun.**

CAMPECHE: Mexico – Campeche.

CAMPIONARIA DI TRIPOLI: Tripolitania, Libya.

CANAL ZONE on stamps of Colombia, Panama, or United States: **Canal Zone.**

CANARIAS on stamps of Spain: **Spain – Canary Islands.**

CANTON on stamps of Indo-China: **France – Offices in China – Canton.**

CARCHI on stamps of Italy: **Italy – Aegean Islands – Karki.**

CASO on stamps of Italy: **Italy – Aegean Islands – Caso.**

CASTELLORISO, CASTELLORIZO or **CASTELROSSO** on stamps of France, French Colonies, or Italy: **Castellorizo.**

CAUCA: Colombia – Cauca.

CAVALLE: France – Offices in Turkey – Cavalle.

C C C P (abbreviation for "Union of Soviet Socialist Republics"): **Russia.**

C. CH. on stamps of French Colonies: **Cochin China.**

C. or **CS. DE PESO: Philippines.**

ĈECHY A MORAVA: Czechoslovakia – Bohemia and Moravia.

C.E.F. (Cameroon Expeditionary Force) on stamps inscribed "Kamerun": (British) **Cameroons**; (Chinese Expeditionary Force) on stamps of India: **India** – military stamps.

CENT or **CENTS** on stamps of France: **France – Offices in China**; on stamps of Russia: **Russia – Offices in China**; with crowns in a circle: **Mongolia**.

CENTENAIRE ALGERIE or **CENTENAIRE DE L ALGÉRIE** ("Algerian Centenary"): **France**.

CENTENAIRE DU GABON: French Equatorial Africa.

CENTESIMI: Italy, many Italian Colonies, **San Marino, Vatican City**; on stamps of Austria or Bosnia and Herzegovina: **Italy – Austrian occupation**.

CENTESIMI DI CORONA in serif letters on stamps of Italy: **Austria – Italian occupation**; in sans-serif letters on stamps of Italy: **Dalmatia**.

CENTIMES on stamps of Germany: **Germany – Offices in Turkey**; on stamps of Austria: **Austria – Offices in Crete**.

CENTIMOS with no country name: **Spain**; on stamps of France: **French Morocco**.

ČESKOSLOVENSKÁ, ČESKOSLOVENSKO: Czechoslovakia.

ČESKO – SLOVENSKO: Czechoslovakia – Slovakia.

CFA on stamps of France: **Reunion**.

C.G.H.S.: Upper Silesia.

CH followed by oriental characters: **Korea**.

CHALA: Peru – Chala.

CHAMBA: India – Chamba.

CHAPEL HILL, N.C.: United States – Chapel Hill, North Carolina.

CHARKHARI: India – Charkhari.

CHARLESTON S.C.: United States – Charleston, South Carolina.

CHATTANOOGA, TEN.: United States – Chattanooga, Tennessee.

CHEMINS DE FER SPOORWEGEN: Belgium.

CHIFFRE TAXE with no country name: **France, French Colonies**.

CHINA on stamps of Hong Kong: **Great Britain – Offices in China**; on stamps of Germany: **Germany – Offices in China**.

CHINE on stamps of France: **France – Offices in China**.

CHRISTMAS ISLAND on stamps of Australia: **Christmas Island**.

CIHS on stamps of Germany: **Upper Silesia**.

CILICIE on stamps of France or Turkey: **Cilicia**.

CINQUANTENAIRE 24 SEPTEMBRE 1853 1903 on postage due stamps of French Colonies: **New Caledonia** – postage due stamps.

CIRENAICA on stamps of Italy or Tripolitania: **Cyrenaica**.

CITY DISPATCH POST: United States – New York, New York.

CITY POST: United States – Charleston, South Carolina.

C.M.T. on stamps of Austria: **Western Ukraine – Romanian occupation**.

CN (for "cheun"): **Korea**.

COAMO: Puerto Rico – Coamo.

COCHIN, COCHIN ANCHAL: India – Cochin.

CO. Ci. on stamps of Yugoslavia: **Yugoslavia – Ljubljana**.

COLIS POSTAL or **POSTAUX** on stamps with no country name: **Belgium**.

COLOMBIA on stamps showing a map of Panama: **Panama – Colombian dominion**.

COLONIA DE RIO DE ORO: Rio de Oro.

COLONIA ERITREA on stamps of Italy or Somalia: **Eritrea**.

COLONIE (or **COLONIALI**) **ITALIANE:** Italian Colonies.

COLONIES DE L'EMPIRE FRANÇAISE: French Colonies.

COMMISSION DE GOUVERNEMENT HAUTE SILÉSIE: Upper Silesia.

COMMISSION INTERALLIÉE MARIENWERDER on stamps of Germany: **Marienwerder.**

COMORES: Comoros Islands.

COMP. or **COMPANHIA DE MOÇAMBIQUE: Mozambique Company:** on stamps of Mozambique: **Mozambique Company.**

COMPANHIA DO NYASSA ("Nyassa Company"): **Nyassa – Mozambique.**

COMUNICAÇIONES: Spain.

CONFEDERATE STATES or **CONFEDERATE STATES OF AMERICA:** United States – **Confederate States.**

CONFŒDERATIO HELVETICA ("Helvetic or Swiss Confederation"): **Switzerland.**

CONGO on stamps with Portuguese inscriptions: **Portuguese Congo;** with "Belge": **Congo Democratic Republic** (ex-Belgian); with **"Française": French Congo;** with **"Française Gabon": Gabon;** with **"Republic du": Congo Democratic Republic** (ex-Belgian) or **Congo People's Republic** (ex-French).

CONGRESO DE LOS DIPUTADOS: Spain.

CONSTANTINOPLE on stamps of Russia: **Russia – Offices in Turkey.**

CONSTANTINOPOL on stamps of Romania: **Romania – Offices in Turkey.**

COO on stamps of Italy: **Italy – Aegean Islands – Coo.**

COOK ISLANDS – NIUE: Niue.

CORDOBA: Argentina – Cordoba.

COREE, COREAN: Korea.

CORFU on stamps of Greece or Italy: **Corfu – Italian occupation.**

CORONA: Dalmatia: on stamps of Italy: **Austria – Italian occupation.**

CORREIO, CORREIOS, or **CORREIOS E TELEGRAPHOS:** with no country name: **Portugal.**

CORREO AEREO with no country name: **Spain.**

CORREO ESPAÑOL MARRUECOS on stamps of Spain: **Spanish Morocco.**

CORREO ESPAÑOL TANGER: Spanish Morocco – Tangier.

CORREO URBANO DE BOGOTA: Colombia – Bogota.

CORREOS with no country name and denominations in CUARTOS, REALES, CS, or CTOS., (i.e., CENTIMOS): **Spain;** with "Real": **Dominican Republic.**

CORREOS with no country name: **Cuba, Peru, Philippines, Dominican Republic, Spain, Uruguay.**

CORREOS ARGENTINOS: Argentina.

CORREOS DE COLOMBIA: Colombia.

CORREOS INTERIOR: Philippines.

CORREOS MEXICO GOBIERNO REVOLUCIONARIO: Mexico – Yucatan.

CORREOS NAÇIONALES: Colombia.

CORREOS NALES: Colombia.

CORREOS OAXACA: Mexico – Oaxaca.

CORREOS SONORA: Mexico – Sonora.

CORREOS Y TELEGEOS or **TELEGs:** Spain.

CORRESPONDENCIA URGENTE: Spain.

CORRIENTES: Argentina – Corrientes

COS on stamps of Italy: **Italy – Aegean Islands – Coo.**

COSTA ATLANTICA B: Nicaragua – Province of Zelaya.

COSTA ATLANTICA C: Nicaragua – Cabo Gracias a Dios.

COSTANTINOPOLI on stamps of Italy: **Italy – Offices in Turkey – Constantinople.**

COTE DE SOMALIS or **COTE FRANÇAIS DES SOMALIS:** Somali Coast.

COTE D'IVOIRE: Ivory Coast.

COURTLAND AL: United States – Courtland, Alabama.

СРБИЈА: Serbia.

СРБСКА: Serbia.

CRUZ ROJA DOMINICA: Dominican Republic.

CRUZ ROJA HONDURENA: Honduras.

CRVENI KRST on stamps of Yugoslavia: **Yugoslavia – Offices Abroad, Montenegro – German Occupation.**

CROISSANT ROUGE TURC: Turkey.

CRUZ VERMELHA PORTUGUESA: Portugal.

CS on stamps of Hungary: **Hungary** (Parcel posts).

C.S. on stamps of South Australia: **South Australia.**

C.S. or **C.S.A. POSTAGE:** United States – Confederate States.

СТОТИНКИ, СТ., СТОТ.: Bulgaria.

CUAUTLA: Mexico – Cuautla.

CUBA on stamps of United States: **Cuba – U.S. Administration.**

CUERNAVACA: Mexico – Cuernavaca.

CUNDINAMARCA: Colombia – Cundinamarca.

CURAÇAO: Netherlands Antilles.

CUZCO on stamps inscribed "Peru" or "Franqueo": **Peru – Cuzco.**

C.X.C. ("Serbs, Croats, and Slovenes"): **Yugoslavia.**

CYPRUS on stamps of Great Britain: **Cyprus.**

D

/d on stamps of Cape of Good Hope: **Griqualand West.**

D (for "dinar") on stamps with Arabic writing: **Persia.**

d (pence), / (shilling), or **£** (pound) preceded by a numeral, on stamps with king's or queen's head but no country name: **Great Britain.**

DAI NIPPON on stamps of Straits Settlements: **Malaya – Japanese occupation;** on various Malaya states: **Malaya States – Japanese occupation** of state overprinted on.

DALTON GA.: United States – Dalton, Georgia.

DANMARK: Denmark.

DANSK-VESTINDISKE or **-VESTINDIEN:** Danish West Indies.

DANVILLE, VA.: United States – Danville, Virginia.

DANZIG on stamps of Germany: **Danzig.**

DARDANELLES on stamps of Russia: **Russia – Offices in Turkey.**

D.B.L. in script letters on stamps of Russia: **Far Eastern Republic;** with three bars: **Siberia.**

DDR: Germany – German Democratic Republic.

DÉDÉAGH: France – Offices in Turkey.

DEFICIT: Peru.

DELEGACOES: Portugal.

DEL GOLFO DE GUINEA: Spanish Guinea.

DEN WAISEN SIROTAM on stamps of Italy: **Yugoslavia – Ljubljana – German occupation.**

DEUTSCH: ("German") followed by NEU-GUINEA: **German New Guinea;** by OSTAFRIKA: **German East Africa;** by SUDWEST AFRIKA: **German Southwest Africa.**

DEUTSCH DEMOKRATISCHE REPUBLIK: Germany – **German Democratic Republic.**

DEUTSCHE BUNDESPOST: **Germany;** inscribed BERLIN: **Germany – Berlin.**

DEUTSCHE FELDPOST: **Germany** – military parcel post stamps.

DEUTSCHE MILITAER–VERWALLUNG MONTENEGRO on stamps of Yugoslavia: **Montenegro – German occupation.**

DEUTSCHE NATIONAL VERSAMMLUNG: **Germany.**

DEUTSCHE POFT or POST: **Germany, Germany – Berlin, Germany – German Democratic Republic.**

DEUTSCHE POST OSTEN on stamps of Germany: **Poland – German occupation.**

Deutfches Reich on stamps of Bavaria: **Bavaria.**

Deutfches Reich: **Germany.**

Deutfchöfterreich: **Austria.**

DEUTSCHES REICH: **Germany.**

DEUTSCHES REICH GENERAL GOUVERNEMENT: **Poland – German occupation.**

DEUTSCHES REICHSPOST: **Germany.**

DEUTSCHLAND: **Germany – Allied occupation.**

DHAR: **India – Dhar.**

D.H. GHASS P.M.: **United States – Lynchburg, Virginia.**

DIEGO–SUAREZ on stamps of French Colonies: **Diego – Suarez.**

DIENST on stamps inscribed "Nederlandsch–Indies": **Dutch Indies.**

DIENST SACHE: **Württemberg** – Official stamps.

DIENSTMARKE: **Bavaria, Danzig, Germany, Prussia, Saar.**

DILIGENCIA: **Uruguay.**

DINAR or DINARS: **Persia.**

DINERO: **Peru.**

DIOS, PATRIA, REY: **Spain.**

DISTRITO: **Peru – Cuzco.**

DJ or DJIBOUTI on stamps of Obock: **Somali Coast.**

DOLLAR on stamps of Russia: **Russia – Offices in China.**

DOPŁATA: **Central Lithuania, Poland.**

DOPLATIT or DOPLATNÉ with no country name: **Czechoslovakia.**

DRŽAVA, DRŽAVNA on stamps of Bosnia and Herzegovina: **Yugoslavia – Bosnia and Herzegovina.**

DUC. DL. PARMA: **Parma.**

DUITSCH OOST AFRIKA BELGISCHE BEZETTING on stamps of Congo Democratic Republic (ex-Belgian): **German East Africa – Belgian occupation.**

105

DURAZZO on stamps of Italy: **Italy – Offices in Turkey – Durazzo.**
DUTTIA: India – Duttia.

E

E.A. on stamps of Algeria: on stamps of Greece: **Greece – Aegean Islands – Chios.**
E.A.F. on stamps of Great Britain: **Great Britain – Offices in East Africa – Somalia.**
EAST AFRICA & UGANDA PROTECTORATES with portrait of King George V: if watermarked Multiple Crown and C.A.: **East Africa and Uganda;** if watermarked Multiple Crown and Script C.A.: **Kenya, Uganda, and Tanzania.**
EAST INDIA POSTAGE: India; on stamps with Crown and new denominations: **Straits Settlements.**
EATONTON GEO.: United States – Eatonton, Georgia.
ECUADOR on stamps of Colombia: **Ecuador.**
E.E.F. ("Egyptian Expeditionary Force"): **Palestine.**
EESTI on stamps of Russia: **Estonia.**
EE. UU. DE C.: Colombia – Tolima.
EGEO on stamps of Italy: **Italy – Aegean Islands.**
EGYPTE: Egypt.
EINZUZIEHEN: Danzig – Postage due stamps.
EIRE: Ireland.
EJERCITO RENOVADOR: Mexico – Sinaloa.
EL PARLAMENTO A CERVANTES: Spain – Official stamps.
ELSAẞ (Alsace) on stamps of Germany: **France – German occupation.**
EL SALVADOR: Salvador.
ELUA KENETA: Hawaii.
ΕΛΕΥΘΕΡΑ ΓΟΛΙΤΕΙΑ: Greece – Aegean Islands – Icaria.
ΕΛΛΑΧ, ΕΛΛΑΣ ("Hellas"): **Greece;** on stamps of Italy: **Italy – Ionian Islands – German occupation;** on stamps of Crete: **Crete.**
ΕΛΛΗΝΙΚΗ on stamps of Bulgaria: **Greece – Aegean Islands – Cavilla, Dedaegatch, North Epirus, and Occupied Territories.**
ΕΛΛΗΝΙΚΗ: Greece.
ΕΛΛΗΝΙΚΗ ΔΙΟΚΣΙΣ on stamps of Greece: **Greece – Aegean Islands – Icaria.**
Έλληνική Κατοχή Μυτιλήν on stamps of Greece: **Greece – Aegean Islands – Mytilene.**
EMORY: United States – Emory, Virginia.
EMP. OTTOMAN: Eastern Rumelia, Turkey.
EMPIRE CENTRAFRICAIN: Central Africa.
EMPIRE FRANC (or **FRANÇAIS): France, French Colonies.**
ΕΝΑΡΙΘΜΟΝ: Greece.
ΕΘΝΙΚΗ: Greece.
ЕРМАК or **ЕРМАКЪ: South Russia.**
EQUATEUR: Ecuador.
E.R. ("Elizabeth Regina") on stamps with queen's head: **Great Britain.**

ESCUELAS: Venezuela.
ESPAÑA, ESPAÑOLA: Spain.
ESPAÑA SAHARA: Spanish Sahara.
ESTADO DA INDIA: Portuguese India.
ESTADO ESPAÑOL ("Spanish State"): Spain.
ESTADOS UNIDOS DE NUEVA GRENADA: Colombia.
EST AFRICAIN ALLEMAND OCCUPATION BELGE on stamps of Congo
      Democratic Republic (ex-Belgian): German East Africa.
ESTERO on stamps of Italy: Italy – Offices Abroad.
ÉTABLISSEMENTS DANS L'INDE or DE L'INDE: French India.
ÉTABLISSEMENTS DE L'OCÉANIE: French Polynesia.
ÉTAT DU CAMEROUN: Cameroun.
ÉTAT FRANÇAIS: France.
ÉTAT IND. (or INDEPENDANT) DU CONGO ("Independent State of Congo"):
      Congo Democratic Republic (ex-Belgian).
ETIOPIA, ETHIOPIE, ETHIOPIENNES: Ethiopia.
ÉTS. FRANÇS. DE L'OCÉANIE: French Polynesia.
E.U. DE COLOMBIA ("United States of Colombia"): Colombia.
EUPEN or EUPEN & MELMEDY on stamps of Belgium: Germany – Belgian
      occupation.
EXPED. SCIENT. on stamps with oriental characters: China.
EXPOSICIÓN DE BARCELONA, EXPOSICION GENERAL ESPAÑOLA or
      EXPOSICIÓN GRAL SEVILLA BARCELONA: Spain.
EXPOSITION COLONIALE INTERNATIONALE PARIS 1931 with no country
      name: France.
EXPOSITION INDUSTRIELLE DAMAS 1929 ("Damascus Industrial "Exhibition"):
      Syria.
ΣAMOY: Greece – Aegean Islands – Samos.
ΣΔΔ on stamps of Greece: Greece – Aegean Islands – Dodecanese Islands.

F

FACTAJ on stamps of Romania: Romania – Parcel post stamps.
FARIDKOT: India – Faridkot.
FCFA: Reunion.
FDO. POO: Fernando Po.
FEDERATA DEMOKRATIKE NDERKOMBETARE E GRAVE: Albania.
FEDERATED MALAY STATES: Malaya.
FEDERATION DU MALI: Mali.
FEDERATION OF MALAYA: Malay.
FELDPOST on stamps of Germany: Germany – Military stamps; with 2kg: Germany
      – Military Parcel Posts.
FEN, FN: Manchukuo; FEN on stamps of Poland: Poland.
FERNANDO POO (or PÓ): Fernando Poo (or Pó).
FESTIVAL OF BRITAIN 1851-1951: Great Britain.

FEZZAN or **FEZZAN-GHADAMES**: Libya – French occupation.

FIERA DI TRIESTE on stamps of Italy: **Trieste.**

FILIPAS-IMPRESOS or **FILIPINAS**: **Philippines.**

FILLÉR: **Hungary.**

FILS on stamps with no country name: **Iraq, Jordan.**

FINCASTLE: United States – Fincastle, Virginia.

FIUME on stamps of Hungary: **Fiume.**

FLÜCHTLINGSHILFE MONTENEGRO on stamps of Yugoslavia: **Montenegro – German occupation.**

FLUGPOST ("Airmail"): **Austria, Danzig, Germany.**

FORCES FRANÇAISES LIBRES-LEVANT: Syria – Free French Administration.

FØROYAR: Faroe Islands.

fr. on stamps of Senegal: **French West Africa.**

FRANC on stamps of Austria: **Austria – Offices in Crete.**

FRANCA on stamps of Peru: **Peru – Ancachs, Chiclayo.**

FRANÇAISE: France.

FRANCE D'OUTRE-MER or **D'OUTREMER**: French Colonies.

FRANCO: Philippines, Spain, Switzerland.

FRANCO BOLLO with no country name on perforated stamps: **Italy;** on imperforated stamps: **Sardinia.**

FRANCO BOLLO DI STATO: Italy – Official stamps.

FRANCO BOLLO POSTALE with denominations in BAJ, SCUDO, CENT. or CENTESIMI: **Roman States.**

FRANCO SCRISOREI: Romania – Moldavia – Walachia.

FRANK: Austria.

FRANKLIN, N.C.: United States – Franklin, North Carolina.

FRANQUICIA: Spain.

FREDERICKSB'G: United States – Fredericksburg, Virginia.

FREI DURCH ABLÖSUNG ("Free because of prepayment"): **Germany.**

FREIE STADT DANZIG: Danzig.

FREIMARKE with no country name: **Baden, Prussia, Thurn and Taxis, Württemberg.**

Freiftaat Bayern on stamps of Germany: **Bavaria.**

FRIMÆRKE KGL POST: Denmark.

FÜNF GROTE: Bremen.

FÜRSTENTUM or **FVERSTENTUM LIECHTENSTEIN**: Liechtenstein.

G

G or **GW** on stamps of Cape of Good Hope: **Griqualand West.**

GAB. or **GABON** on stamps of French Colonies: **Gabon.**

GALVESTON TEX.: United States – Galveston, Texas.

GARCH: Saudi Arabia.

GARZÓN: Colombia – Tolima.

G.E.A. on stamps of East Africa and Uganda: **German East Africa – British occupation;** on stamps of Kenya: **Tanganyika.**

GENERAL GOVERNMENT: Poland – German occupation.

GENÈVE: Switzerland – Geneva.

Gen.-Gouv. Warfchau on stamps of Germany: **Poland – German occupation.**

GEORGIE, GEORGIENNE: Georgia.

GEORGETOWN S.C.: United States – Georgetown, South Carolina.

GERUSALEMME on stamps of Italy: **Italy – Offices in Turkey – Jerusalem.**

GHADAMÈS TERRITOIRE MILITAIRE: Libya – French occupation.

GHANA INDEPENDENCE on stamps of Gold Coast: **Ghana.**

GIBRALTAR on stamps of Bermuda: **Gibraltar.**

GILBERT & ELLICE PROTECTORATE on stamps of Fiji: **Gilbert and Ellice Islands.**

GIORNALI STAMPE: Sardinia.

GOLFE DE BÉNIN: Benin.

GOLIAD: United States – Goliad, Texas.

GONZALES TEXAS: United States – Gonzales, Texas.

GOVERNMENT CITY DISPATCH: United States – Baltimore, Maryland.

GOVERNO MILITARE ALLEATO on stamps of Italy: **Italy – Allied occupation.**

GOYA: Spain.

G.P.E. or **G.&D.** on stamps of French Colonies: **Guadeloupe.**

GRAHAM LAND on stamps of Falkland Islands: **Falkland Islands – Graham Land.**

GRANA: Two Sicilies.

GRANADINA: Colombia.

GRANDE COMOREC: Grand Comoro.

GRAND LIBAN: Lebanon.

GREENSBORO ALA.: United States – Greensboro, Alabama.

GREENSBORO N.C.: United States – Greensboro, North Carolina.

GREENVILLE, ALA.: United States – Greenville, Alabama.

GREENVILLE C.H.S.C.: United States – Greenville Court House, South Carolina.

G.R.I. on stamps inscribed "Deutsch New Guinea": **New Britain;** on stamps of Samoa: **Samoa – German Administration.**

GRIFFIN GA.: United States – Griffin, Georgia.

GRØNLAND: Greenland.

GROSSDEUTSCHES REICH ("Great Germany"): **Germany;** with **BÖHMEN UND MÄHREN: Czechoslovakia – Bohemia and Moravia.**

GROSSDEUTSCHES REICH GENERALGOUVERNEMENT: Poland – German occupation.

GROUCH: Turkey.

GROVE HILL ALA.: United States – Grove Hill, Alabama.

GUADALAJARA: Mexico – Guadalajara.

GUADELOUPE on stamps of French Colonies: **Guadeloupe.**

GUAM on stamps of United States: **Guam.**

GUANACASTE: Costa Rica – Guanacaste.

GUERNSEY: Great Britain – Guernsey.

GUINE or **GUINE PORTUGUESA: Cape Verde, Portuguese Guinea.**

GUINE BISSAU: Guinea – Bissau.

109

GUINEA followed by **CONTINENTAL, CORREOS,** or **ESPAÑOLA: Spanish Guinea;** by **ECUATORIAL: Equatorial Guinea.**
GUINEE or **GUINEE FRANÇAIS: French Guinea.**
GÜLTIG 9 ARMEE on stamps of Germany: **Romania – German occupation.**
GUYANA on stamps of British Guinea: **Guyana.**
GUYANE FRANÇAISE: **French Guiana.**
GWALIOR: **India – Gwalior.**

H

HABILITADO on stamps of Cuba: **Cuba – U.S. Administration.**
HALLETTSVILLE TEX.: **United States – Hallettsville, Texas.**
HAMBURG S.C.: **United States – Hamburg, South Carolina.**
HARPER: **Liberia.**
HASHEMITE KINGDOM OF JORDAN: **Jordan.**
HATAY DEVLETI: **Hatay.**
HAUTE SILESIE: **Upper Silesia.**
HAUTE VOLTA: **Upper Volta.**
HAUT-SÉNÉGAL-NIGER: **Upper Senegal and Niger.**
H.E.H. THE NIZAM'S: **India – Hyderabad.**
HEDJAZ & NEDJDE, HEJAZ & NEJD: **Saudi Arabia.**
HELENA: **United States – Helena, Texas.**
HELLER: **Austria, Bosnia – Herzegovina, Liechtenstein.**
HELVETIA: **Switzerland.**
H.H. NAWAB SHAH JAHANBECAM: **India – Bhopal.**
H.I. or HAWAIIAN ISLANDS POSTAGE: **Hawaii.**
H.I. & U.S.: **Hawaii.**
HIRLAPJEGY: **Hungary.**
Новч., Новчич: **Montenegro.**
HOI HAO on stamps of Indo-China: **France – Offices in China – Hoi Hao.**
HOLKAR STATE: **India – Indore.**
HOLSTEIN: **Schleswig – Holstein.**
HONDOUR'S: **United States – Charleston, South Carolina.**
HOUSTON TXS.: **United States – Houston, Texas.**
Н.Р. БЪЛГАРИЯ: **Bulgaria.**
ΗΠΕΙΡΟΣ: **Epirus.**
HRVATSKA: **Croatia, Yugoslavia.**
H.R.Z.G.L.: **Schleswig – Holstein.**
HT-SÉNÉGAL-NIGER: **Upper Senegal and Niger.**
HUNTSVILLE TEX.: **United States – Huntsville, Texas.**
HYDERABAD: **India – Hyderabad.**

I

ICC on stamps of India: **India – International Commission in Indochina – Laos and Vietnam.**

IDAR: India – Idar.

I.E.F. ("Indian Expeditionary Force"): **India.**

I.E.F. 'D' on stamps of Turkey: **Mesopotamia.**

IERUSALEM on stamps of Russia: **Russia – Offices in Turkey.**

ILE DE LA RÉUNION: Reunion.

ILE ROUAD on stamps of French offices in the Levant: **Rouad.**

ILES WALLIS ET FUTUNA: Wallis and Futuna Islands.

IMPERIAL BRITISH EAST AFRICA COMPANY: British East Africa.

IMPERIAL CHINESE POST, CHINESE IMPERIAL POST or **CHINESE EMPIRE: China.**

IMPERIAL JAPANESE POST: Japan.

IMPERIAL KOREAN POST: Korea.

IMPÉRIO COLONIAL PORTUGUES with no colony name: **Portuguese Africa.**

IMPTO or **IMPUESTO DE GUERRA: Spain.**

INCI YIL DÖNÜMÜ: Turkey.

INDE, INDIE: French India.

INDEPENDENCE, TEX.: United States – Independence, Texas.

INDIA with inscriptions in Portuguese or words **REIS, TANGAS,** or **RUPIA: Portuguese India.**

INDIA PORT. or **PORTUGUEZA: Portuguese India.**

INDO-CHINE: Indo-China.

INDONESIA not preceded by **"REPUBIK": Dutch Indies – Indonesia.**

INDORE: India – Indore.

INDUSTRIELLE KRIEGSWIRTSCHAFT: Switzerland.

INHAMBANE on stamps of Mozambique: **Inhambane.**

INKERI: North Ingermanland.

INLAND: Liberia.

INSELPOST on stamps of Germany: **Germany – military stamps.**

INSTRUCAO on stamps of Portuguese India: **Timor.**

INSTRUCCION: Venezuela.

INSUFFICIENTLY PREPAID POSTAGE DUE: Zanzibar.

IONIKON ΚΡΑΤΟΣ: Ionian Islands – Kratos.

I.O.V.R.: Romania.

I.R. OFFICIAL on stamps of Great Britain: **Great Britain – Official stamps.**

IRAN: Persia.

IRANIENNES ("Iranien"): **Persia.**

IRAQ on stamps of Turkey: **Mesopotamia.**

IRIAN BARAT: West New Guinea.

ÍSLAND: Iceland.

ISLAS GALAPAGOS: Ecuador – Galapagos Islands.

ISLE OF MAN: Great Britain –Isle of Man.

111

ISOLE ITALIANE DELL'EGEO on stamps of Italy: **Italy – Aegean Islands.**
ISOLE JONIE on stamps of Italy: **Ionian Islands – Italian occupation.**
ISTRA or ISTRIA: Yugoslavia – **Issues for Istria and the Slovene Coast.**
ΙΤΑΛΙΑΣ-ΕΛΛΑΔΣ-ΤΟΥΡΚΙΑΣ: **Greece.**
ITÄ-KARJALA on stamps inscribed "SUOMI-FINLAND": **Karelia – Finnish administration.**
ITALIA, ITALIANE, ITALIANO: **Italy.**
ITALIAN SOMALILAND: **Somalia.**
ITALIA OCCUPAZIONE MILITARE ITALIANA ISOLE CEFALONIA E ITACA on stamps of Greece: **Ionian Islands – Italian occupation.**
I-U-KA: **United States – Iuka, Mississippi.**
IZMIR HİMAYEİ ETFAL: **Turkey.**

J

JAFFA on stamps of Russia: **Russia – Offices in Turkey.**
JAIPUR: **India – Jaipur.**
JAM. DIM. SOOMAALIYA: **Somalia.**
JAMES M BUCHANAN: **United States – Baltimore, Maryland.**
JAMHURI ZANZIBAR TANZANIA: **Zanzibar.**
JANINA on stamps of Italy: **Italy – Offices in Turkey – Janina.**
JAPANESE EMPIRE: **Japan.**
JAVA on stamps inscribed "Nederlandsch–Indie": **Dutch Indies.**
J.D. SOOMAALIYEED: **Somalia.**
JEEND, JHIND, or JIND STATE: **India – Jhind.**
JERSEY: **Great Britain – Jersey.**
JERUSALEM on stamps of Russia: **Russia – Offices in Turkey.**
JOHOR or JOHORE: **Malay States – Johore.**
JONESBORO T.: **United States – Jonesboro, Tennessee.**
JOURNAUX DAGBLADEN on stamps of Belgium: **Belgium – Newspaper stamps.**
J.P. JOHNSON, P.M.: **United States – Pittsylvania Court House, Virginia.**
JUBILE DE L'UNION POSTALE UNIVERSELLE: **Switzerland.**
JUGOSLAVIJA: **Yugoslavia.**
ЈУГОСЛАВИЈА: **Yugoslavia.**

K

K with no country name (abbreviation for "krone"): **Bosnia and Herzegovina.**
K-numeral-K on stamps of Russia: **Far Eastern Republic.**
K 60 K on stamps of Russia: **Armenia.**
KAIS. KÖN: **Austria.**
KALAALLIT NUNAAT: **Greenland.**

KALAYAAN NANG PILIPINAS: Philippines – Japanese occupation.

KAMERUN: Cameroun.

KAP.: Latvia.

КАРПАТСЬКА-УКРАІНА on stamps inscribed "Česko-Slovensko": **Czechoslovakia – Carpath-Ukraine.**

KARJALA: Karelia.

KARKI on stamps of Italy: **Italy – Aegean Islands – Karki.**

KARLFONDS: Austria, Bosnia & Herzegovina.

KAROLINEN: Caroline Islands.

KÄRNTEN ABſTIMMUNG ("Carinthian Plebiscite") on stamps of Austria: **Austria.**

KEDAH: Malay States – Kedah.

KELANTAN: Malaya – Kelantan.

KEMAHKOTAAN or **KETAHKOTAAN** on stamps inscribed "Johore": **Malay States – Johore.**

KENTTÄ-POSTI FÄLTPOST or **KENTTÄPOSTIA:** Finland – Military stamps.

KENYA & UGANDA: Kenya, Uganda, and Tanzania.

KENYA UGANDA TANZANIA: Kenya, Uganda, and Tanzania.

KERASSUNDE on stamps of Russia: **Russia – Offices in Turkey.**

K.G.C.A. on stamps of Yugoslavia: **Yugoslavia.**

K.G.L. or **KONGELIG:** Danish West Indies, Denmark.

KHMER REPUBLIC: Cambodia.

KHOR FAKKAN: Sharjah and Dependencies.

KIAUTSCHOU: Kiauchau.

KIBRIS CUMHURIYETI: Cyprus.

KINGSTON GA.: United States – Kingston, Georgia.

KIONGA on stamps of Lourenco Marques: **Kionga.**

KISHANGARH or **KISHENGARH:** India – Kishengarh.

K.K. or **KAISERLICHE KÖNIGLICHE ÖSTERREICHISCHE POST** ("Imperial and Royal Austrian Post"): **Austria.**

K.K.POST-STEMPEL with values in **KREUZER:** Austria; with values in **CENTES:** Austria – Lombardy – Venetia.

KLAIPĖDA: Memel – Lithuanian occupation.

KNOXVILLE: United States – Knoxville, Tennessee.

KORCA or **KORCE:** Albania.

KOREAN POST: Korea.

KORONA: Hungary.

KOUANG-TCHÉOU or **KOUANG TCHÉOU-WAN** on stamps of Indo-China: **France – Offices in China – Kwangchowan.**

KPHTH: Crete.

KR., KREUZER: Austria, Baden, Bavaria, Germany, Hungary, Württemberg.

KRALJEVSTVO (or **KRALJEVINA**) **SRBA, HRVATA I SLOVENACA** ("Kingdom of the Serbs, Croats and Slovenes"): **Yugoslavia.**

KRONE, KRONEN: Austria.

K.S.A.: (Kingdom of) Saudi Arabia.

K.u.K. ("Imperial and Royal"): **Austria, Bosnia and Herzegovina.**

K-U-K-FELDPOST: Austria; with values in "BANI" or "LEI": **Romania.**

K-U-K-MILITÄRPOST: Bosnia and Herzegovina.

K. und K. FELDPOST: Austria.

KUWAIT on stamps of India or Great Britain: **Kuwait.**

K. WÜRTT: **Württemberg.**

К.С. ПОШТА, К.СРБСКА ПОШТА: **Serbia.**

КИТАЙ on stamps of Russia: **Russia – Offices in China.**

КОН, КОП, КON, КOP: Batum, Far Eastern Republic, Finland, Latvia, Russia, South Russia.

КРАЉ ЦРНА ГОРА: **Montenegro.**

КРАЉЕВСТВО СРБА, ХРВАТА, И СЛОВЕНАЦА or С.Х.С. ("Kingdom of the Serbs, Croats and Slovenes"): **Yugoslavia.**

L

LA AGÜERA: **La Aguera.**

LABUAN on stamps of North Borneo: **Labuan.**

LA CANEA on stamps of Italy: **Italy – Offices in Crete.**

LA GEORGIE: **Georgia.**

LA GRANGE TEX.: **United States – La Grange, Texas.**

LAIBACH: **Yugoslavia – Ljubljana – German occupation.**

LAKE CITY FLA.: **United States – Lake City, Florida.**

LANDSTORMEN: **Sweden.**

LANSA: **Colombia.**

L.A.R. (Libyan Arab Republic): **Libya.**

LAS BELA: **India – Las Bela.**

LATTAQUIE on stamps of Syria: **Latakia.**

LATVIJA, LATWIJAS: **Latvia.**

LAVACA: **United States – Port Lavaca, Texas.**

LEI on stamps of Austria: **Romania – Austrian occupation.**

LENOIR N.C.: **United States – Lenoir, North Carolina.**

LERO or LEROS on stamps of Italy: **Italy – Aegean Islands – Leros.**

LESOTHO on stamps of Basutoland: **Lesotho.**

LEVA: **Bulgaria.**

LEVANT: **France – Offices in Turkey;** on stamps of Great Britain: **Great Britain – Offices in Turkey;** on stamps of Poland: **Poland – Offices in Turkey.**

LEVANTE on stamps of Italy: **Italy – Offices in Turkey.**

LEXINGTON, MISS.: **United States – Lexington, Mississippi.**

LIBAN, LIBANAISE: **Lebanon.**

LIBAU on stamps of Germany: **Latvia – German occupation.**

LIBIA, LIBYE: **Libya;** on stamps of Cyrenaica: **Libya.**

LIETUVA, LIETUVOS: **Lithuania;** on stamps of Russia: **Lithuania – South District.**

LIGNES AERIENNES DE LA FRANCE LIBRE (or F.A.F.L.): **Syria – Free French Administration.**

LIMA: **Peru.**

LIMBAGAN 1543-1943 on stamps of Philippines: **Philippines.**

LIPSO, LISSO on stamps of Italy: **Italy – Aegean Islands – Lisso.**

LIRE on stamps of Austria: **Italy – Austrian occupation.**

LISBOA: Portugal.

LITAS: Lithuania.

LITWA ŚRODKOWA, LITWY ŚRODKOWEI: Central Lithuania.

LIVINGSTON: United States – Livingston, Alabama.

LJUBLJANSKA: Yugoslavia – Ljubljana – German occupation.

L. MARQUES on stamps of Mozambique: Lourenço Marques.

LOCKPORT N.Y.: United States – Lockport, New York.

LÖSEN: Sweden.

LOTHRINGEN on stamps of Germany: France – German occupation.

L.P. on stamps of Russia: Latvia.

LTSR 1940 VII 21on stamps of Lithuania: Lithuania – Russian occupation.

LUBIANA on stamps of Yugoslavia: Yugoslavia – Ljubljana – Italian occupation.

LUFTFELDPOST: Germany – Military air post stamps.

LUXEMBURG: Luxembourg; on stamps of Germany: Luxembourg – German occupation.

M

MACAU or MACAV: Macao.

MACON: United States – Macon, Georgia.

MADEIRA on stamps of Portugal: Madeira.

MADRID: Spain.

MAGYAR ("Hungarian"): Hungary.

MAGYAR KIR.: Hungary.

MAGYAR KIRÁLYI or MAGY. KIR: Hungary.

MAGYAR NEMZETI KORMÁNY SZEGED on stamps of Hungary: Hungary – Serbian occupation – Szeged.

MAGYARORSZÁG: Hungary.

MALACCA: Malay States – Malacca.

MALAGA on stamps of Spain: Spain – Malaga.

MALAGASY: Madagascar.

MALAYA with no further inscriptions, over portrait of Sultan: Malaya States – Kelantan, Negri Sembilan, Pahang, Perak, Perlis, Selangor, Trengganu; over picture of mosque: Selangor; over picture of State Arms: Negri Sembilan.

MALAYA PERLIS: Malaya – Perlis.

MALAYA POSTAL UNION: Malaya.

MALAYA SINGAPORE: Singapore.

MALGACHE: Madagascar.

MALDIVES: Maldives Islands.

MALMÉDY on stamps of Belgium: Germany – Belgian occupation.

MANAMA: a dependency of Ajman.

MAPKA: Finland, Russia, Serbia.

MARCA DA BOLLO: Italy.

MARIANEN on stamps of Germany to 1900 or engraved: Mariana Islands.

MARIANAS ESPAÑOLAS on stamps inscribed "Filipinas": **Mariana Islands – Spanish Dominion.**

MARIETTA: United States – Marietta, Georgia.

MARION VA.: United States – Marion, Virginia.

MARK: Finland, Germany.

MARKA: Estonia.

MARKKAA: Finland.

MAROC: French Morocco, Morocco.

MAROCCO, MAROKKO on stamps of Germany: **Germany – Offices in Morocco.**

MARREUCOS: Morocco – Northern Zone, Spanish Morocco.

MARSCHALL-INSELN on stamps of Germany to 1900: **Marshall Islands.**

MARSHALL-INSELN on stamps of Germany to 1900 or engraved: **Marshall Islands.**

MARTINIQUE on stamps of French Colonies: **Martinique.**

MAURITANIE: Mauritania.

M.B.D. on stamps inscribed "Raj Nandgaon": **India – Nandgaon.**

MBLEDHAJA on stamps of Albania: **Albania – Italian dominion.**

MBLEDHJA KUSHTETUËSE, MBRETNIA SHQIPTARE, MBR. SHQIPTARE, MBRETNIJA SHQIPTARE: Albania.

M.C. GALLAWA: United States – Memphis, Tennessee.

MECKLENB. SCHWERIN: Mecklenburg – Schwerin.

MEDELLIN: Colombia, Colombia – Antioquia.

MEDIA ONZA: Spain.

MEDIO REAL: Dominican Republic.

M.E.F. on stamps of Great Britain: **Great Britain – Offices in Africa.**

MEJICO: Mexico.

MELAKA: Malay States – Malacca.

MEMELGEBIET ("Memel Territory"): **Memel.**

MEMPHIS TENN.: United States – Memphis, Tennessee.

METELIN on stamps of Russia: **Russia – Offices in Turkey.**

MEXICANO ("Mexican"): **Mexico.**

MICANOPY FLA.: United States – Micanopy, Florida.

MILITÄRPOST EILMARKE: Bosnia and Herzegovina – Special handling stamps.

MILITÄRPOST or **MILIT. PORTOMARKE:** Bosnia and Herzegovina – Military post postage due stamps.

MILL., MILLIEMES on stamps of France: **France – Offices in Egypt.**

MILLEDGEVILLE GA.: United States – Milledgeville, Georgia.

M. KIR. ("Magyar Kirly"): **Hungary.**

MN: Korea.

MOBILE ALA.: United States – Mobile, Alabama.

MOÇAMBIQUE: Mozambique.

MONGTZE, MONG-TSEU, or **MONGTSEU** on stamps of Indo-China: **France – Offices in China – Mongtseu.**

MONROVIA: Liberia.

MONT ATHOS on stamps of Russia: **Russia – Offices in Turkey.**

MONTENEGRO on stamps of Austria: **Montenegro – Austrian occupation;** on stamps of Yugoslavia: **Montenegro – Italian occupation.**

MONTEVIDEO: Uruguay.

MONTGOMERY: United States – Montgomery, Alabama.

MONTSERRAT on stamps of Antigua: **Montserrat.**

MOQUEGUA on stamps inscribed "Peru" or "Franqueo": **Peru – Moquegua.**

MOГA: Ukraine.

MOROCCO AGENCIES on stamps of Great Britain: **Great Britain – Offices in Morocco.**

MORVI: India – Morvi.

MOYEN CONGO or **MOYEN-CONGO: Middle Congo.**

MQE on stamps of French Colonies: **Martinique.**

MULTA: Portugal and Portuguese Colonies – Postage due stamps.

MUSCAT & OMAN: Oman.

M.V.i.R. on stamps of Germany or Romania: **Romania – German occupation.**

N

NABHA: India – Nabha.

NACIONES UNIDAS: United Nations.

NANDGAON: India – Nandgaon.

NAPOLETANA: Two Sicilies.

NASHVILLE: United States – Nashville, Tennessee.

NA SLASK: Central Lithuania.

NATIONALER VERWALTUNGSAUSSCHUSS on stamps of Montenegro: **Montenegro – German occupation.**

NATIONS UNIES: United Nations – Offices in Geneva.

NAURU on stamps of Great Britain: **Nauru.**

N.C.E. on stamps of French Colonies: **New Caledonia.**

N.D. HRVATSKA: Croatia.

NED or **NEDERLANDS NIEUW GUINEA: Netherlands Dutch New Guinea.**

NED or **NEDERLANDSE ANTILLEN: Netherlands Antilles.**

NED-INDIE, NEDERL-INDIE, NEDERLANDSCH-INDIE: Dutch Indies.

NEDERLAND: Netherlands.

NEGERI, NEGRI or **N. SEMBILAN: Malay States – Negri Sembilan.**

NEW HAVEN CT.: United States – New Haven Connecticut.

NEW HEBRIDES CONDOMINIUM on stamps of Fiji: **New Hebrides.**

NEW ORLEANS or **N.O.P.O.: United States – New Orleans, Louisiana.**

NEW YORK: United States – New York, New York.

NEZAVISNA DRŽAVA HRVATSKA: Croatia.

NEZ. DRŽ. HRVATSKA: Croatia.

N.F. on stamps of Nyasaland Protectorate: **German East Africa – British occupation.**

NIEUW GUINEA: Dutch New Guinea.

NIEUWE REPUBLIEK: New Republic.

NIPPON: Japan.

NISIRO or **NISIROS** on stamps of Italy: **Italy – Aegean Islands – Nisiro.**

NIUE on stamps of New Zealand: **Niue.**

NLLE CALÉDONIE: New Caledonia.

NO HAY ESTAMPILLAS: Colombia – many states.

NORDDEUTSCHER POSTBEZIRK or **POST.** ("North German Postal District"): **Germany – North German Confederation.**

NOREG and **NORGE: Norway.**

NORTHERN COOK ISLANDS: Penrhyn Island.

NOSSI-BE on stamps of French Colonies: **Nossi-Be.**

NOUVELLE CALEDONIE: New Caledonia.

NOUVELLES HEBRIDES: New Hebrides – French Issues.

NOWANUGGUR: India – Nowanuggur.

N.S.B. on stamps of French Colonies: **Nossi-Be.**

N. SEMBILAN: Malay States – Negri Sembilan.

N.S.W.: New South Wales.

N.W. PACIFIC ISLANDS on stamps of Australia: **North West Pacific Islands.**

NYASALAND: Nyasaland Protectorate.

NYASSA on stamps of Mozambique: **Nyassa.**

N.Z.: New Zealand.

ОДНА МАРКА: Finland.

OAXACA: Mexico – Oaxaca.

OBOCK on stamps of French Colonies: **Obock.**

OCCUPATION FRANÇAISE on stamps of Hungary: **Hungary – French occupation.**

OCÉANIE: French Polynesia.

OESTERR or **ŒSTERR POST: Austria;** with name Liechtenstein: **Liechtenstein – Austrian postal administration.**

OEUVRES or **ŒUVRES DE SOLIDARITÉ FRANÇAISE: French Colonies.**

OFFENTLIG or **OFF. SAK: Norway – Official stamps.**

OFFICIAL on stamps of Kenya, Uganda, and Tanzania: **Tanganyika.**

OFFISIEEL ("Official"): **South Africa, South West Africa.**

ÖſTERREICH: Austria.

OIL RIVERS: Niger Coast Protectorate.

ОКСА: Russia – Army of the North.

OLTRE GIUBA on stamps of Italy: **Oltre Giuba.**

O.M.F. SYRIE on stamps of France: **Syria.**

ORANGE RIVER COLONY on stamps of Cape of Good Hope: **Orange River Colony.**

ORANJE VRIJ STAAT ("Orange Free State"): **Orange River Colony.**

ORCHA: India – Orcha.

ØRE: Denmark, Norway.

ÖRE: Sweden.

ORTS-POST: Switzerland.

O.S.: Norway – Official stamps.

ÖSTERREICH: Austria.

ÖSTERR-POST, ÖSTERREICHISCHE POST: Austria.

OSTLAND ("Eastland") on stamps of Germany: **Russia – German occupation.**

OTVORENIE SLOVENSKÉHO on stamps of Czechoslovakia: **Czechoslovakia – Slovakia.**

OUBANGUI-CHARI: Ubangi.

OUBANGUI-CHARI-TCHAD on stamps of Middle Congo: **Ubangi.**

O.W. OFFICIAL on stamps of Great Britain: **Great Britain – Official stamps.**

ΟΛΥΜ., ΟΛΥΜΠ., or **ΟΛΥΜΠΙΑΚΟΙ ΑΓΩΝΕΣ** ("Olympic Games"): **Greece.**

ΟΛΥΜΠΙΑ ("Olympia"): **Greece.**

P

p (pence) or **£** (pound) preceded by a numeral, on stamps with king's or queen's head but no country name: **Great Britain.**

PACCHI POSTALI ("Parcel Post"): **Italy;** with value in diagonal band: **San Marino;** with star and crescent emblem: **Somalia.**

PACKHOI or **PAK-HOI** on stamps of Indo-China: **France – Offices in China – Packhoi.**

PAHANG: Malay States – Pahang.

PAID with value in cents: **United States – various provisionals.**

PAISA, PICE: Nepal.

PAITA on stamps of Peru: **Peru – Paita.**

PAKISTAN on stamps of India: **Pakistan.**

PAKKE-PORTO: Greenland.

PALESTINE on stamps of Egypt: **Egypt – Palestine occupation;** on stamps of Egypt with "E.E.F.": **Palestine – British Mandate;** on stamps of Trans-Jordan: **Palestine.**

PAPUA on stamps of British New Guinea: **Papua New Guinea.**

PAPUA & NEW GUINEA: Papua New Guinea.

PARA: Yugoslavia.

PARA(S): Egypt, Mesopotamia, Turkey; on stamps of Austria: **Austria – Offices in Turkey;** on stamps of France: **France – Offices in Turkey;** on stamps of Germany: **Germany – Offices in Turkey;** on stamps of Great Britain: **Great Britain – Offices in Turkey;** on stamps of Italy: **Italy – Offices in Turkey;** on stamps of Romania: **Romania – Offices in Turkey;** on stamps of Russia: **Russia – Offices in Turkey.**

PASCO on stamps of Peru: **Peru – Pasco.**

PATIALA: India – Patiala.

PATMO or **PATMOS** on stamps of Italy: **Italy – Aegean Islands – Patmo.**

P.C.Φ.C.P. (abbreviation for "Russia Soviet Socialist Republic"): **Russia.**

P.E. inscribed on stamps with Arabic overprints: **Egypt.**

PECHINO on stamps of Italy: **Italy – Offices in China – Peking.**

PEN, PENNI, PENNIA: Finland.

PENNY: United States – various provisionals.

PENRHYN ISLAND on stamps of Cook Islands or New Zealand: **Penrhyn Island.**

PEOPLE'S DEMOCRATIC REPUBLIC OF YEMEN: Yemen, People's Democratic Republic.

PERAK: Malay States – Perak.
PERLIS: Malay States – Perlis.
PERSANE: Persia.
PERSEKUTUAN TANAH MELAYU: Malaya.
PERUANA: Peru.
PERU-AEREO: Peru – air post.
PESA on stamps of Germany: **German East Africa.**
PESETA (PTA) or **PESETAS (PTAS): Cuba, Peru, Spain;** with no country name:
    Spain.
PETERSBURG VIRGINIA: United States – Petersburg, Virginia.
PF or **PFG** on stamps of Germany: **Germany – Offices in China – Kiauchau;** on
    stamps of Russia: **Estonia – German occupation.**
PFENNIG: Bavaria, Germany, Württemberg.
P.G.S. on stamps of Strait Settlements: **Malaya – Perak.**
PHILIPPINES on stamps of United States: **Philippines – U.S. Administration.**
PIASTER: Austria – Offices in Turkey; Germany – Offices in Turkey.
PIASTRA, PIASTRE, PIASTRES on stamps of France: **France – Offices in Turkey;**
    on stamps of Great Britain: **Great Britain – Offices in Turkey;** on stamps of
    Italy: **Italy – Offices in Crete** or **in Turkey;** on stamps of Russia: **Russia –**
    Offices in Turkey.
PIES: India.
PILGRIM TERCENTENARY with no country name: **United States.**
PILIPINAS: Philippines.
PINSIN: Ireland.
PISCO on stamps of Peru: **Peru – Pisco.**
PISCOPI on stamps of Italy: **Italy – Aegean Islands – Piscopi.**
PIURA on stamps of Peru: **Peru – Piura.**
PLEASANT SHADE: United States – Pleasant Shade, Virginia.
PLÉBISCITE OLSZTYN ALLENSTEIN on stamps of Germany: **Allenstein.**
PLEBISCIT SLESVIG: Schleswig.
P.M. on stamps of Italy: **Italy – Military stamps.**
РОССІЯ: Russia, South Russia.
POCZTA: Poland.
POCZTA POLSKA ("Polish postage"): **Poland;** on stamps of Austria: **Poland;** on
    stamps of Germany: **Germany – Polish occupation;** on stamps inscribed
    "Waszara": **Poland.**
POHJOIS INKERI: North Ingermanland.
POLSKA: Poland.
POLYNESIE FRANÇAISE: French Polynesia.
PONCE, P.R.: Puerto Rico – Ponce.
Р.О.П.и.Т. on stamps of Russia: **Russia – Offices in Turkey, Ukraine.**
PORTEADO: Portugal.
PORTE DE CONDUCCIÓN: Peru.
PORTE DE MAR: Mexico.
PORTE FRANCO: Peru, Portugal.
PORT GDAŃSK on stamps of Poland: **Poland – Offices in Danzig.**
PORT-LAGOS on stamps of French colonies: **France – Offices in Turkey – Port
    Lagos.**

PORT-SAID: France – Offices in Egypt – Port Said.

PORTO on stamps with no country name: **Austria;** with "piaster": **Austria – Offices in Turkey.**

PORTO GAZETEI: Romania – Moldavia.

PORTOMARKE: Bosnia & Herzegovina.

PORTO RICO on stamps of United States: **Puerto Rico.**

POSTA ROMANA CONSTANTINOPOL on stamps of Romania: **Romania – Offices in Turkey.**

POŠTA ČESKOSLOVENSKA on stamps of Austria: **Czechoslovakia.**

POSTAGE with value in pies, annas or rupees: **India – Hyderabad;** with **CAMB. AUST. CIGILLUM NOV** in a circle: **New South Wales.**

POSTAGE, POSTAGE & REVENUE with denominations in d or p (pence)/(shilling) or £ (pound) and portraits of a king or queen, but no country name: **Great Britain;** with denominations in annas: **India – Kishengarh.**

POSTAGE I.E.F.'D' on stamps of Turkey: **Mesopotamia.**

POSTAGE DUE with denominations in d or p (pence)/(shilling), or £ (pound): **Australia, Great Britain.**

POSTAGE TWO CENTS with portrait of Andrew Jackson, and initials C.S. in lower corners: **United States – Confederate States.**

POSTALI: Italy; with value in diagonal band: **San Marino;** with star and crescent emblem: **Somalia.**

POSTAS LE HÍOC or **N'ÍOC** ("postage due"): **Ireland.**

POSTE AÉRIENNE on stamps with no country name: **Persia.**

POSTE CENTIME with numeral in center of stamp covered with a network of colored lines: **France – Alsace and Lorraine – German occupation.**

POSTE ESTENSI: Modena.

POSTE KHEDEVIE EGIZIANE: Egypt.

POSTE LOCALE: Switzerland – various cantons.

POSTE VATICANE: Vatican City.

POSTES: Belgium, France, French Colonies, Luxembourg.

POSTES followed by **EGYPTIENNES:** Egypt; followed by **HEDJAZ AND NEDJDE:** Saudi Arabia; followed by **OTTOMANES:** Mesopotamia, Turkey; followed by picture of crescent: **Afghanistan.**

POSTES PERSANES: Bushire, Persia.

POSTGEBIET OB. OfT C on stamps of Germany: **Lithuania – German occupation.**

POST OFFICE DISPATCH: United States – Baltimore, Maryland.

POSTZEGEL with no country name: **Netherlands.**

POUL: Afghanistan.

PREUSSEN: Prussia.

PRINCE FAROUK: Egypt.

PRINCIPAUTE DE MONACO ("Principality of Monaco"): **Monaco.**

PRO TACNA Y ARICA, PRO PLEBISCITO TACNA Y ARICA: Peru.

PROJECT MERCURY: United States.

PROTECTORADO ESPAÑOL or with **EN MARRUECOS** on stamps of Spain: **Spanish Morocco.**

PROTECTORAT FRANÇAIS on stamps inscribed "Chiffre Taxe": **French Morocco.**

PROTECTORATE on stamps of Bechuanaland: **Bechuanaland Protectorate.**

PRO TUBERCULOSOS POBRES: Spain.

PRO UNION IBEROAMERICANA ("For the Spanish American Union"): **Spain.**

PROVINCIE MODONESI: Modena.

PROVINZ LAIBACH: Yugoslavia – Ljubljana – German occupation.

PROVISIONAL 1881-1882 on stamps inscribed "Peru" or "Franqueo": **Peru –** Arequipa.

PROV. R.I.: United States – Providence, Rhode Island.

PS or **SP:** Colombia – Cauca (Provincial Post).

P.S.N.C. ("Pacific Steam Navigation Co.") letters on four corners: **Peru.**

PTO. RICO, PUERTO RICO: Puerto Rico.

PUL: Afghanistan.

PUNO on stamps inscribed "Peru" or "Franqueo": **Peru – Puno.**

PUTTIALLA on stamps of India: **India – Patiala.**

РУБ or **руб:** Finland, Russia, Siberia, South Russia.

РУССКАЯ ПОЧТА or on stamps of Russia or Ukraine: **Russia – Offices in Turkey –** Wrangel Issues.

ПАРА, ПАРЕ: Montenegro, Serbia, Yugoslavia (ПАРА only).

ПОРТО СКРИСОРИ: Romania – Moldavia.

ПОРТО МАРКА: Serbia.

ПОРТО PORTO ("postage due"): **Serbia.**

ПОЩА ВЪ РОМЖНИЯ: Romania – Bulgarian occupation.

ПОШТА or **ПОЩТА:** Serbia.

ПОЧТ МАРКА on stamps with no country name: **Azerbaijan.**

ПОЧТА ("postage"): **Russia.**

ПОЧТА РУССКОЙ АРМИИ or on stamps of Russia or Ukraine: **Russia – Offices in** Turkey – Wrangel Issues.

ПОЧТОВАЯ МАРКА: Finland.

ΠΡΟΣΩΡΙΝΟΝ ("temporary") on stamps of Crete: **Crete.**

ΠΡΟΣΩΡΙΝΟΝ ΤΑΧΥΔΡΟΜΕΙΟ (or **ΤΑΧΥΔΡΟΜ**) with **ΗΡΑΚΛΕΙΟΥ:** Crete.; with **ΡΕΘΥΜΝΗΣ:** Rethymnon – Russian Offices; with **ΣΑΜΟΥ:** Samos.

Q

QATAR on stamps of Great Britain: **Qatar.**

QARKU: Albania.

QINDAR, QINTAR: Albania.

QUELIMANE on stamps of various Portuguese Colonies: **Quelimane.**

R

R on stamps of Colombia: **Panama.**

R (for "rial") on stamp with Arabic lettering, but no country name: **Persia.**

R. COMMISSARIATO, etc. on stamps of Yugoslavia: **Yugoslavia – Ljubljana –
Italian occupation.**

RAJASTHAN on stamps of Jaipur: **India – Rajasthan.**

RALEIGH N.C.: United States – Raleigh, North Carolina.

RAPPEN: Switzerland.

RECARGO: Spain.

REGATUL ROMANIEI ("Romanian Kingdom") on stamps of Hungary: **Hungary –
Romanian occupation.**

REGENCE DE TUNIS: Tunisia.

REGNO D'ITALIA ("Kingdom of Italy"): **Italy;** on stamps of Austria with words
VENEZIA GIULIA or with **TRENTINO: Austria – Italian occupation;** on
stamps inscribed **FIVME** or **FIUME: Fiume.**

REICH, REICHPOST: Germany.

REIS or **RÉIS** with no country name: **Portugal.**

REP. or **REPUB. DI S. MARINO: San Marino.**

REPOBLIKA MALAGASY: Madagascar.

REPUBBLICA ITALIANA: Italy.

REPUBBLICA SOCIALE ITALIANA: Italy – Italian Socialist Republic.

REPUBLIC OF BOTSWANA on stamps of Bechuanaland Protectorate: **Botswana.**

REPUBLIC OF CHINA: China – Taiwan.

REPUBLICA DA GUINE-BISSAU: Guinea – Bissau.

REPUBLICA DE COLOMBIA: Colombia, Panama.

REPUBLICA DOMINICANA: Dominican Republic.

REPUBLICA ESPAÑOLA: Spain.

REPÚBLICA ORIENTAL ("Eastern Republic"): **Uruguay.**

REPÚBLICA PERUANA: Peru.

REPUBLICA POPULARA ROMANA: Romania.

REPUBLICA PORTUGUESA: Portugal.

REPUBLICA QUELIMANE on stamps of various Portuguese Colonies: **Quelimane.**

REPUBLICA TETE on stamps of various Portuguese Colonies: **Tete.**

REPUBLIEK VAN SUID-AFRIKA: South Africa.

REPUBLIK INDONESIA: Indonesia.

REPUBLIKA NG. PILIPINAS: Philippines – Japanese occupation.

REPUBLIKA POPULLORE SOCIALISTE E SHQIPERISE: Albania.

REPUBLIQUE ARABE SYRIENNE: Syria.

REPUBLIQUE ARABE UNIE-SYRIE: Syria – United Arab Republic.

REPUBLIQUE AUTONOME DU TOGO: Togo.

REPUBLIQUE CENTRAFRICAINE: Central African Republic.

REPUBLIQUE d'AZERBAIDJAN: Azerbaijan.

REPUBLIQUE D'HAITI or **RÉPUBLIQUE D'HAÏTI: Haiti.**

RÉPUBLIQUE DE CÔTE d'IVOIRE: Ivory Coast.

REPUBLIQUE DE DJIBOUTI: Djibouti.

RÉPUBLIQUE DE GUINÉE: Guinea.

REPUBLIQUE DE HAUTE VOLTA: Upper Volta.

**RÉPUBLIQUE DEMOCRATIQUE DU CONGO: Congo Democratic Republic (ex-
Belgian).**

RÉPUBLIQUE DÉMOCRATIQUE POPULAIRE LAO: Laos.

REPUBLIQUE DU CAMEROUN: Cameroon.

REPUBLIQUE DU CONGO: Congo Democratic Republic (ex-Belgian), Congo People's Republic (ex-French).

REPUBLIQUE DU DAHOMEY: Dahomey.

REPUBLIQUE DU MALI: Mali.

REPUBLIQUE DU NIGER: Niger.

REPUBLIQUE DU SENEGAL: Senegal.

REPUBLIQUE DU TCHAD: Chad.

REPUBLIQUE DU TOGO: Togo.

REPUBLIQUE DU ZAIRE: Congo Democratic Republic (ex-Belgian).

REPUBLIQUE FEDERALE DU CAMEROUN: Cameroon.

REPUBLIQUE FEDERALE ISLAMIQUE DES COMORES: Comoro Islands.

REPUBLIQUE FRANÇAISE or REPUB. FRANÇ if perforated: **France;** if imperforated: **French Colonies.**

REPUBLIQUE GABONAISE: Gabon.

REPUBLIQUE ISLAMIQUE DE MAURITANIE: Mauritania.

REPUBLIQUE LIBANAISE: Lebanon.

REPUBLIQUE MALGACHE: Madagascar.

REPUBLIQUE POPULAIRE DU BENIN: Benin.

REPUBLIQUE POPULAIRE DU CONGO: Congo People's Republic (ex-French).

REPUBLIQUE RWANDAISE: Rwanda.

REPUBLIQUE TOGOLAISE: Togo.

REPUBLIQUE TUNISIENNE: Tunisia.

RESPUBLICA HUNGARICA: Hungary.

RETYMNO (as "ΡΕΘΥΜΝΟΝ": **Crete.**

REUNION on stamps of French Colonies: **Reunion.**

R.F. (Abbreviation for "Republic of France") with no country name: **France, French Colonies.**

R.H. (Abbreviation for "Republic of Haiti"): **Haiti.**

RHEATOWN: United States – Rheatown, Tennessee.

RHEINLAND-PFALZ: Germany – Rhine Palatinate – French occupation.

RIAL or RIALS: Persia.

RIALTAR SEALADAČ NA HÉIREANN ("Provisional Government of Ireland") on stamps of Great Britain: **Ireland.**

RIAU on stamps of Indonesia: **Indonesia – Riau Archipelago.**

RICHMOND TEXAS: United States – Richmond, Texas.

RINGGOLD GEORGIA: United States – Ringgold, Georgia.

RIN, RN: Japan.

RIO DE ORO on stamps inscribed "TERRITORIOS DEL AFRICA OCCIDENTAL ESPAÑOLA": **Rio de Oro.**

RIS on stamps of Dutch Indies: **Indonesia.**

RIZEH on stamps of Russia: **Russia – Offices in Turkey.**

RL. PLATA F.: Cuba, Philippines.

R.O. on stamps of Turkey: **Eastern Rumelia.**

RODI: Italy – Aegean Islands – Rhodes.

ROMAGNE: Italian States – Romagna.

ROMANA or ROMINA: Romania.

ROSS DEPENDENCY: New Zealand – Ross Dependency.

ROUMELIE ORIENTALE on stamps of Turkey: **Eastern Rumelia.**

ROYAUME DE L'ARABIE SAOUDITE: Saudi Arabia.

ROYAUME DE YEMEN: Yemen.

ROYAUME DU BURUNDI: Burundi.

ROYAUME DU CAMBODGE: Cambodia.

ROYAUME DU LAOS: Laos.

ROYAUME DU MAROC: Morocco.

RP. (rappen): **Liechtenstein, Switzerland.**

R.P.E. SHQIPERISE: Albania.

RPF on stamps of Luxembourg: **Luxembourg – German occupation.**

R.P. ROMINA: Romania.

R.R. with value in opposite corners: **Switzerland – Zurich.**

R.S.A.: South Africa.

R.S.M.: San Marino.

RUANDA on stamps inscribed "CONGO": **German East Africa – Belgian occupation.**

RUANDA-URUNDI on stamps of Congo Democratic Republic (ex-Belgian): **Ruanda-Urundi.**

RUMÄNIEN on stamps of Germany: **Romania – German occupation.**

Ruſſiſch-Polen ("Russisch-Polen") on stamps of Germany: **Romania – German occupation.**

RUTHERFORDTON N.C.: United States – Rutherfordton, North Carolina.

RYUKYUS: Ryukyu Islands.

S

S.A.: Saudi Arabia.

SAARGEBIET ("Saar Territory"): **Saar.**

SAARLAND, SAARPOST: Saar.

SABAH on stamps of North Borneo: **Sabah.**

SACHSEN: Saxony.

SAHARA ESPAÑOL or **SAHARA OCCIDENTAL: Spanish Sahara.**

ST. CHRISTOPHER NEVIS ANGUILLA: St. Kitts – Nevis.

SAINT LOUIS: United States – St. Louis, Missouri.

SAINT-PIERRE ET MIQUELON: St. Pierre and Miquelon.

S.A.K.: Saudi Arabia.

SALEM N.C.: United States – Salem, North Carolina.

SALISBURY N.C.: United States – Salisbury, North Carolina.

SALONICCO on stamps of Italy: **Italy – Offices in Turkey – Salonika.**

SALONIQUE on stamps of Russia: **Russia – Offices in Turkey.**

SAMOA on stamps of Germany or New Zealand: **Samoa.**

SAN ANTONIO TEX.: United States – San Antonio, Texas.

SANDJAK D'ALEXANDRETTE on stamps of Syria: **Alexandretta.**

SANTANDER: Colombia – Santander.

SAORSTÁT ÉIREANN ("Free State of Ireland") on stamps of Great Britain: **Ireland.**

SARKARI: India – Soruth.

SARRE on stamps of Germany: **Saar.**

SASENO on stamps of Italy: **Saseno.**

SAURASHTRA: India – Soruth.

SCARPANTO on stamps of Italy: **Italy – Aegean Islands – Scarpanto.**

SCHLESWIG: Schleswig – Holstein.

SCINDE DISTRICT DAWK: India – South District.

SCUTARI DI ALBANIA on stamps of Italy: **Italy – Offices in Turkey – Scutari.**

SCUDO: Roman States.

S.d.N BUREAU INTERNATIONAL du TRAVAIL: Switzerland; official stamps for International Labor Bureau.

SEGNATASSE with no country name: **Italy – Postage due.**

SEJM WILNIE: Central Lithuania.

SELANGOR: Malay States – Selangor.

SEN, SN.: Japan, Ryukyu Islands.

SÉNÉGAL on stamps of French Colonies: **Senegal.**

SÉNÉGAMBIE ET NIGER: Senegambia and Niger.

SERBIEN on stamps of Austria or Bosnia and Herzegovina: **Serbia – Austria occupation;** on stamps of Yugoslavia: **Serbia – German occupation.**

SERVICE: Official stamps of **India,** various Indian states, **Nepal, Pakistan.**

SERVICIO POSTAL MEXICANO: Mexico.

SEVILLA-BARCELONA: Spain.

S.H. in upper corners with no country name, eagle, and shield: **German states – Schleswig-Holstein.**

SHANGHAI CHINA on stamps of United States: **United States – Offices in China.**

SHQIPENIA on stamps of Turkey, **SHQIPENIE, SHQIPERIA, SHQIPÈRIÉ, SHQIPERIJA, SHQIPERISE, SHQIPÉTARE, SHQIPNI, SHQIPNIJA, SHQIPONIES, SHQIPTARE, SHQYPNIS, SHQYPTARE: Albania.**

S.H.S. (Abbreviation for "Serbs, Croats, Slovenes"): **Yugoslavia.**

SIEGE DE LA LIGUE ARABE: Morocco.

SIEGE OF MAFEKING: Cape of Good Hope.

SIMI on stamps of Italy: **Italy – Aegean Islands – Simi.**

SINGAPORE MALAYA: Singapore.

SIRMOOR: India – Sirmoor.

SKILLING: Denmark, Norway.

SLD.: Austria – Offices in Turkey.

SLESVIG: Schleswig.

SLOVENSKÁ POŠTA or **SLOVENSKO: Czechoslovakia – Slovakia.**

SLOVENSKÝ ŠTÁT, SLOVENSKO on stamps of Czechoslovakia: **Czechoslovakia – Slovakia.**

S. MARINO: San Marino.

SMIRNE on stamps of Italy: **Italy – Offices in Turkey – Smyrna.**

SMYRNE on stamps of Russia: **Russia – Offices in Turkey.**

S.O. 1920 on stamps of Czechoslovakia or Poland: **Eastern Silesia.**

SOBRETASA AEREA: Colombia.

SOCIALIST PEOPLE'S LIBYAN ARAB JAMAHIRIYA: Libya.

SOCIEDAD COLOMBO-ALEMANA DE TRANSPORTES AEREOS ("SCADTA"): **Colombia.**

SOCIEDADE DE GEOGRAFIA DE LISBOA: Portugal.

SOCIÉTÉ CDES NATIONS ("League of Nations"): **Switzerland – Official Stamps for the League of Nations.**

SOL: Peru.

SOLDI: Austria–Lombardy–Venetia.

SOLIDARITÉ FRANÇAISE: French Colonies.

SOMALI DEMOCRATIC REPUBLIC: Somalia.

SOMALIA on stamps of Italy: **Somalia.**

SOMALIA ITALIANA on stamps of Italy: **Somalia.**

SONORA: Mexico.

SOOMAALIYA: Somalia.

SORUTH: India – Soruth.

S.O. TRSTA-VUJA: Trieste – Zone B.

SOUDAN on stamps of Egypt, Niger, and Upper Senegal: **Sudan;** on stamps of French Colonies: **French Sudan.**

SOUDAN FRANÇAIS: French Sudan.

SOURASHTRA: India – Soruth.

SOUTH GEORGIA on stamps of Falkland Islands: **Falkland Islands Dependencies.**

SOUTH ORKNEYS on stamps of Falkland Islands: **Falkland Islands Dependencies.**

SOUTH SHETLANDS on stamps of Falkland Islands: **Falkland Islands Dependencies.**

SOUTH WEST AFRICA on stamps of South Africa: **South West Africa.**

SOUTHERN RHODESIA on stamps of Great Britain: **Southern Rhodesia.**

SOWJETISCHE BESATZUNGS ZONE on stamps of Germany: **Germany – Russian occupation.**

SPARTA GEO.: United States – Sparta, Georgia.

SPARTANBURG S.C.: United States – Spartanburg, South Carolina.

SPM on stamps of French Colonies: **St. Pierre and Miquelon.**

ŚRODKOWA LITWA: Central Lithuania.

ST, STG ("stang"): **Siam.**

STAMPALIA on stamps of Italy: **Italy – Aegean Islands – Stampalia.**

STATE OF SINGAPORE: Singapore.

STATI PARM or **PARMENSI: Parma.**

S. TOMÉ E PRÍNCIPE: St. Thomas and Prince Islands.

STOCKHOLM: Sweden.

СТОТИНКИ: Bulgaria.

ST.PIERRE M-ON on stamps of French Colonies: **St. Pierre and Miquelon.**

STRAITS SETTLEMENT on stamps of Labuan: **Straits Settlements.**

S.T. TRSTA-VUJA: Trieste – Zone B.

STT VUJA or **VUJNA: Trieste – Zone B;** on stamps of Yugoslavia: **Trieste – Zone B.**

S.U. on stamps of Straits Settlements: **Malay States – Sungei Ujong.**

SUIDAFRIKA: South Africa.

SUIDWES AFRIKA: South West Africa.

S. UJONG: Malay States – Sungei Ujong.

SUL BOLLETTINO or **SULLA RICEVUTA: Italy,** unless additionally overprinted for the various **Italian Colonies;** on stamps with star and crescent emblem: **Somalia.**

SULTANAT D'ANJOUAN: Anjouan.

SULTANATE OF OMAN on stamps of Muscat and Oman: **Oman.**

SUNGEI UJONG: Malay States – Sungei Ujong.

SUOMI: Finland.

SURINAME: Surinam.

SVERIGE: Sweden.

S.W.A.: South West Africa.

SWAZIELAND: Swaziland.

SWAZILAND on stamps of South Africa: **Swaziland.**

SYRIAN ARAB REPUBLIC: Syria.

SYRIE, SYRIENNE: Syria.

T

T with lion, F, and numeral: **Belgium;** in four corners of stamp with numeral in center: **Dominican Republic;** enclosed in a circle: **Peru – Huacho.**

TAHITI on stamps of French Colonies: **Tahiti.**

TAKCA: Bulgaria.

TAKSE: Albania.

TALBOTTON GA.: United States – Talbotton, Georgia.

TANGANYIKA, KENYA, UGANDA: Kenya, Uganda, and Tanzania.

TANGANYIKA & ZANZIBAR: Tanzania.

TANGER with "Correo Español" or on stamps of Spain: **Spanish Morocco – Tangier;** on stamps of France: **French Morocco.**

TANGIER: on stamps of Great Britain: **Great Britain – Offices in Morocco.**

TANZANIA, KENYA, UGANDA: Kenya, Uganda, and Tanzania.

TASSA GAZZETTE: Modena.

TAXA DE GUERRA ("War tax") with values in AVOS: **Macao;** with values in O$: **Portuguese Africa;** with values in REIS: **Portuguese Guinea;** with values in RP: **Portuguese India.**

TAXE: Albania.

TC on stamps of India or Cochin: **India – Travancore – Cochin.**

T.Ç.E.K.: Turkey.

TCHAD: Chad.

TCHONGKING or **TCHONG KING** on stamps of Indo-China: **France – Offices in China – Tchongking.**

T.C. POSTALARI: Turkey.

TE BETALEN: Dutch Indies, Netherlands, Netherlands Antilles, Suriname; preceded by "A PAYER": **Belgium.**

TE BETALEN PORT on red or carmine stamps: **Dutch Indies;** on vermillion stamps: **Dutch New Guinea;** on blue stamps: **Netherlands;** on green stamps: **Netherlands Antilles;** on lilac or purple stamps: **Surinam.**

TELEGRAFOS: Philippines.

TELLICO PLAINS TENN.: United States – Tellico Plains, Tennessee.

T.E.O. ("Occupied Territories of the Enemy") with denominations in milliemes on stamps of France: **Syria;** on stamps of **France – Offices in Turkey:** Cilicia.

TERRES AUSTRALES ET ANTARCTIQUES FRANÇAISES: French Southern and Antarctic Territories.

TERRITOIRE DE IFNI on stamps of Spain: **Ifni.**

TERRITOIRE DE L'ININI: Inini.

TERRITOIRE DU FEZZAN: Libya – Fezzan – French occupation.

TERRITOIRE DU NIGER: Niger.

TERRITOIRE FRANÇAIS DES AFARS ET ISSAS: Afars and Issas.

TERRITORIO DE IFNI (ESPAÑA): Ifni.

TERRITORIOS DEL AFRICA OCCIDENTAL ESPAÑOLA: Spanish West Africa.

TERRITORIOS (or TERRS.) ESPAÑOLES DEL GOLFO DE GUINEA: Spanish Guinea.

TETUAN: Spanish Morocco – Tetuan.

THAILAND or **THAI:** Siam.

THAILAND with values in cents: **Malaya – Siamese occupation.**

THOMASVILLE GA.: United States – Thomasville, Georgia.

THRACE INTERALLIÉE or **THRACE OCCIDENTALE** on stamps of Bulgaria: Thrace.

TIENTSIN on stamps of Italy: **Italy – Offices in China – Tientsin.**

TIMBRE IMPERIAL JOURNAUX: France.

TIMBRE POSTE on stamps of France: **French Morocco.**

TIMBRE TAXE with numeral and no country name: **French Colonies.**

TIMOR on stamps of Macao or Mozambique: **Timor.**

TJENEST-FRIMÆRKE: Denmark.

TJENESTEFRIMERKE: Norway.

T.L.TRIESTE-VUJA: Trieste – Zone B.

TOGA: Tonga.

TOGO on stamps of Dahomey, Germany, or Gold Coast: **Togo.**

TOLIMA: Colombia – Tolima.

TO PAY: Great Britain – Postage due.

TOSCANO: Tuscany.

TOU: Persia.

TOUVA: Tannu Tuva.

TRAITE DE VERSAILLES: Germany – Allenstein.

TRANS-JORDAN: Jordan.

TRASPORTO PACCHI IN CONCESSIONE: Italy – Authorized delivery stamps.

TRAVANCORE (also with **-ANCHAL, -ANCHEL,** or **-COCHIN**): India – Travancore – Cochin.

TREBIZONDE on stamps of Russia: **Russia – Offices in Turkey.**

TRENGGANU: Malay States – Trengganu.

TRIPOLI: Tripolitania; preceded by **FIERA CAMPIONARIA:** Libya.

TRIPOLI DI BARBERIA on stamps of Italy: **Italy – Offices in Africa – Tripoli.**

TRIPOLITANIA on stamps of Italy: **Tripolitania.**

TRISTAN DA CUNHA on stamps of St. Helena: **Tristan da Cunha;** with RESETTLEMENT 1963: St. Helena.

T. Ta. C.: Turkey.

TULLAHOMA TEN.: United States – Tullahoma, Tennessee.

TUNIS, TUNISIE: Tunisia.

TÜRKİYE CUMHURİYETİ (also with **POSTALARI**): Turkey.

TÜRKİYE, TURK POSTALARI: Turkey.
TUSCUMBIA (also with "ALA"): **United States – Tuscumbia, Alabama.**
TWO PENCE under an enthroned queen: **Great Britain – Victoria.**

U

U.A.R.: United Arab Republic; with values in "M" or "£": **Egypt;** with values in "P":
    Syria – United Arab Republic.
U.G. (typewritten): **Uganda.**
UGANDA on stamps of British East Africa: **Uganda;** with **EAST AFRICA** or **KENYA:**
    Kenya, Uganda, and Tanzania.
UGANDA, KENYA, TANGANYIKA: Kenya, Uganda, and Tanzania.
UGANDA, KENYA, TANZANIA: Kenya, Uganda, and Tanzania.
UKRAINE on stamps of Germany: **Russia – German occupation.**
ULTRAMAR ("Beyond the Sea") with a year date: **Cuba, Puerto Rico;** with
    denominations in "AVOS": **Macao;** with denominations in "REIS":
    Portuguese Guinea – war tax stamps.
UNEF on stamps of India: **India – Military stamps – Gaza.**
U.N. FORCE (INDIA) CONGO on stamps of India: **India – Military stamps – Congo.**
UNION CITY, TENNESSEE: United States – Union City, Tennessee.
UNITED ARAB EMIRATES on stamps of Abu Dhabi: **United Arab Emirates.**
UNITED REPUBLIC OF TANYANIKA & ZANZIBAR: Tanzania.
UNITED POSTAL UNION 1949: Great Britain.
UNTEA on stamps of Dutch New Guinea: **West New Guinea.**
URUNDI on stamps of Congo Democratic Republic (ex-Belgian): **German East Africa**
    – Belgian occupation.
US or **U.S.A.: United States.**
U.S. PENNY POST: United States – St. Louis, Missouri.
U.S.P.O.: United States.
ЦАРСТВО: Bulgaria.
ЦАРСТВО БЪЛГАРИЯ: Bulgaria.
ЦРНА ГОРА: Montenegro – Italian occupation.

V

VALDOSTA GA.: United States – Valdosta, Georgia.
VALLEES D'ANDORRE: Andorra.
VALONA on stamps of Italy: **Italy – Offices in Turkey.**
VALPARAÍSO MULTADA: Chile.
VANCOUVER ISLAND: British Columbia and Vancouver Island.
VAN DIEMEN'S LAND: Tasmania.
VATHY: France – Offices in Turkey.

VATICANA or **VATICANE:** Vatican City.

VENEZ, VENEZOLANO: Venezuela.

VENEZIA GIULIA, VENEZIA TRIDENTINA on stamps of Austria or Italy: **Austria – Italian occupation.**

VEREINTE NATIONEN: United Nations – Offices in Vienna.

VICTORIA: United States – Victoria, Texas.

VIỆT-NAM CỘNG HÒA: Viet Nam.

VIVA ESPAÑA CORREOS AERO on stamps of Spain: **Spain – various states.**

VOJNA UPRAVA JUGOSLOVENSKE ARMIJE on stamps of Yugoslavia: **Yugoslavia – Issues for Istria and the Slovene Coast.**

VOM EMPFÄNGER EINZUZIEHEN: Danzig.

V.R. SPECIAL POST on stamps of Transvaal: **Cape of Good Hope.**

VUJA STT or **VUJNA STT** on stamps of Yugoslavia: **Trieste – Zone B.**

W

WADHWAN STATE: India – Wadhwan.

WARRENTON GA.: United States – Warrenton, Georgia.

WEST or **WESTERN AUSTRALIA:** Western Australia.

W.D. COLEMAN: United States – Danville, Virginia.

WENDEN or **WENDENSCHEN:** Russia – Wenden.

WESTERN SAMOA: Samoa.

WHARTON'S: United States – Louisville, Kentucky.

WILLIAMS: United States – Cincinnati, Ohio.

WINNSBORO S.C.: United States – Winnsboro, South Carolina.

WON or **WN** ("weun"): **Korea.**

WÜRTTEMBERG: Württemberg; also **Germany – Württemberg – French Occupation.**

WYTHEVILLE VA.: United States – Wytheville, Virginia.

X

ΧΑΡΤΟΣΗΜΟΝ: Greece.

ХЕЛЕР or **ХЕЛЕРА:** Montenegro.

XII CAMPIONARIA TRIPOLI ("12th Tripoli Fair"): **Libya.**

Y

YCA on stamps of Peru: **Peru – Yca – Chilean occupation.**

Y.C.C.P.: Ukraine; on stamps of Russia: **Ukraine.**

YEMEN ARAB REPUBLIC: Yemen.

YEMEN PDR: Yemen People's Republic.

YEN, YN.: Japan, Manchukuo, Ryukyu Islands.

YUNNAN FOU on stamps of Indo-China: **France – Offices in China – Yunnan Fou.**

YUNNANSEN on stamps of Indo-China: **France – Offices in China – Yunnan Fou.**

УСТАВ: Montenegro.

Укр Н. Р. or **Укр Н. Реп** on stamps of Austria: **Western Ukraine.**

УКРАЇНСЬКА: Ukraine.

Z

Z. AFR. REPUBLIEK, ZUID AFRIKAANSCHE REPUBLIEK, or **ZUID AFRIKAANSE REPUBLIEK** ("South African Republic"): **Transvaal.**

ZANZIBAR on stamps of British East Africa or India: **Zanzibar;** on stamps of France: **France – Offices in Zanzibar.**

ZANZIBAR TANZANIA: Zanzibar.

ZEGELREGT: Transvaal.

ZELAYA: Nicaragua – Zelaya.

ZENTRALER KURIERDIENST: Germany – German Democratic Republic.

ZONA DE OCUPATIE ROMANĂ on stamps of Hungary: **Hungary – Romanian occupation.**

ZONA (also with **DE**) **PROTECTORADO ESPAÑOL** on stamps of Spain: **Spanish Morocco.**

ZONE FRANÇAISE: Germany – French occupation.

ZRAČNA P. or **POŠTA: Trieste – Zone B.**

ZUIDWEST or **ZUID-WEST AFRIKA: South West Africa.**

ZULULAND on stamps of Great Britain or Natal: **Zululand.**

ZÜRICH: Switzerland.

MISCELLANEOUS

বাংলা দে শ: **Bangladesh**.

ЛЕВА or **ЛЕВЪ:** Bulgaria.

З.У.Н.Р. ("Z.U.N.R") **West Ukrainian People's Republic** with trident and shield on stamps of Austria: **Western Ukraine.**

OTHER HARD-TO-IDENTIFY STAMPS

A class of stamps very difficult to identify are those which are not inscribed with any recognizable words and therefore cannot be indexed in the preceding word list. Such stamps should be checked in this section of STAMPS IDENTIFIER.

It is impossible, because of limited space to illustrate all stamps of this kind. We have tried to show a sufficient number so that you can identify virtually all the others.

AFGHANISTAN

Tiger's head and crudely drawn mosque encircled in wreath or ornament identify many of the early issues.

ARMENIA

ARMENIA

Inscription resembling "ZULZ" and "N.F.L." and national emblem — a star, sometimes enclosing a hammer and sickle — identify many stamps of Armenia.

AUSTRIA

AZERBAIJAN

BANGLADESH

BATUM

BOSNIA & HERZEGOVINA

These stamps, if imperforate, belong under Bosnia & Herzegovina: if perforate, under Yugoslavia.

= JUGOSLAVIA

136

BRAZIL

BULGARIA

Country name in various forms

overprinted: ROMANIA — Bulgarian Occupation

BURMA
under Japanese Occupation

**overprinted
under
Japanese Occupation**

137

CHINA

The typical Chinese characters and the sun emblem in a circle, identify many stamps of China.

REPUBLIC OF CHINA

PEOPLE'S REPUBLIC OF CHINA

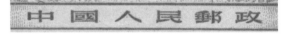

CRETE

Country name and postage in various forms

CUBA
under Spanish Occupation

overprinted: PUERTO RICO

NETHERLANDS INDIES
under Japanese Occupation

EGYPT

EPIRUS

Country name and postage in various forms

ETHIOPIA

FAR EASTERN REPUBLIC

Country name

FAR EASTERN REPUBLIC

**overprinted:
SIBERIA**

FINLAND

Country name

FRENCH COLONIES

—Offices in China

—French Morocco

FRANCE

The stamps shown, if perforated, are France, if imperforate, French Colonies.
The stamps shown are French Colonies.

141

FRENCH COLONIES

Stamps of the type shown were issued for general use in all the French Colonies. To suit local postal needs, various colonies surcharged these stamps with new denominations. The surcharged issues were thereafter classified under the heading of the colony which surcharged and used them. Each colony's surcharges were printed in a characteristic style of type as shown. In some cases denominations additional to those pictured here were used but the style of type remains constant and makes identification possible.

overprinted:

RÉUNION	ANNAM and TONKIN	CONGO

GERMANY

overprinted: FRANCE under German Occupation

AUSTRIA	Lothringen	Elsaß

overprinted: POLAND under German Occupation

GERMANY

overprinted: ROMANIA under German Occupation

GEORGIA

GREAT BRITAIN

overprinted:
IRELAND

overprinted:
OMAN

GREECE

Country name and postage in various forms

GREECE

overprinted: THRACE

HUNGARY

INDIA

GWALIOR

MUSCAT

INDIAN NATIVE STATES

ALWAR

BHOPAL

BUNDI

overprinted: Rajasthan

DHAR

FARIDKOT

JAMMU & KASHtMIR

INDIAN NATIVE STATES

JASDAN	JHALAWAR	JHIND	KISHANGARH	RAJPEEPLA

NANDGAON	POONCH	NOWANUGGUR

IRELAND

ISRAEL

JAPAN

A stylized chrysanthemum, the national emblem of Imperial Japan, was included in virtually all stamp designs produced by this country through 1947. Nearly all subsequent issues bear the name of Japan in four Japanese characters, arranged either vertically or horizontally.

JAPAN

HONG KONG under Japanese Occupation	NORTH BORNEO under Japanese Occupation	KOREA under U.S. Military Rule
 	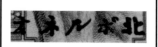	

JORDAN

KOREA

The national emblem of Korea and the characteristic letters under the initials "CH" will enable you to identify most issues.

LEBANON

LIBYA

LOURENCO MARQUES

overprinted:

MALAYA

under Japanese Occupation

MALAY STATES

Kelantan

Pahang

Perak

Negri Sembilan

Selangor

Trengganu

MANCHUKUO

MAURITANIA

overprinted:
FRENCH WEST AFRICA

148

MONGOLIA

MONTENEGRO

Country names in varitous forms

Postage in various forms

NEPAL

PAKISTAN

PAKISTAN
Bahawalpur

PALESTINE

**overprinted:
TRANS-JORDAN**

PANAMA

PERSIA (IRAN)

The heraldic lion brandishing a sword before the rising sun is the national emblem of Persia and identifies many early issues. Many later issues of Persia may be idenitfied by the Arabic lettering shown in the lower central portion of the last stamp pictured.

PHILIPPINES

under Japanese Occupation

RUSSIA

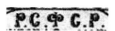

Country names in various forms

All Russian stamps issued since 1922 bear the initials "CCCP", the Russian abbreviation for "Union of Soviet Republics."

151

RUSSIA
overprinted:
ARMENIA

FAR EASTERN REPUBLIC   ## SIBERIA

GEORGIA

SOUTH RUSSIA

TRANSCAUCASIAN FEDERATED REPUBLICS

RUSSIA

overprinted:
UKRAINE

HOW TO IDENTIFY EARLY
ISSUES OF RUSSIA AND FINLAND

Stamps of Finland are identical to stamps of Russia except for the dots in circles worked into the background.

Stamps of Finland are lettered for Finnish currency, penna and markaa. Closely similar Russian stamps are lettered in Kopeks and rubles.

RYUKYU ISLANDS

The country named its own language, arranged horizontally or vertically as shown, and denominations in $ and ¢, will identify most of the issues.

SAUDI ARABIA

SAUDI ARABIA - HEJAZ

SAUDI ARABIA

overprinted:
NEJD

SAUDI ARABIA
overprinted: TRANS-JORDAN

154

SAUDI ARABIA - NEJD

overprinted:
TRANS-JORDAN

SAUDI ARABIA

overprinted: NAJD │ NEJD

SENEGAL
overprinted: FRENCH WEST AFRICA

SERBIA

Country name and postage in various forms

overprinted: JUGOSLAVIA

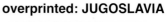

SIAM (THAILAND)

SIBERIA

**overprinted:
FAR EASTERN REPUBLIC**

156

SOUTH RUSSIA

SWITZERLAND

SYRIA

SYRIA   overprinted:
UNITED ARAB REPUBLIC

TANNU TUVA

THRACE

TRANSCAUCASIAN FEDERATED REPUBLICS

TURKEY

Many early issues of Turkey are identified by the "tughra" or sultan's monogram or by the star and crescent, Turkish national emblem. But — caution! — the star and crescent is also the national emblem of Tunisia and of Pakistan; and the tughra appears on some of the early issues of Saudi Arabia.

GREECE overprinted: — Mytilene

158

overprinted: THRACE

overprinted: SYRIA

UKRAINE

FOREIGN NUMERICAL TABLES

ENGLISH	CHINESE	
	Simple	Formal
0	〇	零
½	半	半
1	一	壹
2	二	貳
3	三	參
4	四	肆
5	五	伍
6	六	陸
7	七	柒
8	八	捌
9	九	玖
10	十	拾
100	百	佰
1,000	千	仟
10,000	万	萬
Cent	分	
Dollar	圓	
EXAMPLES $200	貳 佰 圓	
$500	伍 佰 圓	

160

FOREIGN NUMERICAL TABLES

	ARABIC					BURMESE
	Alpha/ Abjad	Eastern	Gobar	Hyderabad	Turkey	
0		٥		٠	٠	၀
1	١	١	ل	١	١	၁
2	ب	٢	ﻉ	٢	٢	၂
3	ج	٣	ﻉ	٣	٣	၃
4	د	ﻉ	ﻉ	٣	٤	၄
5	ه	ﻉ	ﻉ	۵	٥	၅
6	و	٦	ﻉ	۶	٦	၆
7	ز	٧	٧	٧	٧	၇
8	ح	٨	٨	٨	٨	၈
9	ط	٩	٩	٩	٩	၉
10	ي	١٠		١٠	١٠	၁၀
100	ق	١٠٠		١٠٠	١٠٠	၁၀၀

161

FOREIGN NUMERICAL TABLES

	CYRILLIC (RUSSIAN-SLAVONIC)	ETHIOPIAN	HEBREW	INDIAN	KOREAN	KUTCH
0				০	영	૦
1	а̃	፩	א	૧	일	૧
2	в̃	፪	בּ	૨	이	૨
3	г̃	፫	ג	૩	삼	૩
4	д̃	፬	ד	૪	사	૪
5	е̃	፭	ה	૫	오	૫
6	ѕ̃	፮	ו	૬	육	૬
7	з̃	፯	ז	૭	칠	૭
8	и̃	፰	ח	૮	팔	૮
9	ѳ̃	፱	ט	૯	구	૯
10	і̃	፲	י	૧૦	십	૧૦
100	р̃	፻	ק	૧૦૦	백	૧૦૦

162

FOREIGN NUMERICAL TABLES

	MALAY-PERSIAN	MONGOLIAN	NEPALESE	ROMAN	THAI-LAO	TIBETAN
0	٠	0	o		o	၁
1	١	𝒥	٩	I	๑	�
2	٢	𝑎	२	II	๒	२
3	٣	𝑚	३	III	๓	३
4	۴	٥	४	IV	๔	८
5	۵	٨	५	V	๕	५
6	٦ ۶	𝐺	६	VI	๖	७
7	٧	𝑛	७	VII	๗	७
8	٨	𝑙	८ ८	VIII	๘	८
9	٩	𝑙	९	IX	๙	९
10	١٠	𝒥0	٩0	X	๑๐	ৄ০
100	١٠٠	𝒥00	٩00	C	๑๐๐	ৄ০০

PHILATELIC HISTORY

In this section, you will find a capsule history of most countries as they affect the issuance of stamps. A title in CAPITAL LETTERS signifies that it was or is a stamp-issuing entity under that name. A name in parentheses ( ) shows the name of the country whose stamps were used during that time period.

The next section contains a list of countries, islands, protectorates, etc., that no longer issue stamps under those names, although in some cases the country has gained independence and now issues stamps under its new name (Example: Ceylon, now Sri Lanka.)

CURRENT STAMP ISSUING COUNTRIES

AFGHANISTAN
1871-1973	KINGDOM
1973-1979	REPUBLIC
1979-1992	COMMUNIST REPUBLIC
1992-	ISLAMIC REPUBLIC

AITUTAKI
Prior to 1903	Part of Cook Islands
1903-1932	NEW ZEALAND DEPENDENCY
1932-1972	Part of Cook Islands
1972-	POSTAL REGION OF COOK ISLANDS

ALBANIA
1913-1920	PROVISIONAL GOVERNMENTS & OCCUPATION ISSUES
1920-1925	REGENCY
1925-1928	REPUBLIC
1928-1939	KINGDOM
1939-1943	ITALIAN DOMINION
1943-1944	GERMAN OCCUPATION
1944-1946	PROVISIONAL GOVERNMENT
1946-1992	COMMUNIST REPUBLIC
1992-	DEMOCRATIC REPUBLIC

ALGERIA
1849-1871	French Colony (France)
1871-1924	French Overseas Department (France)
1924-1958	FRENCH OVERSEAS DEPARTMENT
1958-1962	French Overseas Department (France)
1962-	REPUBLIC

ANDORRA
1877-1928	Principality (France & Spain)
1928-	PRINCIPALITY (1928-on Spanish Issues) (1931-on French Issues)

ANGOLA
1870-1935	PORTUGUESE COLONY
1935-1951	OVERSEAS PART OF PORTUGAL
1951-1975	PORTUGUESE OVERSEAS PROVINCE
1975-	INDEPENDENT STATE

ANGUILLA
Prior to 1967	Part of St. Kitts-Nevis
1967-1969	SEMI-AUTONOMOUS STATE
1969-1976	BRITISH ADMINISTRATION
1976-1980	SELF-GOVERNING PART OF ST. CHRISTOPHER, NEVIS & ANGUILLA
1980-	SELF-GOVERNING BRITISH COLONY

ANTIGUA
1862-1890	BRITISH COLONY
1890-1903	Part of Leeward Islands
1903-1956	LEEWARD ISLAND PRESIDENCY
1967-1981	BRITISH WEST INDIES ASSOCIATED STATE
1981-	INDEPENDENT STATE

ARGENTINA
1858-1862	CONFEDERATION
1862-	REPUBLIC

Provinces:
1858-1864	BUENOS AIRES
1858-1865	CORDOBA
1856-1880	CORRIENTES

ARMENIA
Prior to 1918	Part of Russia
1918-1919	National Republic (Russia)
1919-1921	NATIONAL REPUBLIC
1921-1922	SOVIET REPUBLIC

164

1922-1923	PART OF TRANSCAUCASIAN FEDERATED REPUBLIC
1923-1991	Part of T.F.R. / Russia
1991-	REPUBLIC

ARUBA
| 1986- | INDEPENDENT PART OF NETHERLANDS KINGDOM |

ASCENSION
| 1867-1922 | British Colony (Great Britain) |
| 1922- | ST. HELENA DEPENDENCY |

AUSTRALIA
Prior to 1901	Separate British Colonies of New South Wales, Queensland, South Australia, Tasmania, Victoria, and Western Australia
1901-1913	INDEPENDENT DOMINION – Postage Due Stamps plus issues of separate states
1913-	INDEPENDENT DOMINION

Australian Antarctic Territory
| 1957- | Australia Post |

AUSTRIA
1850-1871	DUAL MONARCHY: Austria-Hungary
1871-1918	DUAL MONARCHY: for Austria only
1918-1938	REPUBLIC
1938-1945	Part of Germany
1945	ALLIED & U.S.S.R. OCCUPATION ISSUES
1945-1955	REPUBLIC — Under Allied Occupation
1955-	REPUBLIC

AZERBAIJAN
Prior to1918	Part of Russia
1918-1919	National Republic (Russia)
1919-1920	NATIONAL REPUBLIC
1920-1922	SOVIET REPUBLIC
1922-1923	PART OF TRANSCAUCASIAN F.R.
1923-1991	Part of T.F.R. / Russia
1991-	REPUBLIC

BAHAMAS
| 1859-1973 | BRITISH COLONY |
| 1973- | INDEPENDENT COMMONWEALTH |

BAHRAIN
1884-1933	BRITISH PROTECTORATE (India)
1933-1948	BRITISH PROTECTORATE– Indian Postal Administration
1948-1966	BRITISH PROTECTED SHEIKDOM – British Postal Administration
1966-1971	BRITISH PROTECTED SHEIKDOM – Independent Postal Administration
1971-	INDEPENDENT SHEIKDOM

BANGLADESH
Prior to 1947	Part of India
1947-1971	Part of Pakistan
1971-1975	INDEPENDENT STATE
1975-	REPUBLIC

BARBADOS
1852-1962	KINGDOM
1962-1966	SELF-GOVERNING BRITISH COLONY
1966-	PARLIAMENTARY DEMOCRACY

BARBUDA
Prior to 1922	Part of Antigua
1922	ANTIGUA DEPENDENCY
1922-1968	Part of Antigua
1968	ANTIGUA DEPENDENCY

BELARUS
Prior to1918	Part of Russia
1918-1919	National Republic (Russia)
1919-1920	NATIONAL REPUBLIC
1920-1922	SOVIET REPUBLIC
1922-1923	PART OF SOVIET SOCIALIST REPUBLIC
1923-1990	Part of S.S.R. / Russia
1990-	REPUBLIC

BELGIUM
1849-1915	KINGDOM
1914-1918	GOVERNMENT-IN-EXILE/GERMAN OCCUPATION
1918-1940	KINGDOM
1940-1944	GERMAN OCCUPATION
1944-	KINGDOM

BELIZE
Prior to 1973	See *British Honduras* (Vanished Lands)
1973-1981	SELF-GOVERNING BRITISH COLONY
1981-	INDEPENDENT COMMONWEALTH

BENIN
1892-1894	FRENCH PROTECTORATE
1894-1975	See *Dahomey* (Vanished Lands)
1975-	PEOPLE'S REPUBLIC

BERMUDA

1848-1865	BRITISH COLONY– Postmasters Provisionals
1865-1968	BRITISH COLONY
1968-	SEMI-AUTONOMOUS BRITISH COLONY

BHUTAN

1910-1947	British Protected Kingdom (India)
1947-1962	Kingdom (India)
1962-	KINGDOM

BOLIVIA

1867-	REPUBLIC

BOSNIA & HERZEGOVINA

Prior to 1879	Part of Turkey
1879-1908	PROVINCE OF TURKEY UNDER AUSTRIAN OCCUPATION
1908-1918	AUSTRIAN PROVINCE
1918-1921	YUGOSLAV PROVINCE
1921-1992	Part of Yugoslavia
1992-1995	REPUBLIC
1995-	TRIPARTITE PRESIDENCY (Bosniak, Croat, & Serb)

BOTSWANA

Prior to 1966	See *Bechuanaland Protectorate* (Vanished Lands)
1966-	REPUBLIC

BRAZIL

1843-1890	EMPIRE
1890	REPUBLIC

BRITISH ANTARCTIC TERRITORY

Prior to 1963	Part of Falkland Islands Dependencies
1963-	BRITISH TERRITORY

BRITISH INDIAN OCEAN TERRITORY

1847-1965	Part of Mauritius & Seychelles
1965-1976	BRITISH TERRITORY
1976-1990	British Territory (Great Britain)
1990-	BRITISH TERRITORY

BRUNEI

1877-1906	Part of Straits Settlement
1906-1942	BRITISH PROTECTED SULTANATE
1942-1945	JAPANESE OCCUPATION
1945-1947	British Military Administration (Sarawak; North Borneo, Australia)
1947-1983	BRITISH PROTECTED SULTANATE
1983-	INDEPENDENT SULTANATE

BULGARIA

1863-1878	Part of Turkey
1878-1885	PRINCIPALITY UNDER TURKISH DOMINION
1885-1908	PRINCIPALITY
1908-1944	KINGDOM
1944-1946	PROVISIONAL GOVERNMENT
1946-1991	COMMUNIST REPUBLIC
1991-	DEMOCRACY

BURKINA FASO

1906-1920	Part of Upper Senegal & Niger
1920-1933	COLONY OF FRENCH WEST AFRICA
1933-1958	Part of French Sudan, Ivory Coast and Niger Territory
1958-1984	REPULIC OF UPPER VOLTA
1984-	REPUBLIC

BURUNDI

1924-1962	Part of Ruanda-Urundi
1962-1966	MONARCHY
1966-	REPUBLIC

CAMBODIA

Prior to 1946	Part of Indochina
1946-1951	Autonomous Kingdom (Indochina)
1951-1955	KINGDOM OF FRENCH UNION
1955-1970	KINGDOM
1970-1975	KHMER REPUBLIC
1975-1979	COMMUNIST REPUBLIC
1979-1991	KAMPUCHEA REPUBLIC – Vietnamese occupation
1991-	UNDER U.N. MANAGEMENT

NOTE: *Since 1975, it has been illegal to import Cambodian stamps into the United States.*

CAMEROUN

1897-1915	GERMAN PROTECTORATE
1915-1919	FRENCH OCCUPATION
1919-1946	FRENCH MANDATE
1946-1959	FRENCH U.N. TRUSTEESHIP
1960-1961	REPUBLIC
1961-1972	FEDERAL REPUBLIC
1972-	UNITED REPUBLIC

See also: *Cameroons* (Vanished Lands).

CANADA

1851-1867	British Colony
1867-	INDEPENDENT DOMINION OF BRITISH COMMONWEALTH

166

CAPE VERDE

1877-1951	PORTUGUESE COLONY
1951-1975	PORTUGUES OVERSEAS PROVINCE
1975-	REPUBLIC

CAYMAN ISLANDS

1889-1900	Dependency of Jamaica (Jamaica)
1900-1962	DEPENDENCY OF JAMAICA
1962-	BRITISH COLONY

CENTRAL AFRICA

Prior to 1958	See *Ubangi-Shari* (Vanished Lands)
1958-1959	Autonomous Republic (French Equatorial Africa)
1959-1960	AUTONOMOUS REPUBLIC
1960-1976	REPUBLIC
1976-1979	EMPIRE
1979-	REPUBLIC

CHAD

1915-1922	Part of Ubangi-Shari-Chad
1922-1936	COLONY OF FRENCH EQUATORIAL AFRICA
1936-1958	Part of French Equatorial Africa
1958-1959	Autonomous Republic (French Equatorial Africa)
1959-1960	AUTONOMOUS REPUBLIC
1960-	REPUBLIC

CHILE

1853-	REPUBLIC

CHINA: People's Republic

Prior to 1949	See *China* (Vanished Lands)
1949-	COMMUNIST REPUBLIC

NOTE: *Starting as early as 1929, regional issues were used in Communist-controlled areas of China.*

CHINA: Taiwan

Prior to 1949	See *China* (Vanished Lands)
1949-	NATIONALIST REPUBLIC

CHRISTMAS ISLAND

Prior to 1948	Part of Straits Settlements
1948-1958	Dependency of Singapore (Singapore)
1958-	AUSTRALIAN TERRITORY

COCOS ISLANDS

1955-1963	Australian Possession (Australia)
1963-	AUSTRALIAN TERRITORY

COLOMBIA

1859-1861	GRANADINE CONFEDERATION
1861-1862	UNITED STATES OF NEW GRANADA
1862-1886	UNITED STATES OF COLOMBIA
1886-	REPUBLIC

States and Departments:
Antioquia, Bolivia, Boyaca, Cauca, Cundinamarca, Panama, Santander, Tolima

COMOROS

Comoro Islands

1892-1914	Issues of separate islands (Anjouan, Grand Comoro, Mayotte, Mohéli)
1914-1946	Part of Madagascar
1946-1950	French Overseas Territory (Madagascar)
1950-1975	FRENCH OVERSEAS TERRITORY

Comoros (without Mayotte)

1975-1978	REPUBLIC
1978-	ISLAMIC REPUBLIC

CONGO REPUBLIC

Prior to 1958	See *Middle Congo* (Vanished Lands)
1958-1959	Autonomous Republic (French Equatorial Africa)
1959-1960	AUTONOMOUS REPUBLIC
1960-1970	REPUBLIC
1970-	PEOPLE'S REPUBLIC

COOK ISLANDS

1892-1901	BRITISH POSSESSION
1901-1919	NEW ZEALAND DEPENDENCY
1919-1932	Rarotonga – NEW ZEALAND DEPENDENCY
1932-1965	NEW ZEALAND DEPENDENCY
1965-	SELF-GOVERNING STATE WITH NEW ZEALAND ASSOCIATION

COSTA RICA

1863-	REPUBLIC

Province Issues:

1885-1891	GUANACASTE

CROATIA

Prior to 1941	Part of Yugoslavia
1941-1945	GERMAN PUPPET REPUBLIC
1945-1991	Part of Yugoslavia
1991-	REPUBLIC

CUBA

Cuba and Puerto Rico:

1855-1873	SPANISH COLONIES – Joint Issues

Cuba:

1873-1898	SPANISH COLONY
1898-1899	U.S. ADMINISTRATION
1899-1902	REPUBLIC UNDER U.S. RULE
1902-1959	REPUBLIC
1959-	COMMUNIST REPUBLIC

NOTE: *Since 1962, it has been illegal to import Cuban stamps into the United States.*

167

CYPRUS

Prior to 1878	Part of Turkey
1878-1880	British Administration (Great Britain)
1880-1925	BRITISH ADMINISTRATION
1925-1960	BRITISH COLONY
1960-	REPUBLIC

NOTE: *Part of Cyprus is under Turkish occupation and issues local stamps for that region.*

CZECH REPUBLIC

Prior to 1918	Part of Austria-Hungary
1918-1939	REPUBLIC OF CZECHOSLOVAKIA
1939-1945	Under German & Hungarian Occupation
	See also *Bohemia & Moravia* (Vanished Lands) and *Slovakia* (Current Stamp Issuing Countries)
1945-1948	REPUBLIC OF CZECHOSLOVAKIA
1948-1968	COMMUNIST REPUBLIC
1968-1992	COMMUNIST FEDERAL REPUBLIC
1993-	REPUBLIC

DENMARK

1851-1940	KINGDOM
1940-1945	GERMAN OCCUPATION
1945-	KINGDOM

DJIBOUTI

1893-1902	FRENCH POSSESSION
1902-1977	See *Somali Coast; Afars & Issas* (Vanished Lands)
1977-	REPUBLIC

DOMINICA

1860-1874	British Colony (Handstamps)
1874-1890	BRITISH COLONY
1890-1903	Part of Leeward Islands
1903-1939	PRESIDENCY OF LEEWARD ISLANDS
1940-1968	BRITISH COLONY
1968-1978	BRITISH WEST INDIES ASSOCIATED STATE
1978-	INDEPENDENT COMMONWEALTH

DOMINICAN REPUBLIC

Santo Domingo:

1861-1865	Spanish Colony (Cuba & Puerto Rico)

Dominican Republic:

1865-	REPUBLIC

ECUADOR

1865-	REPUBLIC

Territory:

1957-1959	GALAPAGOS ISLANDS

EGYPT

1866-1882	TURKISH SUZERAINTY
1882-1914	NOMINAL TURKISH SUZERAINTY UNDER BRITISH ADMINISTRATION
1914-1922	BRITISH PROTECTORATE
1922-1953	KINGDOM
1953-1958	REPUBLIC
1958-1971	UNITED ARAB REPUBLIC
1971-	REPUBLIC

EQUATORIAL GUINEA

Prior to 1968	See *Spanish Guinea* (Vanished Lands)
1968-	REPUBLIC

ERITREA

1893-1936	ITALIAN COLONY
1936-1938	DISTRICT OF ITALIAN EAST AFRICA
1938-1941	Part of Italian East Africa
1941-1942	British Occupation (Great Britain)
1942-1948	British Administration (Great Britain – Middle Eastern Forces)
1948-1951	British Administration (Great Britain – Eritrea)
1952-1991	Part of Ethiopia
1993-	INDEPENDENT STATE

ESTONIA

Prior to 1918	Part of Russia
1918	GERMAN OCCUPATION
1918-1940	REPUBLIC
1940-1941	Russian Occupation (Russia)
1941	GERMAN OCCUPATION
1941-1944	German Occupation (Russia-Ostland)
1944-1991	Part of Russia
1991-	INDEPENDENT REPUBLIC

ETHIOPIA

1894-1936	MONARCHY
1936	ITALIAN OCCUPATION
1936-1938	DISTRICT OF ITALIAN EAST AFRICA
1938-1941	Part of Italian East Africa
1941-1942	British Occupation (Great Britain)
1942-1943	Monarchy (Middle East Forces)
1943-1974	MONARCHY
1974-1991	MARXIST STATE
1991-	REPUBLIC

FALKLAND ISLANDS
1878-	BRITISH COLONY

FALKLAND ISLAND DEPENDENCIES
Prior to 1946	Part of Falkland Islands
1946-1963	DEPENDENCY OF FALKLAND ISLANDS
1963-1980	Divided between British Antarctic Territory & South Georgia
1980-	DEPENDENCY OF FALKLAND ISLANDS

Regional Issues:
1944-1946	GRAHAM LAND; SOUTH GEORGIA; SOUTH ORKNEYS AND SOUTH SHETLANDS

FAROE ISLANDS
1851-1940	Part of Danish Kingdom (Denmark)
1919	LOCAL ISSUES
1940-1945	BRITISH ADMINISTRATION
1945-1975	Part of Danish Kingdom (Denmark)
1975-	AUTONOMOUS DISTRICT OF DANISH KINGDOM

FIJI
1870-1874	BRITISH PROTECTED KINGDOM
1874-1970	BRITISH COLONY
1970-	INDEPENDENT BRITISH DOMINION

FINLAND
1856-1917	RUSSIAN GRAND DUCHY
1917-1919	INDEPENDENT STATE
1919-	REPUBLIC

Regional Issues:
1984-	ALAND ISLANDS

FRANCE
1849-1852	REPUBLIC
1852-1870	EMPIRE
1870-1940	REPUBLIC
1940-1942	GERMAN OCCUPATION (North) & VICHY GOVERNMENT (South)
1942-1944	GERMAN OCCUPATION
1944-1946	PROVISIONAL GOVERNMENT
1946-	REPUBLIC

FRENCH POLYNESIA
French Oceania:
1882-1892	French Colony (Tahiti)
1892-1958	FRENCH COLONY

French Polynesia:
1958-	FRENCH OVERSEAS TERRITORY

FRENCH SOUTHERN & ANTARCTIC TERRITORIES
Prior to 1955	Dependency of Madagascar (Madagascar)
1955-	FRENCH TERRITORIES

GABON
1886-1891	FRENCH COLONY
1891-1904	Part of French Congo
1904-1910	FRENCH COLONY
1910-1936	COLONY OF FRENCH EQUATORIAL AFRICA
1936-1958	Part of French Equatorial Africa
1958-1959	Autonomous Republic (French Equatorial Africa)
1960-	REPUBLIC

GAMBIA
1869-1888	DEPENDENCY OF SIERRA LEONE
1888-1965	BRITISH COLONY
1965-1970	INDEPENDENT STATE
1970-	REPUBLIC

GEORGIA
Prior to 1918	Part of Russia
1918	GERMAN OCCUPATION
1918-1940	REPUBLIC
1940-1941	Russian Occupation (Russia)
1941	GERMAN OCCUPATION
1941-1944	German Occupation (Russia-Ostland)
1944-1991	Part of Russia
1991-	REPUBLIC

GERMANY
Germany:
Prior to 1872	Separate States
1872-1918	EMPIRE
1918-1933	REPUBLIC
1933-1945	NAZI STATE
1990-	FEDERAL REPUBLIC OF GERMANY

West Germany:
1945-1949	VARIOUS U.S., BRITISH & FRENCH OCCUPATION ISSUES

East Germany:
1949-1990	German Democratic Republic (DDR)

GHANA
Prior to 1957	See *Gold Coast* (Vanished Lands)
1957-1960	INDEPENDENT STATE
1960-	REPUBLIC

GIBRALTAR
1857-1885	British Colony (Great Britain)
1885-	BRITISH COLONY

169

GREAT BRITAIN

1840-	CONSTITUTIONAL MONARCHY

Regional Issues:

1958-1969	GUERNSEY
1958-1969	JERSEY
1958-1973	MAN, ISLE OF
1958-	NORTHERN IRELAND
1958-	SCOTLAND
1958-	WALES & MONMOUTHSHIRE

GREAT BRITAIN: Guernsey-Alderney

1840-1940	Part of Great Britain
1940-1945	GERMAN OCCUPATION
1945-1958	Part of Great Britain
1958-1969	REGIONAL ISSUES (Great Britain)
1969-	BAILIWICK OF GUERNSEY

GREAT BRITAIN: Isle of Man

1840-1958	Part of Great Britain
1958-1973	REGIONAL ISSUES (Great Britain)
1973-	AUTONOMOUS REGION OF UNITED KINGDOM

GREAT BRITAIN: Jersey

1840-1940	Part of Great Britain
1940-1945	GERMAN OCCUPATION
1945-1958	Part of Great Britain
1958-1969	REGIONAL ISSUES (Great Britain)
1969-	BAILIWICK OF JERSEY

GREECE

1861-1924	KINGDOM
1924-1935	REPUBLIC
1935-1941	KINGDOM
1941-1944	GERMAN AND ITALIAN OCCUPATION
1944-1946	REGENCY
1946-1967	KINGDOM
1967-1973	MILITARY GOVERNMENT
1973-	REPUBLIC

Regional Issues

2008-	Mount Athos

GREENLAND

Prior to 1905	Danish Colony (Denmark)
1905-1937	DANISH COLONY (Parcel Post Issues plus Denmark)
1938-1940	DANISH COLONY
1940-1945	U.S. PROTECTORATE
1945-1953	DANISH COLONY
1953-1979	PART OF DANISH KINGDOM
1979-	PART OF DANISH KINGDOM WITH HOME RULE

GRENADA

1861-1967	BRITISH COLONY
1967-1974	BRITISH WEST INDIES ASSOCIATED STATE
1974-1979	INDEPENDENT STATE
1979-1983	MARXIST STATE
1983-	INDEPENDENT STATE

Regional Issues:

1973-	GRENADA GRENADINES

GUATEMALA

1871-	REPUBLIC

GUINEA

Prior to 1958	See *French Guinea* (Vanished Lands)
1958-1959	Republic (French West Africa)
1959-	REPUBLIC

GUINEA-BISSAU

Prior to 1974	See *Portuguese Guinea* (Vanished Lands)
1974-	REPUBLIC

GUYANA

Prior to 1966	See *British Guiana* (Vanished Lands)
1966-1970	INDEPENDENT STATE
1970-	REPUBLIC

HAITI

1881-	REPUBLIC

HONDURAS

1866-	REPUBLIC

HONG KONG

1862-1942	BRITISH COLONY
1942-1945	Japanese Occupation (Japan)
1945	JAPANESE OCCUPATION
1945-	BRITISH COLONY

HUNGARY

1850-1871	Part of Austria-Hungary
1871-1918	DUAL MONARCHY – Issues for Hungary only
1918-1919	PEOPLE'S REPUBLIC
1919	SOVIET REPUBLIC
1919-1920	NATIONAL GOVERNMENT
1920-1944	REGENCY
1944-1946	PROVISIONAL GOVERNMENT
1946-1990	COMMUNIST REPUBLIC
1990-	REPUBLIC

ICELAND

1870-1873	Danish Colony (Denmark)
1873-1918	DANISH ADMINISTRATION
1918-1940	KINGDOM UNDER DANISH CROWN

| 1940-1944 | BRITISH & U.S. ADMINISTRATION |
| 1944- | REPUBLIC |

INDIA
1852-1854	SCINDE DISTRICT POST
1854-1860	EAST INDIA COMPANY ADMINISTRATION
1860-1877	BRITISH COLONY
1877-1947	EMPIRE UNDER BRITISH CROWN
1947-1950	INDEPENDENT BRITISH DOMINION
1950-	REPUBLIC

INDONESIA
Prior to 1958	See *Netherlands Indies*
1948-1949	NETHERLANDS COLONY
1949	AUTONOMOUS STATE
1949-1950	UNITED STATES OF INDONESIA
1950-	REPUBLIC

District:
| 1954-1964 | RIOUW ARCHIPELAGO |

IRAN
Persia:
| 1870-1935 | KINGDOM |

Iran:
| 1935-1979 | KINGDOM |
| 1979- | ISLAMIC STATE |

NOTE: *Importation prohibited since Oct. 29, 1987.*

IRAQ
Prior to 1923	See *Mesopotamia* (Vanished Lands)
1923-1932	BRITISH MANDATE
1932-1958	KINGDOM
1958-	REPUBLIC

NOTE: *Importation prohibited since 1992.*

IRELAND
| 1840-1922 | PART OF GREAT BRITAIN |

Irish Free State:
| 1922 | PROVISIONAL GOVERNMENT |
| 1922-1937 | INDEPENDENT BRITISH DOMINION |

Eire:
| 1937-1949 | INDEPENDENT STATE |

Ireland:
| 1949- | REPUBLIC |

ISRAEL
| Prior to 1948 | See *Palestine* |
| 1948- | REPUBLIC |

ITALY
Prior to 1861	Separate States
1861-1862	Kingdom (Sardinia and Neapolitan Provinces)
1862-1922	KINGDOM
1922-1943	FASCIST KINGDOM
1943	ALLIED MILITARY GOVERNMENT
1943-1946	KINGDOM
1946-	REPUBLIC

IVORY COAST
1892-1895	FRENCH COLONY
1895-1941	COLONY OF FRENCH WEST AFRICA
1941-1942	VICHY FRENCH COLONY
1942-1944	COLONY OF FRENCH WEST AFRICA
1944-1958	Part of French West Africa
1958-1959	Autonomous Republic (French West Africa)
1959-1960	AUTONOMOUS REPUBLIC
1960-	REPUBLIC

JAMAICA
| 1860-1962 | BRITISH COLONY |
| 1962- | INDEPENDENT STATE |

JAPAN
1871-1945	EMPIRE
1945-1948	U.S. MILITARY RULE
1948-	CONSTITUTIONAL MONARCHY

JORDAN
Trans-Jordan:
1918-1920	Part of Palestine
1920-1946	KINGDOM UNDER BRITISH MANDATE
1946-1949	KINGDOM

Jordan:
| 1949- | KINGDOM |

KAZAKHSTAN
Prior to 1918	Part of Russia
1918-1919	National Republic (Russia)
1919-1921	NATIONAL REPUBLIC
1921-1922	SOVIET REPUBLIC
1922-1924	REPUBLIC OF RUSSIA
1924-1991	Part of Russia
1991-	REPUBLIC

KENYA
Prior to 1922	See *British East Africa*
1922-1935	British Colony (Kenya & Uganda)
1935-1963	British Colony (Kenya, Uganda & Tanganyika)

| 1963-1964 | INDEPENDENT STATE |
| 1964- | REPUBLIC |

NOTE: *From 1963-1977 Kenya also used stamps of Kenya, Uganda & Tanzania.*

KIRIBATI
| Prior to 1979 | See *Gilbert Islands* (Vanished Lands) |
| 1979- | REPUBLIC |

KOREA: South
Korea:
1884-1897	KINGDOM
1897-1905	EMPIRE
1905-1945	Japanese Rule (Japan)
1945	Divided into North & South

South Korea:
1945-1946	U.S. Occupation (Japan)
1946-1948	U.S. MILITARY RULE
1948-	REPUBLIC

KOSOVO
Prior to 1990	Part of Serbia / Yugoslavia
1990-2007	UNITED NATIONS INTERIM ADMINISTRATION
2008-	REPUBLIC

KUWAIT
1899-1914	British Protected Sheikdom (Turkey)
1914-1923	British Protected Sheikdom (India)
1923-1948	BRITISH PROTECTED SHEIKDOM – Indian Postal Administration
1948-1959	BRITISH PROTECTED SHEIKDOM – British Postal Administration
1959-1961	BRITISH PROTECTED SHEIKDOM – Independent Postal Administration
1961-	INDEPENDENT SHEIKDOM

KYRGYZSTAN
Prior to 1918	Part of Russia
1918-1919	National Republic (Russia)
1919-1920	NATIONAL REPUBLIC
1920-1921	SOVIET REPUBLIC
1922-1923	PART OF SOVIET SOCIALIST REPUBLIC
1923-1990	Part of S.S.R. / Russia
1991-	REPUBLIC

LAOS
1899-1947	Part of Indochina
1947-1951	Autonomous Kingdom (Indochina)
1951-1956	KINGDOM OF FRENCH UNION
1956-1975	KINGDOM
1975-	COMMUNIST REPUBLIC – Vietnamese Occupation

LATVIA
Prior to 1916	Part of Russia
1918-1919	INDEPENDENT STATE
1919	RUSSIAN OCCUPATION
1919-1940	REPUBLIC
1940	RUSSIAN OCCUPATION
1940-1941	Part of Russia
1941-1944	Part of German Eastern Command
1944-1991	Part of Russia
1991-	INDEPENDENT REPUBLIC

LEBANON
1918-1919	Part of Palestine
1919-1924	Part of Syria
1924-1926	FRENCH MANDATE
1926-1941	AUTONOMOUS REPUBLIC UNDER FRENCH MANDATE
1941-	REPUBLIC

LESOTHO
| Prior to 1966 | See *Basutoland* (Vanished Lands) |
| 1966- | KINGDOM |

LIBERIA
| 1860- | REPUBLIC |

LIBYA
Libia:
Prior to 1912	Part of Turkey
1912-1939	ITALIAN COLONY
1939-1942	PROVINCES OF ITALY
1942-1951	Divided into various Occupation Areas

Libya:
1951-1952	Kingdom (Separate Areas)
1952-1969	KINGDOM
1969-	ARAB REPUBLIC

NOTE: *Importation prohibited since Jan. 7, 1986.*

LIECHTENSTEIN
1866-1912	Principality (Austria)
1912-1920	PRINCIPALITY (Austrian Postal Admin.)
1920-1921	PRINCIPALITY (National Postal Admin.)
1921-	PRINCIPALITY (Swiss Postal Admin.)

LITHUANIA
Prior to 1916	Part of Russia
1916-1918	GERMAN OCCUPATION
1918-1919	INDEPENDENT STATE
1919-1940	REPUBLIC
1940	RUSSIAN OCCUPATION

1940-1941	Part of Russia
1941-1944	Part of German Eastern Command
1944-1991	Part of Russia
1991-	INDEPENDENT STATE

LUXEMBOURG

1852-1914	GRAND DUCHY
1914-1918	Part of Germany
1918-1940	GRAND DUCHY
1940-1941	GERMAN OCCUPATION
1941-1944	Part of Germany
1944-	GRAND DUCHY

MACAO

1863-1884	Portuguese Colony (Hong Kong)
1884-1951	PORTUGUESE COLONY
1951-1976	PORTUGUESE OVERSEAS PROVINCE
1976-	AUTONOMOUS PORTUGUESE PROVINCE

MACEDONIA

1913-1941	Part of Serbia / Yugoslavia
1941-1944	Annexed Territory of Bulgaria
1944-1992	Part of Yugoslavia
1992-2019	INDEPENDENT REPUBLIC
2019-	Renamed REPUBLIC OF NORTH MACEDONIA

MADAGASCAR (MALAGASY)

1889-1896	French Protectorate (French Post Offices in Madagascar)
1896-1958	FRENCH COLONY
1958-1960	AUTONOMOUS REPUBLIC
1960-1975	MALAGASY REPUBLIC
1975-	REPUBLIC

MALAWI

Prior to 1964	See *Nyasaland Protectorate* (Vanished Lands)
1964-1966	INDEPENDENT STATE
1966-	REPUBLIC

MALAYSIA

Prior to 1963	See *Malaya, North Borneo,* and *Sarawak* (Vanished Lands)
1963-	FEDERATED MONARCHY

MALDIVES

1887-1906	Dependency of Ceylon (Ceylon)
1906-1948	CEYLON DEPENDENCY
1948-1965	BRITISH PROTECTED SULTANATE
1965-1968	INDEPENDENT SULTANATE
1968-	REPUBLIC

MALI

Prior to 1958	See *French Sudan* (Vanished Lands)
1958-1959	Autonomous Republic (French West Africa)
1959-1960	Part of Mali Federation
1960-	REPUBLIC

MALTA

1857-1860	British Colony (Great Britain)
1860-1964	BRITISH COLONY
1964-1974	INDEPENDENT STATE
1974-	REPUBLIC

MARSHALL ISLANDS

1889-1897	German Protectorate (Germany)
1897-1914	GERMAN PROTECTORATE
1914-1945	Japanese Occupation and Mandate (Japan)
1945-1947	U.S. Occupation (U.S.)
1947-1984	Part of Trust Territories of the Pacific (U.S.)
1984-	AUTONOMOUS STATE OF TERRITORIES OF THE PACIFIC

MAURITANIA

1899-1903	Part of French West Africa (French Soudan)
1903-1906	Part of Fr. West Africa (Senegambia & Niger)
1906-1944	COLONY OF FRENCH WEST AFRICA
1944-1958	Part of French West Africa
1958-1959	Autonomous Republic (French West Africa)
1959-	ISLAMIC REPUBLIC

MAURITIUS

1847-1968	BRITISH COLONY
1968-	INDEPENDENT STATE

MEXICO

1856-1864	REPUBLIC
1864-1867	EMPIRE UNDER BRITISH PROTECTORATE
1867-	REPUBLIC

MICRONESIA

Prior to 1977	Part of Caroline Islands
1977-1984	State of Trust Territories of the Pacific (U.S.)
1984-	AUTONOMOUS STATE OF U.S. TRUST TERRITORIES OF THE PACIFIC

MOLDOVA

Prior to 1918	Part of Russia
1918-1919	National Republic (Russia)
1919-1920	NATIONAL REPUBLIC
1921-1922	SOVIET REPUBLIC
1922-1923	PART OF
	SOVIET SOCIALIST REPUBLIC
1923-1991	Part of S.S.R. / Russia
1991-	REPUBLIC

MONACO

1851-1860	Principality (Sardinia)
1860-1885	Principality (France)
1885-	PRINCIPALITY

MONGOLIA

Prior to 1912	Part of China
1912-1924	Autonomous Republic (China)
1924-1945	AUTONOMOUS SOVIET
	REPUBLIC
1945-	COMMUNIST REPUBLIC

MONTENEGRO

1874-1910	PRINCIPALITY
1910-1916	KINGDOM
1916	GOVERNMENT-IN-EXILE
1917-1918	AUSTRIAN OCCUPATION
1918-1941	Part of Serbia/Yugoslavia
1941-1943	ITALIAN OCCUPATION
1943-1944	GERMAN OCCUPATION
1944-2002	Part of Yugoslavia
2003-2006	Becomes Serbia & Montenegro
2006-	INDEPENDENT STATE

MONTSERRAT

1860-1876	British Colony (Handstamps)
1876-1890	BRITISH COLONY
1890-1903	Part of Leeward Islands
1903-1956	LEEWARD ISLAND
	PRESIDENCY
1956-	BRITISH COLONY

MOROCCO

1891-1912	Kingdom (Various Foreign Post
	Offices)
1912-1956	Divided into French Morocco,
	Spanish Morocco and Tangier
1956-1958	KINGDOM – Issues for Northern &
	Southern Zones
1958-	KINGDOM

MOZAMBIQUE

1877-1951	PORTUGUESE COLONY
1951-1975	PORTUGAL OVERSEAS
	PROVINCE
1975-	PEOPLE'S REPUBLIC

MYANMAR

Prior to 1937	Part of India
1937-1942	BURMA BRITISH DOMINION
1942	BURMA INDEPENDENCE ARMY –
	Japanese controlled areas.
1942-1945	JAPANESE OCCUPATION
1945-1948	BRITISH MILITARY
	ADMINISTRATION
1946-1948	INTERIM GOVERNMENT
1948-1989	REPUBLIC OF BURMA
1989-	REPUBLIC OF MYANMAR

NAMIBIA

1886-1897	German Colony (Germany)
1897-1915	GERMAN COLONY
1915-1923	SOUTH WEST AFRICA –
	Union of South Africa Occupation
	(Union of South Africa)
1923-1946	SOUTH AFRICAN MANDATE
1946-1990	SOUTH AFRICAN
	ADMINISTRATION
1990-	REPUBLIC

NAURU

1889-1914	Part of Marshall Islands
1914-1916	Part of Northwest Pacific Islands
1916-1920	BRITISH ADMINISTRATION
1920-1942	JOINT BRITISH, AUSTRALIAN &
	NEW ZEALAND
	ADMINISTRATION
1942-1945	Japanese Occupation (Japan)
1945-1968	JOINT BRITISH, AUSTRALIAN, &
	NEW ZEALAND
	ADMINISTRATION
1968-	REPUBLIC

NEPAL

1854-1881	Kingdom (India)
1881-	KINGDOM

NETHERLANDS

1852-1940	KINGDOM
1940-1945	GERMAN OCCUPATION
1945-	KINGDOM

NETHERLANDS ANTILLES

Curaçao:

1873-1948	NETHERLANDS COLONY

Netherlands Antilles:

1948-1954	NETHERLANDS COLONY
1954-	AUTONOMOUS PART OF
	NETHERLANDS KINGDOM

Caribbean Netherlands:

Prior to 2010	Part of Netherlands Antilles
2010-	PART OF
	NETHERLANDS KINGDOM

NEVIS

1861-1890	BRITISH COLONY
1890-1903	Part of Leeward Islands
1903-1956	Part of St. Kitts-Nevis Leeward Island
1956-1980	Part of St. Kitts-Nevis
1980-	PART OF ST. KITTS-NEVIS

NEW CALEDONIA

1858-1862	FRENCH COLONY
1862-1881	French Colony (French Colonies)
1881-1946	FRENCH COLONY
1946-	FRENCH OVERSEAS TERRITORY

NEW ZEALAND

1855-1907	BRITISH COLONY
1907-	INDEPENDENT BRITISH DOMINION

NEW ZEALAND:
Ross Dependency

1908-1910	Edward VII Land (New Zealand)
1910-1957	Victoria Land (New Zealand)
1957-1987	ROSS DEPENDENCY
1994-	Ross Dependency Agency (New Zealand)

NICARAGUA

1862-1981	REPUBLIC
1981-	SANDINISTA GOVERNMENT

NIGER

1862-1921	Part of Upper Senegal & Niger
1921-1922	TERRITORY OF FRENCH WEST AFRICA
1922-1944	COLONY OF FRENCH WEST AFRICA
1944-1958	Part of French West Africa
1958-1960	Autonomous Republic (French West Africa)
1960	AUTONOMOUS REPUBLIC
1960-	REPUBLIC

NIGERIA

Prior to 1914	See *Northern & Southern Nigeria* (Vanished Lands)
1914-1960	BRITISH COLONY & PROTECTORATE
1960-1963	FEDERATED STATE
1963-	FEDERAL REPUBLIC

NIUE

1892-1902	Part of Cook Islands
1902-1974	NEW ZEALAND DEPENDENCY
1974-	SELF-GOVERNING STATE WITH NEW ZEALAND ASSOCIATION

NORFOLK ISLAND

1914-1947	Australian Dependency (Australia)
1947-	AUSTRALIAN DEPENDENCY

NORWAY

1855-1905	KINGDOM UNDER SWEDISH RULE
1905-1940	KINGDOM
1940-1945	GERMAN OCCUPATION
1945-	KINGDOM

OMAN
Muscat & Oman:

1864-1944	British Protected Sultanate (India)
1944-1947	BRITISH PROTECTED SULTANATE
1947-1948	Br. Protected Sultanate (Pakistan)
1948-1966	BRITISH PROTECTED SULTANATE
1966-1970	SULTANATE

Oman:

1970-	SULTANATE

PAKISTAN

Prior to 1947	Part of India
1947-1956	INDEPENDENT BRITISH DOMINION
1956-	REPUBLIC

PALAU

Prior to 1977	Part of Trust Territory of the Pacific (Caroline Islands)
1977-1983	State of Trust Territory of the Pacific
1983-	AUTONOMOUS STATE UNDER U.S. TRUSTEESHIP

PALESTINIAN AUTHORITY

1994-	PALESTINIAN NATIONAL AUTHORITY

PANAMA

Prior to 1878	Part of Colombia
1878-1886	STATE OF COLOMBIA
1886-1903	DEPARTMENT OF COLOMBIA
1903-	REPUBLIC

PAPUA NEW GUINEA
Papua & New Guinea:

Prior to 1952	Separate Territories
1952-1971	AUSTRALIAN TERRITORIES

Papua New Guinea:

1971-1975	AUSTRALIAN TERRITORY
1975-	INDEPENDENT STATE

PARAGUAY

1870-	REPUBLIC

175

PENRHYN ISLAND:
Northern Cook Islands
Penrhyn Island:

1892-1902	Part of Cook Islands
1902-1932	NEW ZEALAND DEPENDENCY
1932-1973	Part of Cook Islands

Northern Cook Islands

1973-	COOK ISLAND POSTAL REGION

PERU

1857-	REPUBLIC

PHILIPPINES

1854-1898	SPANISH DOMINION
1898-1899	PROVISIONAL GOVERNMENT
1899-1935	U.S. ADMINISTRATION
1935-1941	U.S. COMMONWEALTH
1941-1944	JAPANESE OCCUPATION
1944-1946	U.S. COMMONWEALTH
1946-	REPUBLIC

PITCAIRN ISLANDS

1898-1940	British Colony (Fiji)
1940-	BRITISH COLONY

POLAND

1860-1865	DUCHY OF RUSSIA
1865-1915	Duchy of Russia (Russia)
1915-1918	GERMAN OCCUPATION
1918-1919	INDEPENDENT STATE
1919-1939	REPUBLIC
1939-1944	POLISH GENERAL GOVERNMENT (German Occupation)
1944-1945	PROVISIONAL GOVERNMENT
1945-1990	COMMUNIST REPUBLIC
1990-	REPUBLIC

PORTUGAL

1853-1910	MONARCHY
1910-	REPUBLIC

PORTUGAL: Azores

1868-1931	PORTUGUESE COLONY
1931-1980	Part of Portugal
1980-	REGIONAL ISSUES – Part of Portugal

PORTUGAL: Madeira

1868-1881	PORTUGUESE COLONY
1881-1892	Port. Colony (Portugal)
1898	SPECIAL ISSUES
1905-1931	Port. Colony (Azores)
1925-1928	SPECIAL ISSUES
1931-1980	Part of Portugal
1980-	REGIONAL ISSUES – Part of Portugal

QATAR

Prior to 1916	Part of Turkey
1916-1950	British Protected Sheikdom (India)
1950-1957	British Protected Sheikdom (Muscat & Oman)
1957-1971	BRITISH PROTECTED SHEIKDOM
1971-	INDEPENDENT SHEIKDOM

ROMANIA
Moldavia:

1858-1861	PRINCIPALITY

Moldavia-Wallachia:

1861-1865	PRINCIPALITY

Romania:

1865-1881	PRINCIPALITY
1881-1947	KINGDOM
1948-1991	COMMUNIST REPUBLIC
1991-	REPUBLIC

RUSSIA

1852-1917	EMPIRE
1917	PROVISIONAL GOVERNMENT
1917-1922	SOVIET REPUBLIC
1922-1992	COMMUNIST REPUBLIC
1992-	REPUBLIC

RWANDA

Prior to 1962	Part of Rwandi-Urundi
1962-	REPUBLIC

ST. HELENA

1856-	BRITISH COLONY

ST. KITTS-NEVIS
St. Kitts-Nevis:

Prior to 1903	Separate Colonies
1903-1952	LEEWARD ISLAND PRESIDENCY

St. Christopher, Nevis & Anguilla:

1952-1956	LEEWARD ISLAND PRESIDENCY
1956-1967	BRITISH COLONY
1967-1980	BRITISH WEST INDIES ASSOCIATED STATE

St. Kitts-Nevis / Nevis:

1980-	British West Indies Associated State (Separate Local Issues for St. Kitts and Nevis)

ST. LUCIA

1869-1967	BRITISH COLONY
1967-1979	BRITISH WEST INDIES ASSOCIATED STATE
1979-	INDEPENDENT STATE

ST. PIERRE & MIQUELON
1885-1946	FRENCH COLONY
1946-1976	FRENCH OVERSEAS TERRITORY
1976-1985	French Overseas Department (France)
1985-2003	FRENCH TERRITORIAL COLLECTIVITY
1985-2003	FRENCH OVERSEAS COLLECTIVITY

ST. VINCENT
1861-1969	BRITISH COLONY
1969-1979	BRITISH WEST INDIES ASSOCIATED STATE
1979-	INDEPENDENT COMMONWEALTH

ST. VINCENT GRENADINES
1973-1994	PART OF ST. VINCENT

Regional Issues
1984-	BEQUIA
1997-	CANOUAN
2006-	MAYREA
1997-	MUSTIQUES
1984-	UNION ISLANDS

SALVADOR, EL
1867-	REPUBLIC

SAMOA: Western Samoa
Samoa:
1877-1899	KINGDOM
1900	Divided into Western Samoa and American Samoa

Western Samoa:
1900-1914	GERMAN PROTECTORATE
1914-1920	NEW ZEALAND OCCUPATION
1920-1962	NEW ZEALAND MANDATE
1962-	INDEPENDENT STATE

SAN MARINO
1862-1877	Republic (Italy)
1877-1943	REPUBLIC
1943-1944	GERMAN OCCUPATION
1944-	REPUBLIC

SAUDI ARABIA
Hejaz:
Prior to 1916	Part of Turkey
1916-1926	KINGDOM

Nejd:
1925-1926	KINGDOM

Hejaz-Nejd:
1926-1932	KINGDOM

Saudi Arabia:
1932-	KINGDOM

SENEGAL
1887-1895	FRENCH COLONY
1895-1944	COLONY OF FRENCH WEST AFRICA
1944-1958	Part of French West Africa
1958-1959	Autonomous Republic (French West Africa)
1959-1960	Part of Mali Federation
1960-	REPUBLIC

SERBIA
1866-1878	AUTONOMOUS PRINCIPALITY
1878-1882	PRINCIPALITY
1882-1916	KINGDOM
1916-1918	GOVERNMENT IN EXILE on Corfu
1916-1918	AUSTRALIAN OCCUPATION
1918-1921	YUGOSLAV PROVINCE
1921-1941	Part of Yugoslavia
1941-1944	GERMAN OCCUPATION
1944-2002	Part of Yugoslavia
2003-2006	Becomes Serbia & Montenegro
2006-	SOVEREIGN STATE

SEYCHELLES
1861-1890	Dependency of Mauritius (Mauritius)
1890-1903	DEPENDENCY OF MAURITIUS
1903-1976	BRITISH COLONY
1976-	REPUBLIC

Regional Issues
1980-1992	ZIL ELWANNYEN SESEL

SIERRA LEONE
1859-1896	BRITISH COLONY
1896-1961	BRITISH COLONY & PROTECTORATE
1961-1971	INDEPENDENT STATE
1971-	REPUBLIC

SINGAPORE
1867-1946	Part of Straits Settlements
1946-1948	British Colony (Straits Settlements)
1948-1959	BRITISH COLONY
1959-1963	AUTONOM0US STATE
1963-1965	Part of Malaysia
1965-	REPUBLIC

SLOVAKIA
Prior to 1918	Part of Austria-Hungary
1918-1939	Part of Czechoslovakia
1939-1945	GERMAN PUPPET REPUBLIC
1945-1992	Part of Czechoslovakia.
1993-	INDEPENDENT REPUBLIC

SLOVENIA
Prior to 1991	Part of Yugoslavia
1991-	REPUBLIC

SOLOMON ISLANDS
British Solomon Islands:

1896-1907	British Protectorate (New South Wales)
1907-1975	BRITISH PROTECTORATE

Solomon Islands:

1975-1978	BRITISH PROTECTORATE
1978-	INDEPENDENT STATE

SOMALIA
Italian Somalia:

1903-1905	ITALIAN COLONY – Benadir
1905-1936	ITALIAN COLONY
1936-1938	DISTRICT OF ITALIAN EAST AFRICA
1938-1941	Part of Italian East Africa
1941-1950	British Occupation (Offices in Africa)

Somalia:

1950-1960	ITALIAN TRUSTEESHIP
1960-	REPUBLIC

SOUTH AFRICA
Union of South Africa:

Prior to 1910	Separate British Colonies
1910-1961	INDEPENDENT BRITISH DOMINION

South Africa:

1961-	REPUBLIC

SPAIN

1850-1869	KINGDOM
1868-1869	PROVISIONAL GOVERNMENT
1869-1870	DUKE DE LA TORRE REGENCY
1870-1873	KINGDOM
1873-1875	REPUBLIC
1875-1931	KINGDOM
1931-1936	REPUBLIC
1936-1939	CIVIL WAR ISSUES
1939-1977	FASCIST MONARCHY
1977-	CONSTITUTIONAL MONARCHY

SRI LANKA

Prior to 1972	Named Ceylon
1972-	REPUBLIC

SUDAN

1867-1889	British Military Administration (Egypt)
1889-1897	Mahdi Government (No Stamps)
1897-1956	ANGLO-EGYPTIAN CONDOMINIUM
1956-	REPUBLIC

SURINAM

1873-1954	NETHERLANDS COLONY
1954-1975	PART OF NETHERLANDS KINGDOM
1975-	INDEPENDENT STATE

SWAZILAND

1889-1895	KINGDOM
1895-1903	Part of Transvaal
1903-1910	British Colony (Transvaal)
1910-1933	British Colony (Union of South Africa)
1933-1968	BRITISH PROTECTORATE
1968-	KINGDOM

SWEDEN

1855-	KINGDOM

SWITZERLAND

1850-	REPUBLIC

SYRIA

Prior to 1918	Part of Turkey
1918-1919	Part of Palestine
1919-1923	FRENCH OCCUPATION
1923-1934	FRENCH MANDATE
1934-1941	AUTONOMOUS REPUBLIC UNDER FRENCH
1941-1958	REPUBLIC
1958-1961	PART OF UNITED ARAB REPUBLIC- with Egypt
1961-	SYRIAN ARAB REPUBLIC

TAJIKISTAN

Prior to 1918	Part of Russia
1918-1919	National Republic (Russia)
1919-1920	NATIONAL REPUBLIC
1921-1922	SOVIET REPUBLIC
1922-1923	PART OF SOVIET SOCIALIST REPUBLIC
1923-1991	Part of S.S.R. / Russia
1991-	REPUBLIC

TANZANIA

Prior to 1964	See *Tanganyika* (Vanished Lands)

Tanganyika-Zanzibar:

1964	REPUBLIC

Tanzania:

1964-	REPUBLIC

THAILAND
Siam:

1883-1950	KINGDOM

Thailand:

1950-	KINGDOM

TIMOR

1884-1896	DEPENDENCY OF MACAO
1896-1951	PORTUGUESE COLONY
1951-1975	PORTUGUESE OVERSEAS PROVINCE
1975-1976	INDONESIAN OCCUPATION
1976-1999	Part of Indonesia
1999-2002	UNITED NATIONS TRANSITIONAL AUTHORITY (East Timor)
2002-	INDEPENDENT STATE OF TIMOR-LESTE

TOGO

1885-1897	German Protectorate (Germany)
1897-1914	GERMAN PROTECTORATE
1914-1916	BRITISH OCCUP. – Western Part
1914-1919	FRENCH OCCUPATION
1919-1922	FRENCH ADMINISTRATION
1922-1946	FRENCH MANDATE
1946-1955	FRENCH U.N. TRUSTEESHIP
1955-1960	AUTONOMOUS REPUBLIC
1960-	REPUBLIC

TOKELAU ISLANDS

1911-1925	Part of Gilbert & Ellice Islands
1925-1948	Part of Western Samoa
1948-	NEW ZEALAND TERRITORY

TONGA

1886-1900	KINGDOM
1900-1970	BRITISH PROTECTED KINGDOM
1970-	KINGDOM

Regional Issues:

1983-	NIUAFO'OU – Tin Can Island

TRINIDAD & TOBAGO

Prior to 1913	Separate Issues for Trinidad & Tobago
1913-1962	BRITISH COLONY
1962-1976	INDEPENDENT STATE
1976-	REPUBLIC

TRISTAN DA CUNHA

1867-1938	British Colony (Great Britain)
1938-1952	St. Helena Dependency (St. Helena)
1952-1961	ST. HELENA
1961-1963	Uninhabited
1963-	ST. HELENA DEPENDENCY

TUNISIA

1863-1881	Part of Turkey
1881-1888	French Protectorate (France)
1888-1956	FRENCH PROTECTORATE
1956-1957	KINGDOM
1957-	REPUBLIC

TURKEY

1863-1922	OTTOMAN EMPIRE
1922-1923	NATIONALIST GOVERNMENT (Turkey in Asia)
1923-	REPUBLIC

TURKISH REPUBLIC OF NORTHERN CYPRUS

1974-1983	FEDERATED STATE
1983	INDEPENDENT

TURKMENISTAN

Prior to 1918	Part of Russia
1918-1919	National Republic (Russia)
1919-1920	NATIONAL REPUBLIC
1921-1922	SOVIET REPUBLIC
1922-1923	PART OF SOVIET SOCIALIST REPUBLIC
1923-1990	Part of S.S.R. / Russia
1991-	REPUBLIC

TURKS & CAICOS ISLANDS

Prior to 1900	See *Turks Islands* (Vanished Lands)
1900-1959	DEPENDENCY OF JAMAICA
1959-	BRITISH COLONY

TUVALU

Prior to 1975	Part of Gilbert & Ellice Islands
1975-1978	BRITISH COLONY
1978-	INDEPENDENT STATE

UGANDA

1890-1895	Part of British East Africa
1895-1903	BRITISH PROTECTORATE
1903-1922	British Protectorate (East Africa & Uganda)
1922-1935	British Protectorate (Kenya & Uganda)
1935-1962	British Protectorate (Kenya, Uganda & Tanganyika)
1962	BRITISH PROTECTORATE
1962-1967	INDEPENDENT STATE
1967-	REPUBLIC

UKRAINE

Prior to 1918	Part of Russia
1918-1919	NATIONAL REPUBLIC
1919-1920	PETLYURA DIRECTORATE
1920-1922	SOVIET REPUBLIC
1922-1924	PART OF SOVIET SOCIALIST REPUBLIC
1924-1941	Part of S.S.R. / Russia
1941	German Occupation (Germany)

179

1941-1943	GERMAN PUPPET REPUBLIC
1943-1991	Part of S.S.R. / Russia
1991-	REPUBLIC

UNITED ARAB EMIRATES
Prior to 1971	See *Trucial States* (Vanished Lands)
1971-1972	Federation
	(Issues of Separate Sheikdoms)
1972-	FEDERATION OF SHEIKDOMS

UNITED NATIONS
1945-1951	International Organization
	(United States)
1951-	INTERNATIONAL
	ORGANIZATION

Offices Abroad:
| 1969- | GENEVA |
| 1979- | VIENNA |

UNITED STATES
| 1847- | REPUBLIC |

URUGUAY
| 1856-1859 | Republic – Carrier Issues |
| 1859- | REPUBLIC |

UZBEKISTAN
Prior to 1918	Part of Russia
1918-1919	NATIONAL REPUBLIC
1920-1922	SOVIET REPUBLIC
1923-1924	PART OF
	SOVIET SOCIALIST REPUBLIC
1924-1991	Part of S.S.R. / Russia
1991-	REPUBLIC

VANUATU
| Prior to 1980 | See *New Hebrides* (Vanished Lands) |
| 1980- | REPUBLIC |

VATICAN CITY
| 1870-1929 | Part of Italy |
| 1929- | ECCLESIASTIC STATE |

VENEZUELA
| 1859- | REPUBLIC |

VIETNAM
Prior to 1949	Part of Indochina
1949-1951	Autonomous Kingdom (Indochina)
1951-1955	KINGDOM OF FRENCH UNION
1955	Divided into North & South Vietnam

South Vietnam:
1955-1956	INDEPENDENT STATE OF
	FRENCH UNION
1956-1975	REPUBLIC
1975-	Part of Vietnam

NOTE: *It is illegal to import Communist issues of Vietnam into the U.S.*

VIRGIN ISLANDS
1866-1890	BRITISH COLONY
1890-1899	Part of Leeward Islands
1899-1956	PRESIDENCY OF
	LEEWARD ISLANDS
1956-	BRITISH COLONY

WALLIS & FUTUNA ISLANDS
1888-1920	French Protectorate
	(New Caledonia)
1920-1961	FRENCH PROTECTORATE
1961-	FRENCH OVERSEAS TERRITORY

YEMEN
Prior to 1913	Part of Turkey
1913-1918	Autonomous Kingdom (Turkey)
1918-1926	Kingdom (No Stamps)
1926-1962	KINGDOM
1962-1970	ROYALIST REGIME (Part)
1962-1990	YEMEN ARAB REPUBLIC
1990-	REPUBLIC

YEMEN PEOPLE'S REPUBLIC
Prior to 1968	See *Aden* and *South Arabia* (Vanished Lands)
1968-1971	PEOPLE'S REPUBLIC OF
	SOUTHERN YEMEN
1971-	PEOPLE'S REPUBLIC

ZAIRE
Prior to 1971	See *Belgian Congo* and
	Congo Democratic Republic
	(Vanished Lands)
1971-	REPUBLIC

ZAMBIA
Prior to 1964	See *Northern Rhodesia*
	(Vanished Lands)
1964-	REPUBLIC

ZIMBABWE
Prior to 1979	See *Rhodesia* and *Southern Rhodesia*
	(Vanished Lands)
1979-	REPUBLIC

VANISHED LANDS

ENTITIES THAT NO LONGER PRODUCE POSTAGE STAMPS

ABU DHABI
Prior to 1964	Part of Trucial States
1964-1971	BRITISH PROTECTED SHEIKDOM
1971-1972	STATE OF UNITED ARAB EMIRATES
1973-	Part of United Arab Emirates

ADEN
1854-1937	British Possession (India)
1937-1963	BRITISH COLONY & PROTECTORATE
1963-1965	PART OF SOUTH AFRICA
1965-	Part of South Arabia / Southern Yemen

States:
1942-1968	KATHIRI STATE OF SEIYUN
1942-1955	QUAITI STATE OF SHIHR & MUKALLA
1955-1968	QUAITI STATE IN THE HADHRAMAUT

AFARS AND ISSAS
Prior to 1967	Named Somali Coast
1967-1977	FRENCH OVERSEAS TERRITORY
1977-	Name changed to Djibouti

AGUERA, LA
1901-1920	Part of Rio de Oro
1920-1924	SPANISH POSSESSION
1924-	Part of Spanish Sahara / Morocco

AJMAN
Prior to 1964	Part of Trucial States
1964-1971	BRITISH PROTECTED SHEIKDOM
1971-1972	STATE OF UNITED ARAB EMIRATES
1973-	Part of United Arab Emirates

ALAOUITES
1919-1924	Part of Syria
1935-1930	AUTONOMOUS STATE UNDER FRENCH MANDATE
1930	Name changed to Latakia

ALEXANDRETTA
1919-1923	Part of Syria
1923-1938	French Mandate (Syria)
1938	FRENCH MANDATE STATE
1939	Name changed to Hatay

ALLENSTEIN
Prior to 1920	Part of Germany
1920	PLEBISCITE AREA
1920-1945	Part of Germany
1945-	Part of Poland

ANGRA
Prior to 1892	District of Azores
1892-1905	DISTRICT OF AZORES
1905-	District of Azores

ANJOUAN
1892-1898	FRENCH COLONY
1898-1912	FRENCH DEPENDENCY
1912-1914	FRENCH COLONY
1914-	Part of Madagascar / Comoros

ANNAM & TONKIN
1865-1888	French Protectorate (French Colonies)
1888-1892	FRENCH PROTECTORATE
1892-	Part of Indochina / Vietnam

AUSTRIA: Lombardy-Venetia
1850-1859	PROVINCES OF AUSTRIA
1859-1866	VENETIA – PROVINCE OF AUSTRIA
1859	Lombardy – Annexed to Sardinia
1866	Venetia – Kingdom of Italy

AZORES
1853-1868	Portuguese Colony (Portugal)
1868-1931	PORTUGUESE COLONY
1931-	Part of Portugal

BANGKOK
1882-885	BRITISH TREATY PORT
1885-	Part of Thailand

BASUTOLAND
1871-1883	Part of Cape of Good Hope
1883-1910	British Colony (Cape of Good Hope)
1910-1933	British Colony (Union of South Africa)
1933-1966	BRITISH COLONY
1966	Name changed to Lesotho

BATUM
Prior to 1918	Part of Russia
1918-1920	BRITISH OCCUPATION
1920-	Part of Georgia / Russia

BECHUANALAND
1885-1895	BRITISH COLONY
1895-1897	DISTRICT OF CAPE OF GOOD HOPE
1897-	Part of Cape of Good Hope / South Africa

BECHUANALAND PROTECTORATE
1888-1966	BRITISH PROTECTORATE
1966	Name changed to Botswana

BELGIAN CONGO
1886-1908	Congo: SEMI-INDEPENDENT STATE UNDER BELGIAN CROWN
1909-1960	BELGIAN COLONY
1960	Name changed to Congo, then Zaire

BRITISH CENTRAL AFRICA
1891-1907	BRITISH TERRITORY
1908	Name changed to Nyasaland, then Malawi

BRITISH COLUMBIA & VANCOUVER ISLAND
1860-1865	BRITISH COLONIES – Joint Issues
1865-1866	BRITISH COLONIES – Separate Issues for British Columbia & Vancouver Island
1866-1868	BRITISH COLONY – Unified but with separate issues
1868-1871	BRITISH COLONY OF BRITISH COLUMBIA
1871-	Part of Canada

BRITISH EAST AFRICA
1890-1895	BRITISH EAST AFRICA COMPANY ADMINISTRATION
1895-1903	BRITISH PROTECTORATE
1903-1922	Part of East Africa & Uganda
1922	Name changed to Kenya

BRITISH GUIANA
1850-1966	BRITISH COLONY
1966	Name changed to Guyana

BRITISH HONDURAS
1866-1884	JAMAICA DEPENDENCY
1884-1964	BRITISH COLONY
1964-1973	SELF-GOVERNING BRITISH COLONY
1973	Name changed to Belize

BRITISH INDIAN OCEAN TERRITORY
1847-1965	Part of Mauritius & Seychelles
1965-1976	BRITISH TERRITORY
1976-	British Territory (Great Britain)

BURMA
Prior to 1937	Part of India
1937-1942	BRITISH DOMINION
1942-	BURMA INDEPENDENCE ARMY – Japanese controlled areas
1942-1945	JAPANESE OCCUPATION
1945-1948	BRITISH MILITARY ADMINISTRATION
1946-1948	INTERIM GOVERNMENT
1948-	REPUBLIC

BUSHIRE
Prior to 1915	Part of Persia
1915	BRITISH OCCUPATION
1915-	Part of Persia/Iran

CAMEROONS
Prior to 1915	Part of Cameroun
1915-1916	BRITISH OCCUPATION
1916-1922	British Occupation (Nigeria)
1922-1960	Part of Nigeria

Southern Cameroons:
1960-1961	BRITISH MANDATE
1961-	Part of Cameroon

CANAL ZONE
Prior to 1903	Part of Colombia
1903-1980	U.S. LEASED TERRITORY
1980-	Part of Panama – Joint U.S. and Panamanian Administration

182

CABO JUBY (CAPE JUBY)

Prior to 1916	Part of French Morocco
1916-1917	SPANISH POSSESSION
1917-1919	Spanish Possession
	(Rio de Oro and Spanish Morocco)
1919-1949	SPANISH POSSESSION
1949-1950	PART OF SPANISH WEST AFRICA
1950-	Part of Spanish Sahara/Morocco

CAPE OF GOOD HOPE

1853-1910	BRITISH COLONY
1910-1913	PROVINCE OF
	UNION OF SOUTH AFRICA
1913-	Part of South Africa

CAROLINE ISLANDS

1899-1914	GERMAN PROTECTORATE
1914-1945	Japanese Occupation & Mandate
	(Japan)
1945-1977	Part of Trust Territory of Pacific
	(U.S.)
1977-	Divided into Palau and Micronesia

CASTELLORIZO

Prior to 1915	Part of Turkey
1915-1920	French Occupation
	(French Offices in Turkey)
1920	FRENCH OCCUPATION
1920-1922	Italian Dominion (Italy)
1922-1932	ITALIAN DOMINION
1932-	Part of Aegean Islands / Greece

CENTRAL LITHUANIA

1918-1920	Part of Lithuania
1920-1922	POLISH OCCUPATION
1922-1939	Part of Poland
1939-1940	Part of Lithuania
1940-	Part of Russia

CEYLON

1857-1948	BRITISH COLONY
1948-1972	INDEPENDENT
	BRITISH DOMINION
1972	Name changed to Sri Lanka

CHINA

1878-1912	EMPIRE
1912-1949	REPUBLIC

CILICIA

1863-1918	Part of Turkey
1918-1919	Part of Palestine
1919-1921	FRENCH OCCUPATION
1921-	Part of Turkey

COCHIN-CHINA

1865-1886	French Colony (French Colonies)
1886-1892	FRENCH COLONY
1892-	Part of Indochina / Vietnam

CONFEDERATE STATES

Prior to 1861	Part of United States
1861	CONFEDERACY – Provisional Issues
1861-1865	CONFEDERACY
1865-	Part of United States

CONGO DEMOCRATIC REPUBLIC

Prior to 1960	Belgian Congo
1960-1971	REPUBLIC
1971	Name changed to Zaire

CORFU

Prior to 1923	Part of Greece
1923	ITALIAN OCCUPATION
1923-1941	Part of Greece
1941-1944	Italian & German Occupation
1944-	Part of Greece

CRETE

Prior to 1898	Part of Turkey
1898-1900	Joint Administration by Great Britain, France, Italy & Russia – DISTRICT ISSUES
1900-1913	AUTONOMOUS STATE
1913-	Part of Greece

CYRENAICA

Prior to 1923	Part of Libia
1923-1927	DISTRICT OF LIBIA
1927-1934	ITALIAN COLONY
1934-1942	Part of Libia
1943-1950	British Administration (Great Britain – Mid-East Forces)
1950-1951	AUTONOMOUS STATE
1951-	Part of Libya

CZECHOSLOVAKIA

Prior to 1918	Part of Austria-Hungary
1918-1939	REPUBLIC
1939-1945	Divided into various regions under German and Hungarian occupation – see *Bohemia & Moravia* (Vanished Lands), *Slovakia* (Current Stamp Issuing Countries).
1945-1948	REPUBLIC

1948-1968	COMMUNIST REPUBLIC		1903-1922	BRITISH COLONY & PROTECTORATE
1968-	COMMUNIST FEDERAL REPUBLIC		1922	Name changed to Kenya & Uganda

CZECHOSLOVAKIA:
Bohemia & Moravia
1918-1939 Part of Czechoslovakia
1939-1945 GERMAN PROTECTORATE
1945- Part of Czechoslovakia

DAHOMEY
Prior to 1894 Called Benin
1894-1899 French Colony (Benin)
1899-1944 COLONY OF FRENCH WEST AFRICA
1944-1958 Part of French West Africa
1858-1960 Autonomous Republic (French West Africa)
1960 AUTONOMOUS REPUBLIC
1960-1975 REPUBLIC
1975 Name changed to Benin

DALMATIA
Prior to 1918 Part of Austria
1919-1922 ITALIAN OCCUPATION
1922- Part of Yugoslavia

DANISH WEST INDIES
1855-1917 DANISH COLONY
1917- U.S. Territory (United States) – U.S. Virgin Islands

DANZIG
Prior to 1920 Part of Germany
1920-1939 FREE CITY
1939 GERMAN OCCUPATION
1939-1944 Part of Germany
1944- Part of Poland

DIEGO-SUAREZ
1890-1898 FRENCH COLONY
1898- Part of Madagascar

DUBAI
Part to 1963 Part of Trucial States
1963-1971 BRITISH PROTECTED SHEIKDOM
1971-1972 STATE OF UNITED ARAB EMIRATES
1973- Part of United Arab Emirates

EAST AFRICA & UGANDA
1895-1903 Separate issues for Uganda and British East Africa

EASTERN RUMELIA
1863-1880 Part of Turkey
1880-1885 TURKISH PROVINCE
1885 BULGARIAN PROVINCE – South Bulgaria
1885- Part of Bulgaria

EASTERN SILESIA
Prior to 1918 Part of Austria
1918-1920 Czechoslovak Occupation (Czechoslovakia)
1920 PLEBISCITE AREA
1920- Divided between Czechoslovakia & Poland

EGYPT:
Palestine Issues – Gaza Area
Prior to 1948 Part of Palestine
1948-1956 EGYPTIAN OCCUPATION
1956-1957 Israeli Occupation (Israel)
1957-1967 EGYPTIAN OCCUPATION
1967- Israeli Occupation (Israel)

ELOBEY, ANNÓBON & CORISCO
1885-1903 Part of Fernando Po
1903-1909 SPANISH POSSESSION
1909-1960 Part of Spanish Guinea
1960-1968 Divided between Fernando Po & Rio Muni
1968- Part of Equatorial Guinea

EPIRUS
Prior to 1913 Part of Turkey
1914 PROVISIONAL GOVERNMENT
1914-1916 GREEK OCCUPATION
1916-1919 Italian Occupation (Italy)
1919- Part of Albania

FAR EASTERN REPUBLIC
Prior to 1920 Part of Russia
1920-1922 BOLSHEVIK REPUBLIC
1922-1923 REPUBLIC OF RUSSIA
1923- Part of Russia
Priamur & Maritime Districts
1921-1922 ANTI-BOLSHEVIK GOVERNMENT

184

FERNANDO PO

1868	SPANISH COLONY
1868-1879	Spanish Colony (Cuba & Puerto Rico)
1879-1909	SPANISH COLONY
1909-1960	Part of Spanish Guinea
1929	SPECIAL ISSUE
1960-1968	SPANISH OVERSEAS PROVINCE
1968-	Part of Equatorial Guinea

FIUME

Prior to 1918	Part of Austria
1918-1919	ALLIED OCCUPATION
1919-1920	ITALIAN OCCUPATION – D'Annunzio
1920-1924	FREE STATE – Italian Protectorate
1924	PART OF ITALY
1924-1945	Part of Italy
1945-	Part of Yugoslavia

FRANCE: Alsace-Lorraine

Prior to 1870	Part of France
1870-1871	NORTH GERMAN CONFEDERATION OCCUPATION
1872-1918	Part of Germany
1918-1940	Part of France
1940-1941	GERMAN OCCUPATION
1942-1944	Part of Germany
1944-	Part of France

FRENCH COLONIES

1859-1906,	
1943-1945	GENERAL ISSUE FOR USE IN VARIOUS FRENCH COLONIES

FRENCH CONGO

1891-1906	FRENCH COLONY
1906-	Divided into separate colonies

FRENCH EQUATORIAL AFRICA

1910-1936	French Administrative Unit (Separate Colonies)
1936-1958	FRENCH COLONIAL ADMINISTRATIVE UNIT
1958-1960	POSTAL SERVICE FOR SEPARATE AUTONOMOUS REPUBLICS

FRENCH GUIANA

1886-1946	FRENCH COLONY
1946-1947	FRENCH OVERSEAS DEPARTMENT
1947-	French Overseas Dept. (France)

FRENCH GUINEA

1892-1895	FRENCH COLONY
1895-1944	COLONY OF FRENCH WEST AFRICA
1944-1958	Part of French West Africa
1958-	Name changed to Guinea

FRENCH INDIA

1854-1892	French Possession (India)
1892-1954	FRENCH TERRITORY
1954-	Part of India

FRENCH MOROCCO

Prior to 1912	Part of Morocco
1912-1914	French Protectorate (French Post Offices in Morocco)
1914-1956	FRENCH PROTECTORATE
1956-	Part of Morocco

FRENCH SUDAN

1894-1895	FRENCH COLONY
1895-1899	COLONY OF FRENCH WEST AFRICA
1899-1906	Colony dissolved
1906-1920	Part of Upper Senegal & Niger
1920-1921	Colony of French West Africa (Upper Senegal & Niger)
1921-1944	COLONY OF FRENCH WEST AFRICA
1944-1958	Part of French West Africa
1958-	Name changed to Sudanese Republic, then Mali

FRENCH WEST AFRICA

1895-1944	French Administration Unit (Issues of Separate Colonies)
1944-1958	FRENCH ADMINISTRATIVE UNIT
1958-1959	POSTAL SERVICE FOR SEPARATE AUTONOMOUS REPUBLICS

FUJEIRA

Prior to 1964	Part of Trucial States
1964-1971	BRITISH PROTECTED SHEIKDOM
1971-1972	STATE OF UNITED ARAB EMIRATES
1972-	Part of United Arab Emirates

FUNCHAL

Prior to 1892	Part of Madeira
1892-1905	PORTUGUESE COLONY – All of Madeira
1905-	Part of Madeira/Portugal

GERMAN EAST AFRICA

1888-1893	German Protectorate (Germany)
1893-1918	GERMAN PROTECTORATE
1918-	Divided between Britain, Belgium & Portugal

GERMAN NEW GUINEA

1888-1898	German Protectorate (Germany)
1898-1914	GERMAN PROTECTORATE
1914-	New Britain / NW Pacific Islands / New Guinea

GERMAN SOUTH-WEST AFRICA

1886-1897	Germany Colony (Germany)
1897-1915	GERMAN COLONY
1915	Name changed to South West Africa

GERMAN STATES

Baden:

1851-1871	GRAND DUCHY
1872-1945	Part of Germany / German Federal Republic

Bavaria:

1849-1871	KINGDOM
1872-1918	KINGDOM OF GERMAN EMPIRE
1919-1920	AUTONOMOUS REPUBLIC
1920	PART OF GERMANY
1920-	Part of Germany / German Federal Republic

Bergedorf:

1861-1867	JOINT HAMBURG & LUBECK POSSESSION
1867-	Part of Hamburg / German Federal Republic

Bremen:

1855-1867	FREE CITY
1868-	Part of North German Confederation / German Federal. Republic

Brunswick:

1852-1867	GRAND DUCHY
1868-	Part of North German Confederation / German Federal Republic

Hamburg:

1852-1859	Free City (Thurn & Taxis)
1859-1867	FREE CITY
1868-	Part of North German Confederation / German Federal Republic

Hanover:

1850-1866	KINGDOM
1866-1867	Part of Prussia
1868-	Part of North German Confederation / German Federal Republic

Lubeck:

1852-1858	Free City (Thurn & Taxis)
1859-1867	FREE CITY
1868-	Part of North German Confederation / German Federal Republic

Mecklenburg-Schwerin:

1856-1867	GRAND DUCHY
1868-	Part of North German Confederation / German Federal Republic

Mecklenburg-Strelitz:

1864-1867	GRAND DUCHY
1868-	Part of North German Confederation / German Federal Republic

North German Confederation:

Prior to 1867	Issues of separate states
1868-1871	CONFEDERATION OF NORTHERN GERMAN STATES
1872-	Part of Germany

Oldenburg:

1852-1867	GRAND DUCHY
1868-	Part of North German Confederation / German Federal Republic

Prussia:

1850-1867	KINGDOM
1868-1945	Part of North German Confederation / Germany
1945-	Divided by German Federal Republic, German Democratic Republic, Poland, and Russia

Saxony:

1850-1867	KINGDOM
1868-	Part of North German Confederation / German Federal Republic

Schleswig-Holstein:

1850-1851	PROVISIONAL GOVERNMENT
1851-1864	Autonomous Duchies (Denmark)
1864-1865	Schleswig – AUSTRO-PRUSSIAN OCCUPATIONS
1864-1865	Holstein – GERMAN FEDERAL ADMINISTRATION
1865	AUSTRO-PRUSSIAN OCCUPATION
1865-1867	Schleswig – PRUSSIAN ADMINISTRATION
1865-1867	Holstein – AUSTRIAN ADMINISTRATION
1867	Provinces of Prussia
1868-	Part of North German Confederation / German Federal Republic

Thurn & Taxis

1852-1867	PRINCELY POSTAL SYSTEM FOR VARIOUS GERMAN STATES
1868-	Service dissolved

186

Wurttemberg:

1851-1871	KINGDOM
1872-1902	KINGDOM OF GERMAN EMPIRE
1902-1918	KINGDOM OF GERMAN EMPIRE – Officials only plus German stamps
1918-1919	PROVISIONAL GOVERNMENT (plus Germany)
1919-1924	PART OF GERMANY – Officials only
1924-	Part of Germany / German Federal Republic

GERMANY: Berlin (West)

Prior to 1945	Part of Germany
1945-1948	British, French & U.S. Occupation (Issues of General German Occupation)
1948-1950	JOINT BRITISH, FRENCH & U.S. OCCUPATION
1950-	LAND OF GERMAN FEDERAL REPUBLIC UNDER U.S., BRITISH & FRENCH PROTECTION

GERMANY:
German Democratic Republic

Prior to 1945	Part of Germany
1945-1949	U.S.S.R. OCCUPATION – Local & General Issues
1949-	COMMUNIST REPUBLIC

GERMANY: Occupation Issues

Rhineland Area:

1919-1921	BELGIAN OCCUPATION

British & U.S. Zones:

1945-1946	ALLIED MILITARY GOVERNMENT
1946-1948	JOINT ISSUES WITH RUSSIA
1948-1949	JOINT U.S. & BR. ISSUES

French Zone:

1945-1947	FRENCH OCCUPATION
1947-1949	French Occupation (Separate Issues for Baden, Rhineland-Palatinate & Wurttemberg)

Russian Zone:

1945-1946	Russian Occupation (Local issues)
1946-1948	JOINT ISSUES WITH US. & BRITAIN
1948-1949	RUSSIAN OCCUPAITION

GILBERT ISLANDS

Prior to 1975	Part of Gilbert & Ellice Islands
1975-1979	BRITISH COLONY
1979	Name changed to Kiribati

GILBERT & ELLICE ISLANDS

1901-1911	British Protectorate (New South Wales)
1911-1915	BRITISH PROTECTORATE
1915-1975	BRITISH COLONY
1975-	Divided into Gilbert Islands & Tuvalu

GOLD COAST

1875-1957	BRITISH COLONY
1957	Name changed to Ghana

GRAND COMORO ISLAND

1897-1898	FRENCH COLONY
1898-1912	FRENCH DEPENDENCY
1912-1914	FRENCH COLONY
1914-	Part of Madagascar/Comoros

GRIQUALAND WEST

1871-1874	British Administration (Cape of Good Hope)
1874-1880	BRITISH COLONY
1880-	Part of Cape of Good Hope / South Africa

GUADELOUPE

1884-1946	FRENCH COLONY
1947	FRENCH OVERSEAS DEPARTMENT
1947-	French Overseas Dept. (France)

GUAM

Prior to 1899	Part of Marianna Islands
1899-1901	U.S. POSSESSION
1901-1941	U.S. Navy Administration (U.S.)
1941-1944	Japanese Occupation (Japan)
1944-	U.S. Territory (U.S.)

HATAY

Prior to 1939	Named Alexandretta
1939	AUTONOMOUS REPUBLIC UNDER FRENCH PROTECTORATE
1939-	Part of Turkey

HAWAII

1851-1893	KINGDOM
1893-1894	PROVISIONAL GOVERNMENT
1894-1898	REPUBLIC
1899-1900	U.S. ADMINISTRATION
1900-1959	U.S. Territory (U.S.)
1959-	State of United States

187

HELIGOLAND

Prior to 1867	Part of Hamburg
1867-1890	BRITISH POSSESSION
1890-	Part of Germany / German Federal Republic

HUNGARY: Occupation Issues

1919-1920	Arad: FRENCH OCCUPATION
1919-1920	Banat, Bacska – SERBIAN OCCUPATION
1919-1920	Baranya – SERBIAN OCCUPATION
1919-1920	Debrecen: ROMANIAN OCCUPATION
1919	Szeged: ANTI-SOVIET GOVERNMENT
1919	Temesvar: SERBIAN OCCUPATION
1919-1920	Temesvar: ROMANIAN OCCUPATION
1919-1920	Transylvania: ROMANIAN OCCUPATION

IFNI

1860-1941	Spanish Colony (Handstamps)
1941-1949	SPANISH COLONY
1949-1951	PART OF SPANISH WEST AFRICA
1951-1969	SPANISH COLONY
1969-	Part of Morocco

INDIAN NATIVE STATES

Convention States:

1886-1950	CHAMBA
1886-1901	FARIDKOT
1885-1950	GWALIOR
1885-1950	JIND
1885-1950	NABHA
1884-1950	PATIALA

Feudatory States:

1877-1902	ALWAR
1888-1894	BAMRA
1921-1948	BARWANI
1876-1950	BHOPAL
1879-1902	BHOR
1935-1939	BIJAWAR
1894-1949	BUNDI
1895-1901	BUSSAHIR
1894-1950	CHARKHARI
1892-1949	COCHIN
1897-1901	DHAR
1893-1921	DUTTIA
1879-1886	FARIDKOT
1869-1950	HYDERABAD
1939-1944	IDAR
1886-1950	INDORE

1904-1949	JAIPUR
1866-1894	JAMMU & KAHSMIR
1942-1949	JASDAN
1887-1900	JHALAWAR
1874-1885	JIND
1899-1949	KISHANGARH
1931-1949	MORVI
1891-1895	NANDGAON
1877-1895	NOWANUGGUR
1913-1950	ORCCHA
1876-1894	POONCH
1948-1950	RAJASTHAN
1880-1886	RAJPEEPLA
1923-1950	SAURASHTRA
1879-1902	SIRMOOR
1864-1923	SORUTH
1888-1949	TRAVANCORE
1949-1951	TRAVANCORE-COCHIN
1888-1895	WADHWAN

INDOCHINA

1887-1892	French Colonies & Protectorates (French Colonies)
1889-1941	FRENCH COLONY & PROTECTORATE
1941-1945	JAPANESE OCCUPATION
1945-1949	FRENCH COLONY & PROTECTORATE
1949-1951	FOR USE IN SEPARATE STATES
1951-	Divided into Cambodia, Laos & Vietnam

INHAMBANE

Prior to 1895	Part of Mozambique
1895-1920	DISTRICT OF MOZAMBIQUE
1920-	Part of Mozambique

ININI

Prior to 1932	Part of French Guiana
1932-1946	FRENCH TERRITORY
1946-	Part of French Guiana

IONIAN ISLANDS

1859-1864	BRITISH PROTECTORATE
1864-1941	Part of Greece
1941-1943	ITALIAN OCCUPATION
1943-1944	GERMAN OCCUPATION
1944-	Part of Greece

ITALIAN COLONIES

1932-1934	GENERAL ISSUES FOR USE IN ITALIAN COLONIES

188

ITALIAN EAST AFRICA

Prior to 1936	Ethiopia, Eritrea, and Italian Somaliland
1936-1938	Italian Colony – Issues of Ethiopia, Eritrea, & Italian Somaliland
1938-1941	ITALIAN COLONY
1941-	Divided after British Occupation

ITALIAN STATES

Modena:

1852-1859	GRAND DUCHY
1859-1860	PROVISIONAL GOVERNMENT
1860-	Part of Sardinia/Italy

Parma:

1852-1859	GRAND DUCHY
1859-1860	PROVISIONAL GOVERNMENT
1860-	Part of Sardinia/Italy

Romagna:

1852-1859	Part of Roman States
1859-1860	PROVISIONAL GOVERNMENT
1860-	Part of Sardinia/Italy

Roman States:

1852-1870	ECCLESIASTIC STATE
1870-	Part of Italy

Sardinia:

1851-1861	KINGDOM
1861-1862	PART OF ITALY
1862-	Part of Italy

Tuscany:

1851-1859	GRAND DUCHY
1860	PROVISIONAL GOVERNMENT
1860-	Part of Sardinia/Italy

Two Sicilies:

1858-1860	Naples – PART OF TWO SICILIES KINGDOM
1859-1860	Sicily – PART OF TWO SICILIES KINGDOM
1860-1861	PROVISIONAL GOVERNMENT
1861-1862	Neapolitan Provinces – PART OF ITALY
1862-	Part of Italy

ITALY: Aegean Islands

Prior to 1912	Part of Turkey
1912	PROVISIONAL GOVERNMENT
1912	ITALIAN OCCUPATION
1912-1920	Italian Occupation: Issues of separate islands
1920-1929	Italian Dominion – Issues of separate islands
1929-1943	ITALIAN DOMINION
1943-1944	GERMAN OCCUPATION
1944-1947	British Occupation (Middle East Forces)
1947	GREEK OCCUPATION
1947-	Part of Greece

Issues of Separate Islands:

1912-1932	CALCHI; CALIMNO; CASO; COO; LERO; LISSO; NISIRO; PATMOS; PISCOPI; SCARPANTO; SIMI & STAMPALIA
1912-1945	RHODES – Used in all Aegean Islands from 1932-1945

ITALY: Italian Social Republic

1943-1945	REPUBLIC NORTH ITALY UNDER GERMAN OCCUPATION
1945-	Part of Italy

ITALY: Venezia-Guilia

1919-1945	Part of Italy
1945	YUGOSLAV OCCUPATION
1945-1947	ALLIED MILITARY GOVERNMENT
1947-	Divided between Italy & Trieste – Zone A

JORDAN: Palestine Issues – West Bank

Prior to 1948	Part of Palestine
1948-1950	JORDANIAN OCCUPATION
1950-1967	Part of Jordan
1967-	Israeli Occupation (Israel)

KARELIA

Prior to 1922	Part of Russia
1922	AUTONOMOUS REPUBLIC
1922-1941	Part of Russia
1941-1944	Eastern Karelia: FINNISH OCCUPATION
1944-	Part of Russia

KENYA & UGANDA

Prior to 1922	Called East Africa & Uganda
1922-1935	BRITISH COLONY & PROTECTORATE
1935-	Separated – stamps of Kenya, Uganda & Tanganyika

KENYA, UGANDA & TANZANIA

Prior to 1935	Issues for Tanganyika & Kenya-Uganda

Kenya, Uganda, & Tanganyika:

1935-1961	BRITISH POSTAL UNIT
1961-1964	EAST AFRICAN POSTAL UNION – Kenya, Uganda & Tanzania
1964-1976	EAST AFRICAN POSTAL UNION
1976-	Postal Union Dissolved

KIAUCHAU

Prior to 1897	Part of China
1898-1900	German Leased Territory (Germany)
1900-1914	GERMAN LEASED TERRITORY
1914-1922	Japanese Occupation (Japan)
1922-	Part of China

KIONGA

Prior to 1916	Part of German East Africa
1916-1919	PORTUGUESE OCCUPATION
1919-	Part of Mozambique

LABUAN

1860-1867	British Colony (India)
1867-1879	British Colony (Straits Settlements)
1879-1889	DEPENDENCY OF STRAITS SETTLEMENTS
1890-1906	BRITISH NORTH BORNEO COMPANY ADMINISTRATION
1906-1942	Part of Strait Settlements
1942-	Part of North Borneo/Malaysia

LAGOS

1861-1874	Dependency of Sierra Leone (Sierra Leone)
1874-1886	DEPENDENCY OF GOLD COAST
1886-1899	ROYAL NIGER CO. ADMINISTRATION
1899-1906	BRITISH PROTECTORATE
1906-	Part of Southern Nigeria/Nigeria

LATAKIA

Prior to 1930	Called Alaouites
1930-1937	AUTONOMOUS REPUBLIC UNDER FRENCH MANDATE
1937-	Part of Syria

LEEWARD ISLANDS

Prior to 1890	Separate British Colonies of Antigua, Dominica, Montserrat, Nevis, St. Christopher & Virgin Islands
1890-1956	BRITISH COLONY
1956-	Separate British Colonies

LIBIA: Fezzan-Ghadames

1943-1949	FRENCH MILITARY ADMINISTRATION
1948-1950	Fezzan – FRENCH MILITARY ADMINISTRATION
1950-1951	Fezzan – FRENCH CIVIL ADMINISTRATION
1949-1951	Ghadames – FRENCH MILITARY ADMINISTRATION

LOURENCO MARQUES

Prior to 1893	Part of Mozambique
1893-1921	DISTRICT OF MOZAMBIQUE
1921-	Part of Mozambique

MADIERA

1853-1868	Portuguese Colony (Portugal)
1868-1881	PORTUGUESE COLONY
1881-1892	Portuguese Colony (Portugal)
1892-1905	Portuguese Colony (Funchal)
1905-1931	Portuguese Colony (Azores)
1931-	Part of Portugal

MALAYA

Prior to 1943	Issues of Separate States and Sultanates
1943	SIAMESE OCCUPATION – Northern Portion
1943-1945	JAPANESE OCCUPATION – Major Portion
1945-1957	Separate States & Sultanates
1957-1963	INDEPENDENT FEDERATION
1963-	Part of Malaysia

MALAYAN STATES

Federated Malay States:

Prior to 1900	Separate States
1900-1935	BRITISH PROTECTED SULTANATES
1935-	Separate States

Johore:

1876-1914	SULTANATE
1914-1942	BRITISH PROTECTED SULTANATE
1942-1943	JAPANESE OCCUPATION
1943-1945	Japanese Occupation (Malaya)
1945-1948	British Protected Sultanate (Straits Settlements)
1948-1957	BRITISH PROTECTED SULTANATE
1957-1963	STATE OF MALAYA
1963-1965	Part of Malaysia
1965-	STATE OF MALAYSIA

Kedah:

Prior to 1909	Part of Siam
1909-1912	British Protected Sultanate (Fed. Malay States)
1912-1942	BRITISH PROTECTED SULTANATE
1942-1943	JAPANESE OCCUPATION
1943	Siamese Occupation (Siam)
1943-1945	British Protected Sultanate (Straits Settlements)

1948-1957	BRITISH PROTECTED SULTANATE
1957-1963	STATE OF MALAYA
1963-1965	Part of Malaysia
1965-	STATE OF MALAYSIA

Malacca:

Prior to 1942	Part of Straits Settlements
1942	JAPANESE OCCUPATION
1942-1945	Japanese Occupation (Malaya/Straits Sett.)
1945-1949	British Protectorate (Straits Settlements)
1948-1957	BRITISH PROTECTORATE
1957-1963	STATE OF MALAYA
1963-1965	Part of Malaysia
1965-	STATE OF MALAYSIA

Negri Sembilan:

1891-1900	FEDERATION OF BRITISH PROTECTED SULTANATES
1900-1935	Part of Fed. Malay States
1935-1942	FEDERATION OF BRITISH PROTECTED SULTANATES
1942-1943	JAPANESE OCCUPATION
1943-1945	Japanese Occupation (Malaya)
1945-1949	Fed. of British Protected Sultanates (Straits Settlements)
1948-1957	FEDERATION OF BRITISH PROTECTED SULTANATES
1957-1963	STATE OF MALAYA
1963-1965	Part of Malaysia
1965-	STATE OF MALAYSIA

Pahang:

1889-1900	BRITISH PROTECTED SULTANATE
1900-1935	Part of Fed. Malay States
1935-1942	BRITISH PROTECTED SULTANATE
1942-1943	JAPANESE OCCUPATION
1943-1945	Japanese Occupation (Malaya)
1945-1950	British Protected Sultanate (Straits Settlements)
1948-1957	BRITISH PROTECTED SULTANATE
1957-1963	STATE OF MALAYA
1963-1965	Part of Malaysia
1965-	STATE OF MALAYSIA

Penang:

Prior to 1942	Part of Straits Settlements
1942	JAPANESE OCCUPATION
1942-1945	Japanese Occupation (Malaya / Straits Sett.)
1945-1949	British Protectorate (Straits Settlements)
1948-1957	BRITISH PROTECTORATE

1957-1963	STATE OF MALAYA
1963-1965	Part of Malaysia
1965-	STATE OF MALAYSIA

Perak:

1867-1878	British Protected Sultanate (Straits Settlements)
1878-1900	BRITISH PROTECTED SULTANATE
1900-1935	Part of Fed. Malay States
1935-1942	BRITISH PROTECTED SULTANATE
1942-1943	JAPANESE OCCUPATION
1943-1945	Japanese Occupation (Malaya)
1945-1950	British Protected Sultanate (Straits Settlements)
1948-1957	BRITISH PROTECTED SULTANATE
1957-1963	STATE OF MALAYA
1963-	STATE OF MALAYSIA

Perlis:

Prior to 1943	Part of Kedah
1943-1945	Part of Siam
1945-1951	British Protected Sultanate (Straits Settlements)
1948-1857	BRITISH PROTECTED SULTANATE
1957-1963	STATE OF MALAYA
1963-1965	Part of Malaysia
1965-	STATE OF MALAYSIA

Selangor:

1874-1878	British Protected Sultanate (Straits Settlements)
1878-1900	BRITISH PROTECTED SULTANATE
1900-1935	Part of Fed. Malay States
1935-1942	BRITISH PROTECTED SULTANATE
1942-1943	JAPANESE OCCUPATION
1943-1945	Japanese Occupation (Malaya)
1945-1949	British Protected Sultanate (Straits Settlements)
1948-1957	BRITISH PROTECTED SULTANATE
1957-1963	STATE OF MALAYA
1963-1965	State of Malaysia
1965-	STATE OF MALAYSIA

Sunjei Ujong:

| 1878-1895 | BRITISH PROTECTED SULTANATE |
| 1895- | Part of Negri Sembilan/Malaysia |

Trengganu:

| Prior to 1909 | Part of Siam |
| 1909-1910 | British Protected Sultanate (Straits Settlements) |

1910-1942	BRITISH PROTECTED SULTANATE
1942-1943	JAPANESE OCCUPATION
1943	Siamese Occupation (Siam)
1943-1945	Part of Siam
1945-1949	British Protected Sultanate (Straits Settlements)
1948-1957	BRITISH PROTECTED SULTANATE
1957-1963	STATE OF MALAYA
1963-1965	Part of Malaysia
1965-	STATE OF MALAYSIA

MANCHUKUO
Prior to 1932	Part of China
1932-1934	JAPANESE OCCUPATION
1934-1945	JAPANESE PUPPET REPUBLIC
1945-	Part of China

MARIANNA ISLANDS
Prior to 1899	Spanish Colony (Philippines)
1899-1900	SPANISH COLONY
1900-1914	GERMAN PROTECTORATE
1914-1945	Japanese Occupation & Mandate (Japan)
1945-1947	U.S. Occupation (U.S.)
1947-1977	Part of Trust Territory of Pacific (U.S.)
1977-	Northern Marianna – Commonwealth of Trust Territories of Pacific (U.S.)

MARIENWERDER
Prior to 1920	Part of Germany
1920	PLEBISCITE AREA
1920-1945	Part of Germany
1945-	Part of Poland

MARTINIQUE
1886-1946	FRENCH COLONY
1947	FRENCH OVERSEAS DEPARTMENT
1947-	French Overseas Dept. (France)

MAYOTTE
1892-1898	FRENCH COLONY
1898-1912	FRENCH DEPENDENCY
1912-1914	FRENCH COLONY
1914-1976	Part of Madagascar/Comoros
1976-1996	French Overseas Dept. (France)
1997-2011	Philatelic Autonomy
2012-	France

MEMEL
Prior to 1918	Part of Germany
1918-1920	Allied Occupation (Germany)
1920-1923	ALLIED (FRENCH) ADMINISTRATION
1923-1924	LITHUANIAN OCCUPATION
1924-1939	Part of Lithuania
1939-1944	Part of Germany
1944-	Part of Russia

MESOPOTAMIA
1863-1917	Part of Turkey
1917-1918	British Occupation (India)
1917-1918	Baghdad – BRITISH OCCUPATION
1918-1921	Iraq – BRITISH OCCUPATION
1918-1921	Mosul – BRITISH OCCUPATION
1921	Name changed to Iraq

MIDDLE CONGO
Prior to 1904	Part of French Congo
1904-1907	French Colony (French Congo)
1907-1910	FRENCH COLONY
1910-1937	COLONY OF FRENCH EQUATORIAL AFRICA
1937-1958	Part of French Equatorial Africa
1958	Name changed to Congo Republic

MOHÉLI
1906-1912	FRENCH DEPENDENCY
1912-1914	FRENCH COLONY
1914-	Part of Madagascar/Comoros

MOZAMBIQUE COMPANY
Prior to 1892	Part of Mozambique
1892-1942	MOZAMBIQUE COMPANY ADMINISTRATION
1942-	Part of Mozambique

NATAL
1857-1910	BRITISH COLONY
1910-1913	PROVINCE OF UNION OF SOUTH AFRICA
1913-	Part of South Africa

NETHERLANDS INDIES
1864-1942	NETHERLANDS COLONY
1942-1945	Japanese Occupation (Separate Districts)
1945-1948	NETHERLANDS COLONY
1948	Name changed to Indonesia

192

Japanese Occupation Districts:

1943-1945	JAVA & MADURA
1943-1945	SUMATRA
1943-1945	EASTERN INDONESIA

NETHERLANDS NEW GUINEA

Prior to 1950	Part of Netherlands Indies
1950-1962	NETHERLANDS OVERSEAS TERRRITORY
1962	Name changed to West Irian

NEVIS

1861-1890	BRITISH COLONY
1890-1903	Part of Leeward Islands
1903-	Part of St. Kitts-Nevis

NEW BRITAIN

Prior to 1914	Part of German New Guinea
1914-1915	AUSTRALIAN OCCUPATION
1915-	Part of NW Pacific Islands / Papua New Guinea

NEW BRUNSWICK

1851-1867	BRITISH COLONY
1867-	Province of Canada

NEW GUINEA

Prior to 1925	German New Guinea / NW Pacific Islands
1925-1942	AUSTRALIAN TERRITORY
1942-1944	Japanese Occupation (Japan)
1944-1952	Australian Territory (Australia)
1952-	Part of Papua New Guinea

NEW HEBRIDES

1887-1908	British & French Protectorate (New Caledonia)
1908-1980	BRITISH & FRENCH CONDOMINIUM – British & French Currency Issues
1980	Name changed to Vanuatu

NEW REPUBLIC

1881-1886	Part of Natal
1886-1888	BOER REPUBLIC
1888-1903	Part of South African Rep.
1903-	Part of Natal/South Africa

NEW SOUTH WALES

1850-1901	BRITISH COLONY
1901-1913	STATE OF AUSTRALIA
1913-	State of Australia

NEWFOUNDLAND

1857-1933	SELF-GOVERNING BRITISH DOMINION
1933-1949	BRITISH COLONY
1949-	Province of Canada

NIGER COAST PROTECTORATE

1892-1893	Oil River Prot. – BRITISH PROTECTORATE
1893-1900	BRITISH PROTECTORATE
1900-	Part of Southern Nigeria/Nigeria

NORTH BORNEO

1883-1941	BRITISH NORTH BORNEO COMPANY ADMINISTRATION
1942-1945	JAPANESE OCCUPATION
1945-1946	BRITISH MILITARY ADMINISTRATION
1946-1963	BRITISH COLONY
1963	Name changed to Sabah

NORTH INGERMANLAND

Prior to 1920	Part of Russia
1920	PROVISIONAL GOVERNMENT
1920-	Part of Russia

NORTHERN NIGERIA

1900-1913	BRITISH PROTECTORATE
1914-	Part of Nigeria

NORTHERN RHODESIA

Prior to 1924	Part of Rhodesia
1925-1953	BRITISH PROTECTORATE
1954-1963	Part of Rhodesia & Nyasaland
1963-1964	BRITISH PROTECTORATE
1964-	Name changed to Zambia

NORTHWEST PACIFIC ISLANDS

Prior to 1915	German New Guinea/New Britain
1915-1924	AUSTRALIAN MILITARY GOVERNMENT
1952	Name changed to New Guinea

NOSSI-BE

1889-1894	DEPENDENCY OF DIEGO-SUAREZ
1894-1901	FRENCH COLONY
1901-	Part of Madagascar

NOVA SCOTIA

1851-1867	BRITISH COLONY
1867-	Province of Canada

NYASALAND PROTECTORATE

Prior to 1908	was called British Central Africa
1908-1954	BRITISH PROTECTORATE
1954-1963	Part of Rhodesia & Nyasaland
1963-1964	BRITISH PROTECTORATE
1964	Name changed to Malawi

NYASSA

Prior to 1908	Part of Mozambique
1898-1929	NYASSA COMPANY ADMINISTRATION
1929-	Part of Mozambique

OBOCK

1892-1893	FRENCH POSSESSION
1893-1903	USED ONLY IN DJIBOUTI
1903-	Part of Somali Coast/Djibouti

OLTRE GUIBA

Prior to 1925	Part of Kenya & Uganda
1925-1926	ITALIAN PROTECTORATE
1926-	Part of Somalia

ORANGE RIVER COLONY

1868-1900	Orange Free State – BOER REPUBLIC
1900	Orange Free State – BRITISH OCCUPATION
1900-1910	BRITISH COLONY
1910-1913	PROVINCE OF UNION OF SOUTH AFRICA
1913-	Part of South Africa

PAKISTAN: Native States

1945-1949	Bahawalpur: FEUDATORY STATE
1897-1907	Las Bela: FEUDATORY STATE

PALESTINE

Prior to 1918	Part of Turkey
1918-1920	BRITISH MILITARY ADMINISTRATION
1920-1923	BRITISH ADMINISTRATION
1923-1948	BRITISH MANDATE
1948-	Divided into Israel, Gaza & West Bank Areas

PONTA DELGADA

Prior to 1892	Part of Azores
1892-1905	DISTRICT OF AZORES
1905-	Part of Azores/Portugal

PORTUGUESE AFRICA

1898, 1919, 1945	SPECIAL ISSUES FOR PORTUGUESE COLONIES

PORTUGUESE CONGO

1870-1894	Part of Angola
1894-1920	PORTUGUESE COLONY
1920-	Part of Angola

PORTUGUESE GUINEA

1877-1881	Dependency of Cape Verde (Cape Verde)
1881-1951	PORTUGUESE COLONY
1951-1974	PORTUGUESE OVERSEAS PROVINCE
1974	Name changed to Guinea-Bissau

PORTUGUESE INDIA

1871-1951	PORTUGUESE COLONY
1951-1961	PORTUGUESE OVERSEAS PROVINCE
1961-	Part of India

PRINCE EDWARD ISLAND

1861-1873	BRITISH COLONY
1873-	Province of Canada

PUERTO RICO

1855-1873	Spanish Colony (Cuba & Puerto Rico)
1873-1898	SPANISH COLONY
1898-1900	U.S. ADMINISTRATION
1900-1917	U.S. Civil Administration (U.S.)
1917-1952	U.S. Territory (U.S.)
1952-	Autonomous U.S. Commonwealth (U.S.)

QUEENSLAND

1850-1859	Part of New South Wales
1859-1901	BRITISH COLONY
1901-1913	STATE OF AUSTRALIA
1913-	State of Australia

QUELIMANE

Prior to 1893	Part of Mozambique
1893-1913	Part of Zambezia
1913-1914	DISTRICT OF MOZAMBIQUE
1914-1920	Part of Zambezia/Mozambique

RAS AL KHAIMA
Prior to 1964	Part of Trucial States
1964-1971	BRITISH PROTECTED SHEIKDOM
1971-1972	STATE OF
	UNITED ARAB EMIRATES
1973-	Part of United Arab Emirates

RÉUNION
1852-1946	FRENCH COLONY
1946-1975	FRENCH OVERSEAS
	DEPARTMENT
1975-	French Overseas Department (France)

RHODESIA
1890-1909	British South Africa – BRITISH
	TERRITORY
1909-1924	BRITISH TERRITORY
1924-	Divided into
	Northern & Southern Rhodesia

RHODESIA & NYASALAND
Prior to 1953	Separate Colonies & Protectorates
1954-1963	BRITISH FEDERATED STATE
1963-	Separate Countries

RIO DE ORO
1901-1905	Spanish Colony (Spain)
1905-1924	SPANISH COLONY
1924-	Name changed to Spanish Sahara

RIO MUNI
Prior to 1909	Called Spanish Guinea
1909-1960	Part of Spanish Guinea
1960-1968	SPANISH OVERSEAS PROVINCE
1968-	Part of Equatorial Guinea

ROUAD, ILE
Prior to 1916	Part of Turkey
1916-1920	FRENCH OCCUPATION
1920-	Part of Syria

RUANDA-URUNDI
Prior to 1916	Part of German East Africa
1916-1924	Belgian Occupation
	(German East Africa –
	Belgian Occupation)
1924-1968	BELGIAN TRUSTEESHIP
1968-	Divided into Burundi & Rwanda

RUSSIA:
Union of Soviet Socialist Republics
Russian Socialist Federated Soviet Republics:
1917-1922	SOVIET REPUBLIC

Union of Soviet Socialist Republics:
1922-	COMMUNIST REPUBLIC

RUSSIA: Occupation Issues
1916-1918	Baltic Provinces – GERMAN
	OCCUPATION
1919	Aunis – FINNISH OCCUPATION
1941-1944	German Eastern Command –
	GERMAN OCCUPATION

RYUKYU ISLANDS
Prior to 1879	Part of China
1879-1945	Part of Japan
1945-1951	U.S. MILITARY GOVERNMENT
1951-1972	SEMI-AUTONOMOUS UNDER U.S.
	ADMINISTRATION
1972-	Part of Japan

SAAR
Prior to 1920	Part of Germany
1920-1935	LEAGUE OF NATIONS
	ADMINISTRATION
1935-1945	Part of Germany
1945-1947	Part of French Occupation Zone
1947-1948	FRENCH ADMINISTRATION
1948-1951	FRENCH PROTECTORATE
1951-1957	SEMI-INDEPENDENT STATE
	UNDER FRENCH
	PROTECTORATE
1957-1959	GER. FEDERAL REP.
	ADMINISTRATION
1959-	Part of German Federal Republic

SABAH
Prior to 1963	Called North Borneo
1963-	STATE OF MALAYSIA

ST. CHRISTOPHER
1860-1870	British Colony (Handstamps)
1870-1890	BRITISH COLONY
1890-1903	Part of Leeward Islands
1903-	Part of St. Kitts-Nevis

STE. MARIE DE MADAGASCAR
1890-1894	Part of Diego-Suarez
1894-1898	FRENCH COLONY
1898-	Part of Madagascar

SARAWAK

1869-1888	INDPENDENT STATE
1888-1942	BRITISH PROTECTORATE
1942-1945	JAPANESE OCCUPATION
1945-1946	BRITISH MILITARY ADMINISTRATION
1946-1963	BRITISH COLONY
1963-	STATE OF MALAYSIA

SASENO

1914-1923	Italian Occupation (Italy)
1923	ITALIAN POSSESSION
1923-1943	Part of Italy
1943-	Part of Albania

SCHLESWIG

1868-1920	Part of Nth. German Conf. / Germany
1920	PLEBISCITE AREA
1920-	Zone 1 to Denmark, Zone 2 to Germany

SENEGAMBIA & NIGER

Prior to 1899	Part of French Sudan
1899-1903	Protectorate of French West Africa (French Sudan)
1903-1904	PROTECTORATE OF FRENCH WEST AFRICA
1904	Name changed to Upper Senegal & Niger

SHANGHAI

1865-1898	CITY OF CHINA – EUROPEAN POST OFFICES
1898-	City of China

SHARJAH

Prior to 1963	Part of Trucial States
1963-1971	BRITISH PROTECTED SHEIKDOM
1971-1972	STATE OF UNITED ARAB EMIRATES
1973-	Part of United Arab Emirates

SIBERIA

Prior to 1919	Part of Russia
1919-1920	CZECH LEGION POST
1919	ADMIRAL KOLCHAK ISSUES
1920	AMUR – Communist Government
1920	TRANSBAIKAL – Ataman Semyonov Government
1920-	Part of Russia

SOMALI COAST

Prior to 1902	Called Djibouti
1902-1947	FRENCH COLONY
1947-1967	FRENCH OVERSEAS TERRITORY
1967	Name changed to Afars & Issas

SOMALILAND PROTECTORATE

1887-1903	British Somaliland – British Protectorate (India)
1903-1904	British Somaliland – BRITISH PROTECTORATE
1904-1940	BRITISH PROTECTORATE
1940-1941	ITALIAN OCCUPATION
1941-1942	British Protectorate (Aden)
1942-1960	BRITISH PROTECTORATE
1960	REPUBLIC
1960-	United with Somalia

SOUTH AFRICA
Regional Issues:

1977-1994	BOPHUTHATSWANA Self-Governing Homeland
1981-1994	CISKEI Self Governing Homeland
1976-1994	TRANSKEI Self-Governing Homeland
1979-1994	VENDA Self Governing Homeland

SOUTH ARABIA

Prior to 1959	Aden & States
1959-1963	British Federated State (Aden & States)
1963-1967	BRITISH PROTECTED FEDERATION
1968-	Name changed to Southern Yemen

SOUTH AUSTRALIA

1855-1901	BRITISH COLONY
1901-1913	STATE OF AUSTRALIA
1913-	State of Australia

SOUTH GEORGIA

Prior to 1944	Falkland Islands
1944-1946	FALKLAND ISLANDS. DEPENDENCY
1946-1963	Part of Falkland Islands Dependency
1963-1980	FALKLAND ISLANDS DEPENDENCY
1980-	Name changed to Falkland Islands Dependency

SOUTH RUSSIA
Prior to 1918	Part of Russia
1919-1920	GENERAL DENEKIN ISSUES
1919	Crimea – REGIONAL GOVERNMENT
1918-1920	Kuban Area – COSSACK GOVERNMENT
1920	GENERAL WRANGEL ISSUES
1920-	Part of Russia

SOUTH WEST AFRICA
1886-1897	German Colony (Germany)
1897-1915	GERMAN COLONY
1915-1923	SOUTH WEST AFRICA – Union of South Africa Occupation (Union of South Africa)
1923-1946	SOUTH AFRICAN MANDATE
1946-1990	SOUTH AFRICAN ADMINISTRATION
1990-	Name changed to Namibia

SOUTHERN NIGERIA
Prior to 1900	Niger Coast Protectorate
1900-1901	British Protectorate (Niger Coast Prot.)
1901-1906	BRITISH PROTECTORATE
1906-1913	BRITISH COLONY & PROTECTORATE
1914-	Part of Nigeria

SOUTHERN RHODESIA
1909-1924	Part of Rhodesia
1924-1953	SELF-GOVERNING BRITISH COLONY
1954-1963	Part of Rhodesia & Nyasaland
1964-1965	BRITISH COLONY
1965-1979	Rhodesia – INDEPENDENT STATE
1979-	Name changed to Zimbabwe

SPANISH GUINEA
1885-1902	Part of Fernando Po
1902-1960	SPANISH COLONY
1960-1968	Divided into Rio Muni & Fernando Po
1968-	Name changed to Equatorial Guinea

SPANISH MOROCCO
Prior to 1912	Part of Morocco
1912-1914	Spanish Protectorate (Spanish P. Offices)
1914-1956	SPANISH PROTECTORATE
1956-	Part of Morocco

SPANISH MOROCCO: Tetuan
1908-1912	SPANISH POSSESSION

SPANISH SAHARA
Prior to 1924	Rio de Oro
1924-1949	SPANISH COLONY
1949-1951	PART OF SPANISH WEST AFRICA
1951-1958	SPANISH COLONY
1958-1976	SPANISH OVERSEAS PROVINCE
1976-1979	Divided between Morocco & Mauritania
1979-	Moroccan Occupation

SPANISH WEST AFRICA
Prior to 1949	Separate Spanish Colonies
1949-1951	SPANISH ADMINISTRATIVE UNIT
1951-	Divided between Ifni & Spanish Sahara

STELLALAND
1884-1885	BOER REPUBLIC
1885-1897	Part of British Bechuanaland
1897-	Part of Cape of Good Hope/South Africa

STRAITS SETTLEMENTS
1867-1942	BRITISH COLONY
1942-1943	JAPANESE OCCUPATION
1943-1945	Japanese Occupation (Malaya)
1945-1948	BRITISH MILITARY ADMINISTRATION
1948-1950	BRITISH POSTAL AREA
1950-	Separate States/Malaya

TAHITI
1882-1893	FRENCH COLONY
1903,1915	SPECIAL ISSUES
1893-	Part of French Polynesia

TANGANYIKA
Prior to 1921	Part of German East Africa
1921-1935	BRITISH MANDATE
1935-1961	British Mandate (Kenya, Uganda & Tanganyika)
1961-1962	INDEPENDENT STATE
1962-1964	REPUBLIC
1964-	Name changed to Tanzania

197

TANNA TUVA

1878-1912	Part of China
1912-1926	Autonomous Republic (Russia)
1926-1945	AUTONOMOUS SOVIET REPUBLIC
1945-	Part of Russia

TASMANIA

1853-1901	BRITISH COLONY
1901-1913	STATE OF AUSTRALIA
1913-	State of Australia

TETE

Prior to 1893	Part of Mozambique
1893-1913	Part of Zambezia
1913-1914	DISTRICT OF MOZAMBIQUE
1914-	Part of Zambezia / Mozambique

THRACE

Eastern Thrace:

Prior to 1920	Part of Turkey
1920	GREEK OCCUPATION
1920-1923	Part of Greece
1923-	Part of Turkey

Western Thrace:

Prior to 1913	Part of Turkey
1913	GREEK OCCUPATION
1913	AUTONOMOUS GOVERNMENT
1913-1919	Part of Bulgaria
1919-1920	ALLIED OCCUPATION
1920	GREEK OCCUPATION
1920-	Part of Greece

TIBET

Prior to 1911	Part of China
1911-1921	CHINESE POST OFFICES
1912-1951	AUTONOMOUS THEOCRACY
1951-	Part of China

TOBAGO

1860-1879	British Colony (Handstamps)
1879-1889	BRITISH COLONY
1889-1896	WARD OF TRINIDAD
1896-	Part of Trinidad / Trinidad & Tobago

TRANSCAUCASIAN FEDERATED REPUBLICS

Prior to 1922	Separate Republics
1922-1923	Soviet Republic (Armenia, Azerbaijan & Georgia)
1923	SOVIET REPUBLIC
1923-1924	PROVINCES OF RUSSIA
1924-	Part of Russia

TRANSVAAL

1869-1877	South African Rep. – BOER REPUBLIC
1877-1878	BRITISH OCCUPATION
1878-1882	BRITISH COLONY
1882-1901	South African Rep. – BOER REPUBLIC
1900-1902	South African Rep. – BRITISH OCCUPATION
1902-1910	BRITISH COLONY
1910-1913	PROVINCE OF UNION OF SOUTH AFRICA
1913-	Part of South Africa

TRIESTE – Zone A

Prior to 1947	Part of Italy (Venezia-Guilia)
1947-1954	ALLIED MILITARY GOVERNMENT
1954-	Part of Italy

TRIESTE – Zone B

Prior to 1947	Istria & Slovene Coast
1947-1954	YUGOSLAV MILITARY ADMINISTRATION
1954-	Part of Yugoslavia

TRINIDAD

1851-1913	BRITISH COLONY
1913-	Name changed to Trinidad & Tobago

TRIPOLITANIA

1912-1923	Part of Libia
1923-1927	DISTRICT OF LIBIA
1927-1934	ITALIAN COLONY
1934-1942	Part of Libia
1943-1948	British Occupation (Middle East Forces)
1948-1950	BRITISH MILITARY ADMINISTRATION
1950-1951	BRITISH ADMINISTRATION
1951-	Part of Libya

TRUCIAL STATES

Prior to 1961	Separate Sheikdoms using stamps of Oman, India, etc.
1961-1963	UNION OF BRITISH PROTECTED SHEIKDOMS
1963-1971	Issues of separate Sheikdoms
1971-	Name changed to United Arab Emirates

TURKS ISLANDS
1867-1873	BRITISH COLONY
1873-1900	DEPENDENCY OF JAMAICA
1900	Name changed to
	Turks & Caicos Islands

Regional Issues:
1981-1985	CAICOS

UBANGI-SHARI
Prior to 1906	Part of French Congo
	(Ubangi-Shari-Chad)
1906-1910	French Colony (French Congo)
1910-1915	Colony of French Equatorial Africa
	(French Congo)
1915-1922	COLONY OF
	FRENCH EQUATORIAL AFRICA
	(Ubangi-Shari)
1922-1936	COLONY OF
	FRENCH EQUATORIAL AFRICA
1936-1958	Part of French Equatorial Africa
1958-	Name changed to
	Central African Republic

UMM AL QIWAIN
Prior to 1964	Part of Trucial States
1964-1971	BRITISH PROTECTED SHEIKDOM
1971-1972	STATE OF UNITED ARAB
	EMIRATES
1973-	Part of United Arab Emirates

UPPER SENEGAL & NIGER
Prior to 1904	Senegambia & Niger
1904-1906	Colony of French West Africa
	(Senegambia & Niger)
1906-1920	COLONY OF
	FRENCH WEST AFRICA
1920-	Colony dissolved

UPPER VOLTA
1906-1920	Part of Upper Senegal & Niger
1920-1933	COLONY OF
	FRENCH WEST AFRICA
1933-1947	Divided by Niger, French Sudan, and
	Ivory Coast
1947-1958	Part of French West Africa
1958-1959	Autonomous Republic
	(French West Africa)
1959-1960	AUTONOMOUS REPUBLIC
1960-1986	REPUBLIC
1986-	Name changed to Burkina Faso

VICTORIA
1850-1901	BRITISH COLONY
1901-1913	STATE OF AUSTRALIA
1913-	State of Australia

WEST IRIAN
Prior to 1962	Netherlands New Guinea
1962-1963	West New Guinea –
	UNITED NATIONS
	EXECUTIVE AUTHORITY
1963-1970	INDONESIAN ADMINISTRATION
1970-	Part of Indonesia

WESTERN AUSTRALIA
1854-1901	BRITISH COLONY
1901-1913	STATE OF AUSTRALIA
1913-	State of Australia

WESTERN UKRAINE
Prior to 1918	Part of Austria-Hungary
1918-1919	AUTONOMOUS STATE
1919	ROMANIAN OCCUPATION
1919-1939	Part of Poland
1939-1941	Russian Occupation (Russia)
1941-1943	Part of Ukraine
1943-	Part of Russia

YUGOSLAVIA
Prior to 1918	Separate Countries
1918-1921	Kingdom
	(Issues of Separate Provinces)
1921-1941	KINGDOM
1941-1944	Separate Areas under
	German and Italian Occupation
1944-1945	DEMOCRATIC FEDERATION
1945-1992	COMMUNIST REPUBLIC
1992-2002	REPUBLIC

YUGOSLAVIA: Ljubljana
Prior to 1941	Part of Yugoslavia
1941	PROVINCE OF ITALY
1941-1944	Province of Italy (Italy)
1944-1945	GERMAN OCCUPATION
1945-	Part of Yugoslavia

YUGOSLAVIA: Istria & Slovene Coast
Prior to 1945	Part of Italy
1945-1947	YUGOSLAV MILITARY
	ADMINISTRATION
1947-	Divided by Yugoslavia &
	Trieste – Zone B

199

ZAMBEZIA

Prior to 1893	Part of Mozambique
1893-1913	DISTRICT OF MOZAMBIQUE
1913-1914	Divided into Quelimane & Tete
1914-1920	DISTRICT OF MOZAMBIQUE
1920-	Part of Mozambique

ZANZIBAR

1875-1890	Sultanate (India)
1890-1895	British Protected Sultanate (India)
1895-1963	BRITISH PROTECTED SULTANATE
1963-1964	INDEPENDENT SULTANATE
1964	REPUBLIC
1964-1968	PART OF TANZANIA
1968-	Part of Tanzania

ZULULAND

1881-1887	Part of Natal
1887-1888	British Occupation (Natal)
1888-1898	BRITISH COLONY
1898-	Part of Natal/South Africa

Aden

Elobey Annobon & Corsico

Saar

Gold Coast

Tahiti

Tete

Palestine

Heligoland

Allenstein

Bechuanaland Protectorate

Labuan

Zululand

Umm Al Qiwain

Zambezia

Orange River Colony

Inini

MAP INDEX

	Map No.			Map No.
1. ABU DHABI	8	39.	BENIN	9
2. ADEN	8	40.	BERGEDORF	6
2A. AEGEAN ISLANDS	5	41.	BERMUDA	1
3. AFARS & ISSAS	9	42.	BHUTAN	11
4. AFGHANISTAN	11	43.	BOLIVIA	3
5. AGUERA	9	44.	BOSNIA & HERZEGOVINA	5
6. AITUTAKI	12	37.	BOTSWANA	9
7. AJMAN	8	387.	BOUKINA FASO	9
8. ALAOUITES	8	45.	BRAZIL	9
9. ALBANIA	5	46.	BREMEN	6
10. ALEXANDRETTA	8	47.	BRITISH ANTARCTIC TERRITORY	Key Map
11. ALGERIA	9	48.	BRITISH CENTRAL AFRICA	9
12. ALLENSTEIN	5	6A.	BRITISH CHANNEL ISLANDS: GUERNSEY, ISLE OF MAN, JERSEY, ALDERNEY	5,6
13. ANDORRA	5			
14. ANGOLA	9			
15. ANGRA	4	49.	BRITISH COLUMBIA & VANCOUVER ISLANDS	1
15A. ANGUILLA	2			
16. ANJOUAN	10	50.	BRITISH EAST AFRICA	9
17. ANNAM & TONKIN	11	51.	BRITISH GUIANA	3
18. ANTIGUA	2	52.	BRITISH HONDURAS	1
19. ARGENTINA	3	53.	BRITISH INDIAN OCEAN TERRITORY	10
20. ARMENIA	8			
21. ASCENSION	4	54.	BRITISH SOLOMAN ISLANDS	12
22. AUSTRALIA	11	393A.	BRITISH VIRGIN ISLANDS	2
23. AUSTRIA	5	55.	BRUNEI	12
24. AZERBAIJAN	8	56.	BRUNSWICK	6
25. AZORES	4	57.	BULGARIA	5
26. BADEN	6	58.	BURMA	11
27. BAHAMAS	2	59.	BURUNDI	9
28. BAHRAIN	8	60.	BUSHIRE	8
29. BANGKOK	11	61.	CAMBODIA	11
30. BANGLADESH	11	62.	CAMEROUN	9
31. BARBADOS	2	63.	CANADA	1
32. BARBUDA	2	64.	CANAL ZONE	1
33. BASUTOLAND	9	65.	CAPE OF GOOD HOPE	9
34. BATUM	8	66.	CAPE JUBY	9
35. BAVARIA	6	67.	CAPE VERDE	4
36. BECHUANALAND	9	68.	CAROLINE ISLANDS	12
37. BECHUANALAN PROTECTORATE	9	69.	CASTELLORIZO	8
84. BELGIAN CONGO	9	70.	CAYMAN ISLANDS	2
297. BELGIAN EAST AFRICA	9	71.	CENTRAL AFRICAN REPUBLIC	9
38. BELGIUM	5	72.	CENTRAL LITHUANIA	5
52. BELIZE	1	73.	CEYLON (SRI LANKA)	11

201

MAP INDEX

Map No.   **Map No.**

74. CHAD 9
75. CHILE 3
76. CHINA (FORMOSA) 11
77. CHINA –
     PEOPLE'S REPUBLIC 11
78. CHRISTMAS ISLAND 12
79. CILICIA 8
80. COCHIN CHINA 11
81. COCOS (KEELING) ISLANDS 11
82. COLOMBIA 3
83. COMORO ISLANDS 10
84. CONGO –
     DEMOCRATIC REPUBLIC 9
85. CONGO –
     PEOPLE'S REPUBLIC 9
86. COOK ISLANDS 12
87. CORFU 5
88. COSTA RICA 1
89. CRETE 5,8
90. CROATIA 5
91. CUBA 2
236. CURAÇAO –
     NETHERLANDS ANTILLES 2
92. CYPRUS 8
93. CYRENAICA 9
94. CZECHOSLOVAKIA 5
95. DAHOMEY 9
96. DALMATIA 5
97. DANISH WEST INDIES 2
98. DANZIG 5
99. DENMARK 5
100. DIEGO-SUAREZ 10
3. DJIBOUTI 9
101. DOMINICA 2
102. DOMINICAN REPUBLIC 2
103. DUBAI 8
104. DUTCH INDIES 12
105. DUTCH NEW GUINEA 12
106. EAST AFRICA & UGANDA
     PROTECTORATES 9
107. EASTERN RUMELIA 5
108. EASTERN SILESIA 5
109. ECUADOR 3
110. EGYPT 9

111. ELOBEY, ANNOBON &
     CORISCO 9
112. EPIRUS 8
113. EQUATORIAL GUINEA 9
113A. ERITREA 9
114. ESTONIA 5
115. ETHIOPIA 9
116. FALKLAND ISLANDS 3
117. FAR EASTERN REPUBLIC 11
402. FAROE ISLANDS 5
118. FERNANDO PO 9
119. FIJI 12
120. FINLAND 5
121. FIUME 5
122. FRANCE 5
123. FRENCH CONGO 9
124. FRENCH EQUATORIAL AFRICA .. 9
125. FRENCH GUIANA 3
126. FRENCH GUINEA 9
127. FRENCH INDIA 11
128. FRENCH MOROCCO 9
129. FRENCH POLYNESIA 12
130. FRENCH SOUTHERN &
     ANTARCTIC
     TERRITORIES .... *Key Map*
131. FRENCH SUDAN 9
132. FRENCH WEST AFRICA 9
133. FUJEIRA 8
134. FUNCHAL 4
135. GABON 9
136. GAMBIA 9
137. GEORGIA 8
138. GERMAN EAST AFRICA 9
139. GERMAN NEW GUINEA 12
140. GERMAN
     SOUTH-WEST AFRICA 9
141. GERMANY 5
141A. GERMANY – West Berlin 5
142. GERMANY –
     German Democratic Republic 5
143. GHANA 9
144. GIBRALTER 5
145A. GILBERT ISLANDS 12
145. GILBERT & ELLICE ISLANDS 12

202

MAP INDEX

Map No.

143. GOLD COAST 9
146. GRAND COMORO 10
147. GREAT BRITAIN 5
148. GREECE.................................... 5
149. GREENLAND 1
150. GRENADA................................... 2
151. GRIQUALAND WEST 9
152. GUADELOUPE............................ 2
153. GUAM 12
154. GUATEMALA............................... 1
126. GUINEA 9
280. GUINEA-BISSAU 9
51. GUYANA.................................... 3
155. HAITI... 2
156. HAMBURG 6
157. HANOVER 6
10. HATAY 10
159. HAWAII 12
160. HELIGOLAND 5
161. HONDURAS 1
162. HONG KONG 11
163. HORTA 4
164. HUNGARY.................................. 5
165. ICELAND 1
166. IFNI 9
167. INDIA 11
168. INDO-CHINA 11
104. INDONESIA................................ 12
169. INHAMBANE 9
170. ININI... 3
171. IONIAN ISLANDS 5
272. IRAN (PERSIA) 8
172. IRAQ 8
173. IRELAND 5
174. ISRAEL 8
176. ITALIAN EAST AFRICA 9
177. ITALY 5,7
178. IVORY COAST 9
179. JAMAICA 2
180. JAPAN 11
181. JORDAN 8
183. KARELIA.................................... 5
184. KENYA....................................... 9
185. KIAUCHAU 11

Map No.

186. KIONGA..................................... 9
145A. KIRIBATI.................................. 12
187. KOREA 11
188. KUWAIT 8
189. LABUAN 12
190. LAGOS 9
191. LAOS 11
8. LATAKIA 8
192. LATVIA 5
193. LEBANON 8
194. LEEWARD ISLANDS 2
33. LESOTHO 9
195. LIBERIA 9
196. LIBYA 9
197. LIECHTENSTEIN 5
198. LITHUANIA................................. 5
199. LOURENCO MARQUES............... 9
200. LUBECK 6
201. LUXEMBOURG........................... 5
202. MACAO 11
202A. MACEDONIA............................ 5
203. MADAGASCAR (MALAGASY) 10
204. MADEIRA 4
48. MALAWI 9
205. MALAYA, MALAYSIA & STATES 11
    205A.   JOHORE
    205B.   KEDAH
    205C.   KELANTAN
    205D.   MALACCA (MELAKA)
    205E.   NEGRI SEMBILAN
    205F.   PAHANG
    205G.   PENANG (PULAU PINANG)
    205H.   PERAK
    205J.   PERLIS
    251.   SABAH
    313.   SARAWAK
    205K.   SELANGOR
    205L.   SUNGEI UJONG
    205M.   TRENGGANU
206. MALDIVE ISLANDS 10
207. MALI 9
208. MALTA....................................... 5
209. MANCHUKUO 11
210. MARIANA ISLANDS..................... 12
211. MARIENWERDER 5
213. MARSHALL ISLANDS.................. 12

MAP INDEX

Map No.   **Map No.**

214. MARTINIQUE 2
215. MAURITANIA................................9
216. MARITIUS 10
217. MAYOTTE 10
218. MECKLENBURG-SCHWERIN 6
219. MECKLENBURG-STRELITZ..........6
220. MEMEL 5
172. MESOPOTAMIA.............................8
222. MEXICO.....................................1
222A. MICRONESIA 12
 85. MIDDLE CONGO 9
223. MODENA....................................7
224. MOHELI 10
225. MONACO....................................5
226. MONGOLIA 11
227. MONTENEGRO 5
228. MONTSERRAT 2
229. MOROCCO...................................9
230. MOZAMBIQUE 9
231. MOZAMBIQUE COMPANY...........9
232. NATAL 9
233. NAURU 12
234. NEPAL 11
235. NETHERLANDS 5
236. NETHERLANDS ANTILLES
        (CURAÇAO) 2
104. NETHERLANDS INDIES.............12
105. NETHERLANDS NEW GUINEA ..12
237. NEVIS......................................2
140. NEW BRITAIN 8
238. NEW BRUNSWICK 1
239. NEW CALEDONIA 12
240. NEWFOUNDLAND 1
140. NEW GUINEA.............................12
241. NEW HEBRIDES 12
242. NEW REPUBLIC 9
243. NEW SOUTH WALES 12
244. NEW ZEALAND...........................12
245. NICARAUGUA.............................1
246. NIGER 9
247. NIGER COAST
        PROTECTORATE 9
248. NIGERIA 9
249. NIUE 12

250. NORFOLK ISLAND 12
251. NORTH BORNEO 12
252. NORTHERN NIGERIA 9
253. NORTHERN RHODESIA 9
254. NORTH INGERMANLAND 5
255. NORTH WEST
        PACIFIC ISLANDS 12
256. NORWAY 5
257. NOSSI-BE 10
258. NOVA SCOTIA............................1
 48. NYASALAND PROTECTORATE...9
259. NYASSA 9
260. OBOCK......................................9
261. OLDENBURG...............................6
262. OLTRE GIUBA 9
263. OMAN 8
264. ORANGE RIVER COLONY 9
265. PAKISTAN.................................11
265A. PALAU....................................12
266. PALESTINE 8
267. PANAMA 1,3
268. PAPUA NEW GUINEA.................12
269. PARAGUAY 3
270. PARMA......................................7
271. PENRHYN ISLAND.....................12
272. PERSIA (IRAN) 8
273. PERU..3
274. PHILIPPINES 12
275. PITCAIRN ISLANDS 12
276. POLAND....................................5
277. PONTA DELGADA.......................4
278. PORTUGAL................................5
279. PORTUGUESE CONGO...............9
280. PORTUGUESE GUINEA 9
281. PORTUGUESE INDIA.................11
282. PRINCE EDWARD ISLAND..........1
283. PRUSSIA....................................6
284. PUERTO RICO 2
285. QATAR 8
286. QUEENSLAND...........................12
287. QUELIMANE 9
288. RAS AL KHAIMA........................8
289. RÉUNION...................................10
290. RHODESIA.................................9

MAP INDEX

	Map No.			Map No.
291. RIO DE ORO	9		3. SOMALI COAST	9
292. RIO MUNI	9		331. SOMALILAND PROTECTORATE	9
293. ROMAGNA	7		332. SOUTH AFRICA	9
294. ROMANIA	5		333. SOUTH ARABIA	8
295. ROMAN STATES	7		334. SOUTH AUSTRALIA	12
296. ROUAD, ILE	8		335. SOUTH NIGERIA	9
297. RUANDA-URUNDI	9		336. SOUTHERN RHODESIA	9
298. RUSSIA	5,11		337. SOUTH GEORGIA	3
299. RWANDA	9		338. SOUTH RUSSIA	8
300. RYUKYU ISLANDS	11		140. SOUTH-WEST AFRICA	9
301. SAAR	5		340. SPAIN	5
251. SABAH	12		341. SPANISH GUINEA	9
302. ST. CHRISTOPHER	2		342. SPANISH MOROCCO	9
303. STE. MARIE DE			343. SPANISH SAHARA	9
MADAGASCAR	10		344. SPANISH WEST AFRICA	9
304. ST. HELENA	4		73. SRI LANKA (CEYLON)	11
305. ST. KITTS-NEVIS	2		345. STELLALAND	9
306. ST. LUCIA	2		346. STRAITS SETTLEMENTS	11
307. ST. PIERRE & MIQUELON	1		347. SUDAN	9
308. ST. THOMAS & PRINCE			348. SURINAM	3
ISLANDS	9		349. SWAZILAND	9
309. ST. VINCENT	2		350. SWEDEN	5
310. SALVADOR	1		351. SWITZERLAND	5
311. SAMOA	12		352. SYRIA	8
312. SAN MARINO	5		353. TAHITI	12
313. SARAWAK	12		354. TANGANYIKA	9
314. SARDINIA	7		355. TANNU TUVA	11
315. SASENO	5		356. TANZANIA	9
316. SAUDI ARABIA	8		357. TASMANIA	12
317. SAXONY	6		358. TETE	9
318. SCHLESWIG	6		326. THAILAND (SIAM)	11
319. SCHLESWIG-HOLSTEIN	6		359. THRACE	5
320. SENEGAL	9		361. TIBET	11
321. SENEGAMBIA & NIGER	9		362. TIMOR	12
322. SERBIA	5		363. TOBAGO	2
323. SEYCHELLES	10		364. TOGO	9
324. SHANGHAI	11		365. TOKELAU ISLANDS	12
325. SHARJAH & DEPENDENCIES	8		366. TONGA	12
326. SIAM (THAILAND)	11		367. TRANSCAUCASIAN	
327. SIBERIA	11		FEDERATED REPUBLICS	8
328. SIERRA LEONE	9		368. TRANSVAAL	9
329. SINGAPORE	11		369. TRIESTE	5
54. SOLOMON ISLANDS	12		370. TRINIDAD	2
330. SOMALIA	9		371. TRIPOLITANIA	9

205

MAP INDEX

Map No.

372. TRISTAN DA CUNHA 4
373. TRUCIAL STATES 8
374. TUNISIA 9
375. TURKEY 8
376A. TURKS ISLANDS 2
376. TURKS & CAICOS ISLANDS 2
377. TUSCANY 7
145B. TUVALU 12
378. TWO SICILIES 7
379. UBANGI-SHARI 9
380. UGANDA 9
381. UKRAINE 5
382. UMMAL QIWAIN 8
373. UNITED ARAB EMIRATES 8
383. UNITED NATIONS 1
384. UNITED STATES 1
131. UPPER SENEGAL & NIGER 9
386. UPPER SILESIA 5
387. UPPER VOLTA 9
388. URUGUAY 3
241. VANUATU 12

Map No.

389. VATICAN CITY 5
390. VENEZUELA 3
391. VICTORIA 12
17. VIETNAM 11
393. VIRGIN ISLANDS 2
394. WALLIS & FUTUNA ISLANDS 12
395. WESTERN AUSTRALIA 12
311. WESTERN SAMOA 12
396. WESTERN UKRAINE 5
105. WEST IRIAN 12
397. WURTTEMBERG 6
398. YEMEN 8
333. YEMEN– PEOPLE'S
        DEMOCRATIC REPUBLIC 8
182. YUGOSLAVIA 5
84. ZAIRE 9
399. ZAMBEZIA 9
253. ZAMBIA 9
400. ZANZIBAR 9
290. ZIMBABWE 9
401. ZUZULAND 9

KEY MAP

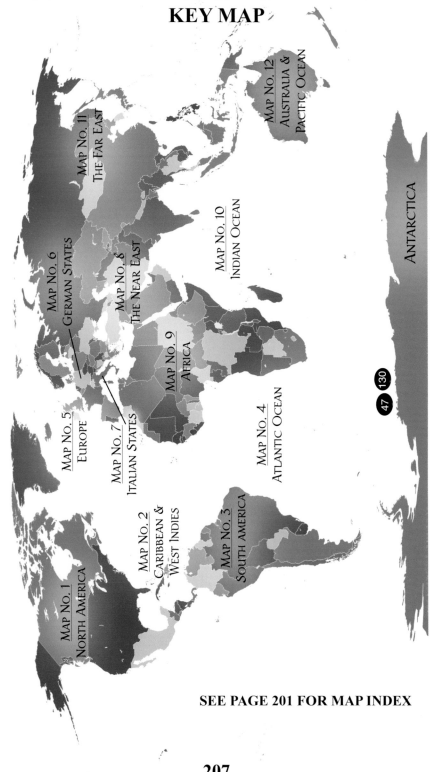

MAP No. 12
AUSTRALIA &
PACIFIC OCEAN

MAP No. 11
THE FAR EAST

MAP No. 10
INDIAN OCEAN

MAP No. 6
GERMAN STATES

MAP No. 8
THE NEAR EAST

MAP No. 9
AFRICA

MAP No. 5
EUROPE

MAP No. 7
ITALIAN STATES

MAP No. 4
ATLANTIC OCEAN

MAP No. 1
NORTH AMERICA

MAP No. 2
CARIBBEAN &
WEST INDIES

MAP No. 3
SOUTH AMERICA

ANTARCTICA

47 130

SEE PAGE 201 FOR MAP INDEX

207

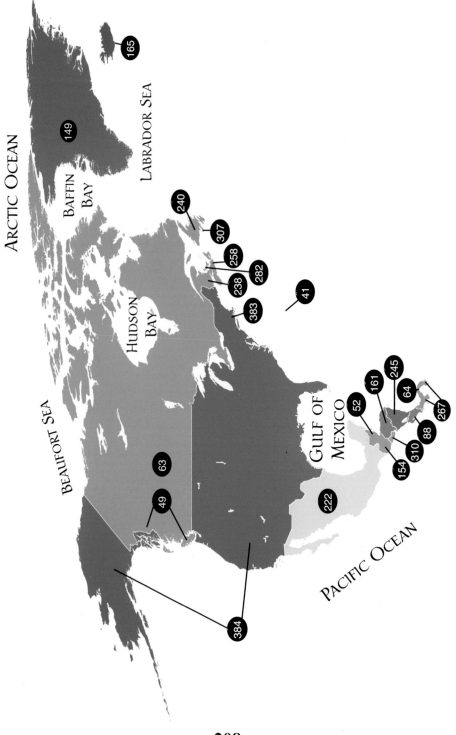

MAP NO. 2: CARIBBEAN SEA & WEST INDIES

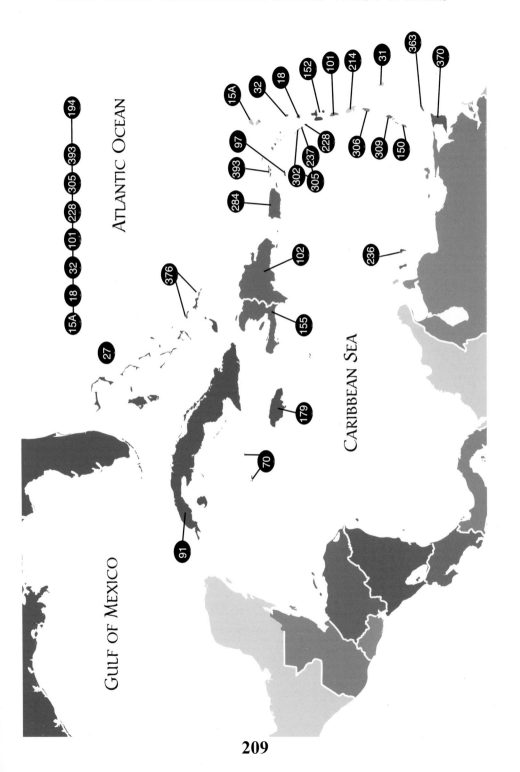

MAP NO. 3: SOUTH AMERICA

MAP NO. 4: ATLANTIC OCEAN

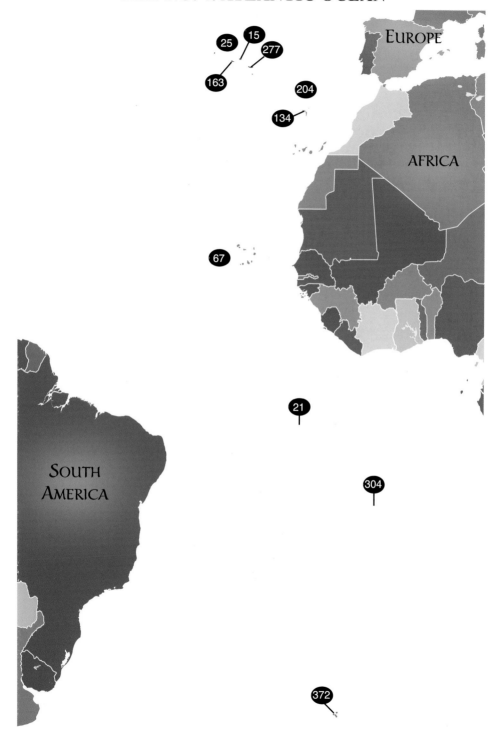

MAP NO. 5: EUROPE

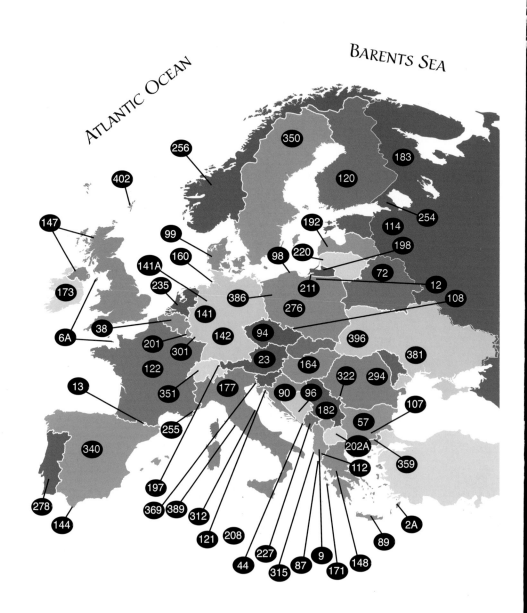

MAP NO. 6: GERMAN STATES

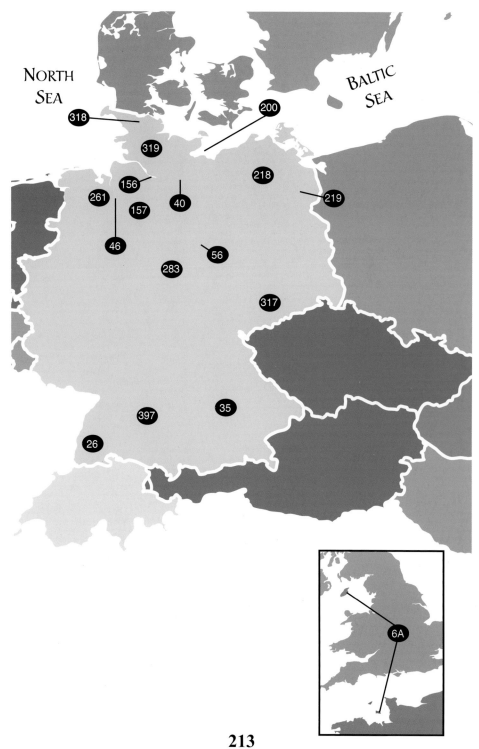

NORTH
SEA

BALTIC
SEA

318

200

319

218

156

261

40

219

157

46

56

283

317

397

35

26

6A

MAP NO. 7: ITALIAN STATES

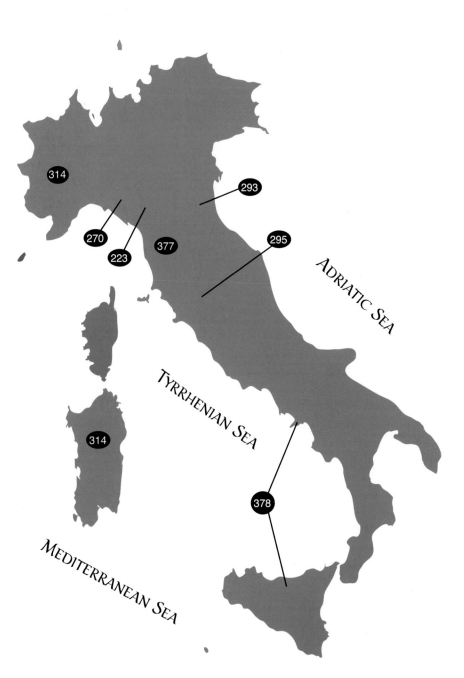

314

293

270

223

377

295

Adriatic Sea

Tyrrhenian Sea

314

378

Mediterranean Sea

MAP NO. 8: THE NEAR EAST

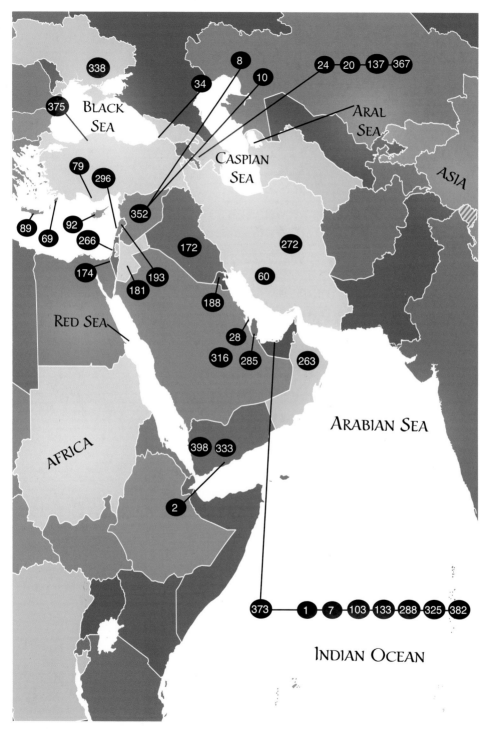

BLACK SEA

ARAL SEA

CASPIAN SEA

ASIA

RED SEA

AFRICA

ARABIAN SEA

INDIAN OCEAN

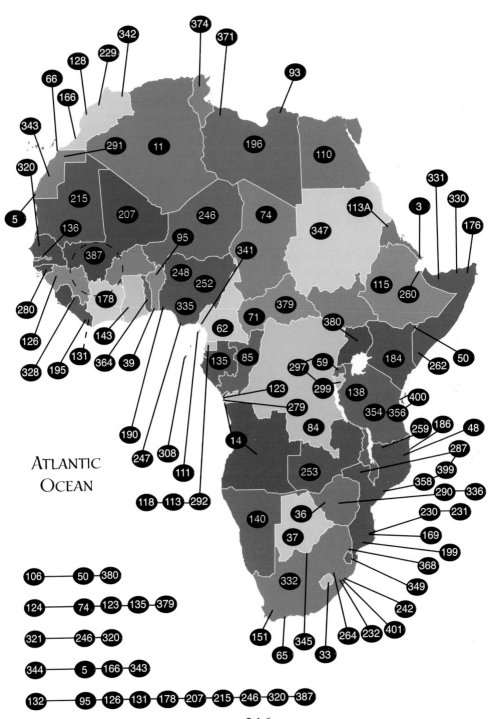

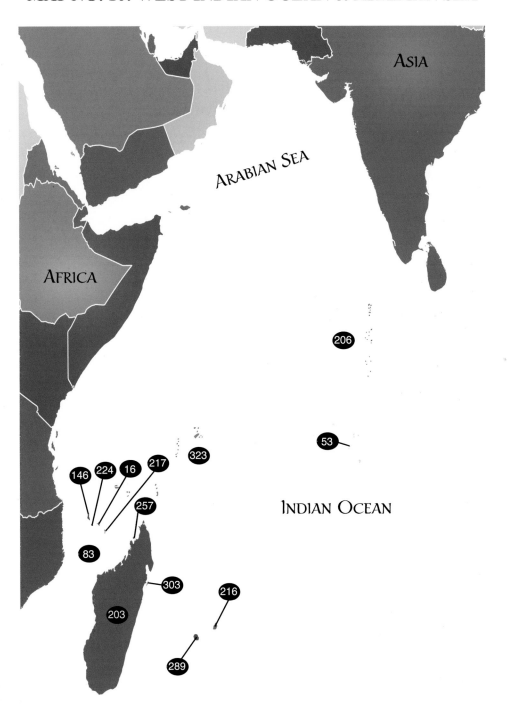

MAP NO. 11: THE FAR EAST

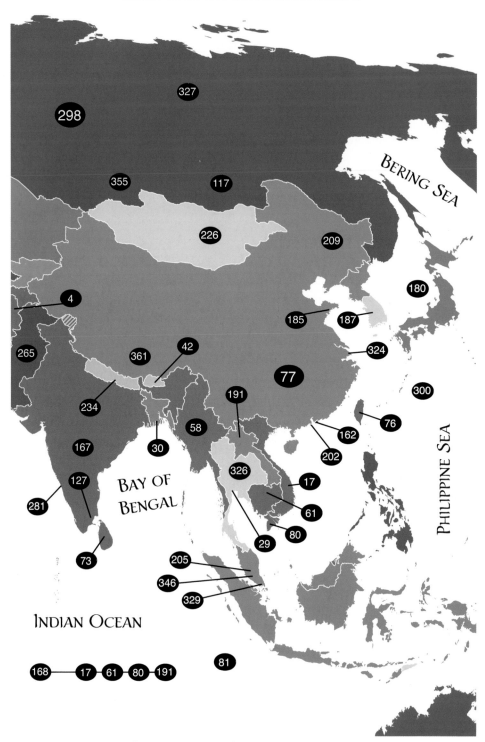

BERING SEA

PHILIPPINE SEA

BAY OF BENGAL

INDIAN OCEAN

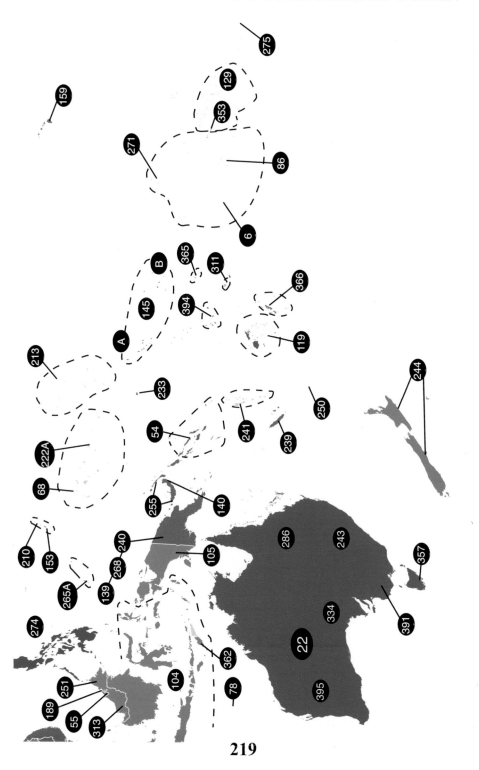

NOTES

NOTES